W9-DAK-774

Cultures of Relatedness

New Approaches to the Study of Kinship

Our understanding of what makes a person a relative has been transformed by radical changes in marriage arrangements and gender relations, and by new reproductive technologies. We can no longer take it for granted that our most fundamental social relationships are grounded in 'biology' or 'nature'. These developments have prompted anthropologists to take a fresh look at idioms of relatedness in other societies, and to review the ways in which relationships are symbolised and interpreted in our own society. Defamiliarising some classic cases, challenging the established analytic categories of anthropology, the contributors to this innovative book focus on the boundary between the 'biological' and the 'social', and bring into question the received wisdom at the heart of the study of kinship.

JANET CARSTEN is Senior Lecturer in Social Anthropology at the University of Edinburgh. She is the author of *The Heat of the Hearth* (1977) and co-editor of *About the House*, published by Cambridge University Press in 1995.

Cultures of Relatedness

New Approaches to the Study of Kinship

Edited by

Janet Carsten
University of Edinburgh

CABRINI COLLEGE LIBRARY
610 King of Prussia Road
Radnor, PA 19087

CAMBRIDGE
UNIVERSITY PRESS

GN
487
.C85
2000

#4136/393

PUBLISHED BY THE PRESS SYNDICATE OF THE UNIVERSITY OF CAMBRIDGE
The Pitt Building, Trumpington Street, Cambridge, United Kingdom

CAMBRIDGE UNIVERSITY PRESS
The Edinburgh Building, Cambridge CB2 2RU, UK   http://www.cup.cam.ac.uk
40 West 20th Street, New York NY 10011–4211, USA   http://www.cup.org
10 Stamford Road, Oakleigh, Melbourne 3166, Australia

© Cambridge University Press 2000

This book is in copyright. Subject to statutory exception and to the provisions of relevant collective licensing agreements, no reproduction of any part may take place without the written permission of Cambridge University Press.

First published 2000

Printed in the United Kingdom at the University Press, Cambridge

Typeset in Plantin 10/12 pt   [CE]

A catalogue record for this book is available from the British Library

Library of Congress cataloguing in publication data

Cultures of relatedness: new approaches to the study of kinship / edited by Janet Carsten.
    p.   cm.
Includes bibliographical references.
ISBN 0 521 65193 X (hardback). – ISBN 0 521 65627 3 (paperback)
1. Kinship Congresses.   I. Carsten, Janet.
GN487.C85   2000
306.83 – dc21   99–15844 CIP

ISBN 0 521 65193 X hardback
ISBN 0 521 65627 3 paperback

Contents

Illustrations

Contributors

RITA ASTUTI is Lecturer in Anthropology at the London School of Economics. She is the author of *Peoples of the Sea: Identity and Descent among the Vezo of Madagascar* (1995). She is currently carrying out research on infant cognition in Madagascar.

BARBARA BODENHORN is College Lecturer in Social Sciences at Pembroke College, Cambridge, and is affiliated with the Social Anthropology Department at the University of Cambridge. She has published on kinship, gender, economic relations, and literacy with reference to northern Alaska.

MARY BOUQUET has held research and teaching posts at the universities of Exeter, Lisbon, Amsterdam, and Oslo; and she has made exhibitions at the Museu de Etnologia (Lisbon), the Nationaal Natuurhistorisch Museum (Leiden), and the Etnografiske Museum (University of Oslo). Her publications include *Reclaiming English Kinship* (1993) and *Sans og samling/Bringing It All Back Home . . . to the Oslo University Ethnographic Museum* (1996). She currently teaches cultural anthropology and museology at Utrecht University and is writing on family photography and exhibitionary practice.

JANET CARSTEN is Senior Lecturer in Social Anthropology at the University of Edinburgh. She has carried out fieldwork in Malaysia. Her research interests include kinship, gender, the house, and migration. She co-edited *About the House: Lévi-Strauss and Beyond* (1995) with Stephen Hugh-Jones and is the author of *The Heat of the Hearth: The Process of Kinship in a Malay Fishing Community* (1997).

JEANETTE EDWARDS is Lecturer in the Department of Sociology and Social Anthropology at the University of Keele. She has conducted fieldwork in north-west England. Her research interests are in kinship, community, reproductive technologies, and social identity. She co-authored *Technologies of Procreation* (1993), and her mono-

graph on kinship and community in north-west England is currently
in press.

SHARON ELAINE HUTCHINSON is Associate Professor of Anthropology
at the University of Wisconsin–Madison. She has conducted extensive fieldwork in the southern Sudan. Her research interests are in
social and cultural change, political economy, ritual and religion, and
gender. Her monograph *Nuer Dilemmas: Coping with Money, War,
and the State* (1996) was awarded the Amaury Talbot Prize for
African anthropology.

HELEN LAMBERT is Senior Lecturer in Medical Anthropology at the
London School of Hygiene and Tropical Medicine, London University. She has conducted extensive fieldwork in Rajasthan, North
India, and in Britain. Her research interests include popular Hinduism and therapeutics, sexual health, and the social construction of
medicine. She is the author of a number of articles on these topics.

KAREN MIDDLETON has conducted fieldwork among the Karembola of
Madagascar. She is the author of several articles on the peoples of
southern Madagascar and is the editor of *Ancestors, Power, and
History in Madagascar* (1999).

CHARLES STAFFORD is Lecturer in Anthropology at the London School
of Economics. His fieldwork has been conducted in south-eastern
Taiwan and north-eastern mainland China, and his research interests
include childhood, education, popular religion, kinship, and historical consciousness. He is the author of *The Roads of Chinese Childhood*
(1995) and is currently completing a monograph on Chinese processes of 'separation' and 'reunion'.

MARILYN STRATHERN is William Wyse Professor of Social Anthropology at the University of Cambridge. Her interests are divided
between Melanesian (*Women in Between*, 1972) and British (*Kinship
at the Core*, 1981) ethnography. *The Gender of the Gift* (1988) is a
critique of anthropological theories of society and gender relations as
they have been applied to Melanesia, while *After Nature* (1992)
comments on the cultural revolution at home. A monograph on the
comparative method is called *Partial Connections* (1991). Her most
recent publications include the co-authored *Technologies of Procreation*
(1993) and the edited volume *Shifting Contexts: Transformations in
Anthropological Knowledge* (1995).

Acknowledgements

The chapters in this volume were all originally presented in October 1996 as a panel which formed part of a 'Boundaries and Identities' conference held to celebrate fifty years of Social Anthropology at the University of Edinburgh. I am grateful to Tony Cohen for providing the space and the occasion, furnishing administrative support, and giving his warm encouragement then and since.

The introduction was written during the tenure of a Nuffield Foundation Social Science Research Fellowship. I am grateful to the Nuffield Foundation, and also to my colleagues in the Department of Social Anthropology at Edinburgh for providing the opportunity for a period of writing and research.

Various people have given me help in the sometimes bumpy process of seeing this book into print. I owe a particular debt to Marilyn Strathern and to Sarah Franklin for giving me detailed comments on an earlier draft of the introduction, and for their encouragement and advice when it was most needed. I am also grateful to Jessica Kuper for her support, and to the anonymous reviewers for Cambridge University Press for their comments.

Jonathan Spencer not only persuaded me to jettison an earlier version of the introduction, he has also been characteristically generous with his ideas, his critical comments, and his support at every stage. Needless to say, I lay claim to the remaining lapses in the editing and introduction.

1   Introduction: cultures of relatedness

Janet Carsten

In recent years new life has been breathed into the anthropological study of kinship. This volume brings together some of the sources of the new vitality by exploring local cultures of relatedness in comparative context. The authors describe what 'being related' does for particular people living in specific localities in Africa, China, India, Madagascar, Alaska, and Europe. Rather than taking the content of 'kinship' for granted, they build from first principles a picture of the implications and the lived experience of relatedness in local contexts. It is a truism that people are always conscious of connections to other people. It is equally a truism that some of these connections carry particular weight – socially, materially, affectively. And, often but not always, these connections can be described in genealogical terms, but they can also be described in other ways.

Consider, for example, the Nuer, who constitute a paradigm of a lineage-based society and, as such, a classic case in the anthropological literature. Nuer are revealed here in very different terms from those in which generations of students have come to understand them (notwithstanding the complexities of Evans-Pritchard's (1940, 1951) original ethnography). In this volume Hutchinson describes how, under the conditions of profound social and political upheaval experienced in southern Sudan, the connections and disconnections of Nuer relatedness have come to be understood not only in terms of blood and cattle but also through the media of money, paper, and guns. That these media are potentially convertible into each other, and that food is convertible into blood, and blood into milk and semen, lends an extraordinary degree of transformability to Nuer idioms of relatedness. This 'unboundedness' not only provides a strong contrast to the classic understandings of Nuer kinship in terms of descent groups, but has important implications for how we consider idioms of relatedness more generally.

Likewise, if we consider Iñupiaq relatedness as described here by Bodenhorn, much anthropological wisdom about what constitutes kinship is called into question. Placing a high value on individual autonomy, Iñupiat strongly deny that ties deriving from procreation exert any overriding moral force. Whereas claims based on different contributions to productive work are described as permanent, 'biology' does not constitute an immutable basis for relations. One of the purposes of this volume is precisely to interrogate the role of biology in local statements and practices of relatedness. In this introductory chapter I situate local practices in a broader comparative context. For the Iñupiat, it is clear that a rejection of biology as constituting the moral bedrock to kinship does not mean that relatedness, as locally constituted, is irrelevant – on the contrary, Bodenhorn makes clear that Iñupiat constantly seek to acquire more ties through naming practices, adoption, and marriage. Crucially, however, these ties are seen as optative rather than given.

The aim of describing relatedness in indigenous terms appears deceptively simple. But it is of course part of a more ambitious project. That project involves assessing where the anthropological study of kinship finds itself at the beginning of the twenty-first century, and where its future might lie. The study of kinship was the very heart of anthropology for nearly a century. In the North American, European, and British schools, from Morgan to Schneider, Durkheim to Lévi-Strauss, Rivers and Malinowski to Radcliffe-Brown and Fortes, the major theorists of anthropology made their mark in the study of kinship (cf. Parkin 1997: 135). It seemed more or less impossible to imagine what anthropology would look like without kinship. And yet from the 1970s on, the position of kinship as a field of study within anthropology has been under question. 'Under question' is something of an understatement. For most anthropologists confronted with the question 'Whatever happened to kinship?', one might say quite simply, as David Schneider did in an interview published shortly before his death, 'the kinds of problems changed' (1995: 193–4).

In Schneider's view, the shift away from kinship was part of a general shift in anthropological understanding from structure to practice, and from practice to discourse. Kinship lost ground – most obviously to gender. But this was part of a wider recasting of the nature of social and cultural life which involved the breaking down of the discrete domains of economics, politics, religion, and kinship which had defined anthropology. This recasting occurred alongside what Schneider termed a 'democratisation of the intellectual enterprise' (1995: 197) in which concerns about social justice, from feminism and the civil rights movement, were crucial. Schneider's view was shaped, of course, by events inside and outside the North American academy. It was more generally true, however, that social stability was no longer the central issue in anthropology. And in one way or another, the study of kinship – whether in evolutionary, functionalist, or structuralist guise – had been bound up with explanations of social stability.

But Schneider also noted that, perhaps surprisingly, kinship in the 1990s had 'risen from its ashes' (1995: 193) – a fact which he attributed to feminist work, to studies of gay and lesbian kinship, and to Marilyn Strathern's *After Nature* (1992). If it is true that kinship has undergone a rebirth, there is no doubt that the 'new kinship' looks rather different from its old-style forebears. It has become standard, in works on kinship published since the 1980s, for gender, the body, and personhood to feature prominently in the analysis, while relationship terminologies are barely referred to, and kinship diagrams scarcely make an appearance. 'The kinds of problems changed.' This volume is one attempt to understand in what ways the problems changed, and how kinship might look as a result.

The present collection is intended as both a new departure and a return to comparative roots. It begins to explore how the issues underlying recent work on kinship in Euro-American cultures, on new reproductive technologies, on gender, and on the social construction of science in the West impinge on the study of relatedness cross-culturally. Much of this recent work has been concerned with a set of issues about 'nature' or 'biology' in Euro-American cultures.

A central theme running through this volume is the relationship between the 'biological' and the 'social'. If 'biology' or 'nature' has been the grounding for the 'social' in the West, and this relationship now appears to have been 'destabilised', can we put our understanding of this process of destabilisation to work in studies of non-Western cultures? What kind of relevance does this breaching of our foundational certainties have for how we understand and compare relatedness cross-culturally? Rather than beginning with a domain of kinship already marked out, the authors in this volume describe relatedness in terms of indigenous statements and practices – some of which may seem to fall quite outside what anthropologists have conventionally understood as kinship. The chapters which follow suggest not only that biology does not everywhere have the kind of foundational function it has in the West, but that the boundaries between the biological and the social which, as Schneider demonstrated, have been so crucial in the study of kinship are in many cases distinctly blurred, if they are visible at all. These new understandings may force us to conclude that kinship needs to be reinvented in a post-modern, or – to use Bruno Latour's (1993) term – 'non-modern' spirit.

A note on 'relatedness'

It should be clear from the outset that this is a book with a particular mission. That mission is to bring together two trends in recent anthropology. One trend involves the investigation not just of kinship, but of 'nature' and wider knowledge practices in the West. The other, taking a broad and imaginative view of what might be included under the rubric 'kinship', describes the ethnographic particularities of being related in a specific cultural context. The authors collected here have all worked on one or both sets of problems.

The particular aim I have sketched necessarily involves constructing a selective version of anthropological history. In this introduction I highlight a set of issues revolving around the separation of biological and social aspects of kinship in anthropology, and I trace one particular thread of continuity in recent work. If in places the argument appears dismissive of previous renditions of kinship, this is unintended. I take it for granted that in order to say something differently one constructs rather partial versions of what went before (I have made this explicit at various points below). But of course the new relies and builds on the old, and I make my full acknowledgement here to the insights and inspiration provided by the scholars I cite as well as many that I do not.

The version of anthropological history which I give below leans heavily on the work of David Schneider and employs a concept of culture which may seem more foreign to British readers than to those trained in the American anthropological tradition. British students (we like to think) have been accustomed to think of kinship in terms of the social – as in social rules, social organisation, social practice (see Bouquet, this volume). American cultural anthropology focuses on meaning. But my sense is that there has for a long time been an implicit rapprochement between these schools which can be attributed as much to the influence of Lévi-Strauss and Dumont as to the writings of American cultural anthropologists.

Particular versions of history sometimes demand different terms. The authors in this volume use the term 'relatedness' in opposition to, or alongside, 'kinship' in order to signal an openness to indigenous idioms of being related rather than a reliance on pre-given definitions or previous versions. In this introduction I have also used 'relatedness' in a more specific way in order to suspend a particular set of assumptions about what is entailed by the terms social and biological. I use 'relatedness' to convey, however unsatisfactorily, a move away from a pre-given analytic opposition between the biological and the social on which much anthropological study of kinship has rested. As a term, it is of course open to criticisms – many of which apply equally to 'kinship'. The obvious problem with relatedness is that either it is used in a restricted sense to convey relations in some way founded on genealogical connection, in which case it is open to similar problems as kinship, or it is used in a more general sense to encompass other kinds of social relations, in which case it becomes so broad that it is in danger of 'becoming analytically vacuous' (Holy 1996: 168).[1] Readers will perceive that 'relatedness' offers no neat solutions for the comparative endeavour – merely that its use has enabled me to suspend one set of assumptions, and to bracket off a particular nexus of problems, in order to frame the questions differently. 'Relatedness' makes possible comparisons between Iñupiat and English or Nuer ways of being related without relying on an arbitrary distinction between biology and culture, and without presupposing what constitutes kinship.

Issues about the natural and the social are of course central to two other areas to which anthropologists have recently given much attention: the body and gender (see, for example, Broch-Due, Rudie, and Bleie 1993; Lambek and Strathern 1998). As I discuss below, the parallel is hardly coincidental. But the study of the body and of gender in anthropology can be seen as part of a shift *away* from kinship in anthropology. One purpose of this volume is to confront these issues head on within the frame of kinship, rather than taking a more circuitous route via gender or the body. The volume thus reiterates in a new way a very old tenet of anthropology – the centrality of kinship.

This collection also reiterates an ambitious commitment to the *comparative* study of kinship in the face of an increasing emphasis on cultural particularism. The reluctance to engage in generalisation is one effect of the sustained attack on the concept of kinship and the increasing attention given by anthropologists to the diversity of the meanings of kinship (cf. Holy 1996: 172–3) – although, as Schneider noted, 'symbols and meanings can be compared just as easily as modes of family organisation, the roles of seniors to juniors, or the methods of agriculture' (1972: 48; cited in Marshall 1977: 656). And, as Andrew Strathern and Michael Lambek (1998: 23) remind us, ethnographic work is always at least implicitly comparative in that the society of the anthropologist is inescapably present. In this volume the analytic language of kinship, as well as certain Euro-American everyday practices and discourses of kinship, explicitly fall within the comparative frame.

It is noteworthy that there has been almost no prominent collection of essays devoted to the cross-cultural comparison of kinship since the publication of Jack Goody's edited volume *The Character of Kinship* in 1973. There have of course been many innovative studies since. But these have either focused on kinship in a local or regional ethnographic context, or have made something else – gender, personhood, houses, bodies, death, procreation – the main object of comparison, with kinship emerging as a prominent subsidiary theme.[2] I address the reasons for this long gap in what follows. But, if nothing else, it may be timely to attempt a fresh look at kinship in comparative perspective.

My introduction is thus clearly not intended to provide a history of the anthropological study of kinship since the nineteenth century. That task has been undertaken by others (e.g. Kuper 1988). Nor do I offer either a new introductory textbook (e.g. Barnard and Good 1984; Holy 1996; Parkin 1997) or a comprehensive survey of the various trends in kinship studies since the 1970s (e.g. Peletz 1995).[3] Instead, I attempt a particular take on 'whatever happened to kinship?' – a take in which David Schneider has a pivotal role, poised as he was, in a unique way, between the old-style kinship and the new.

Whatever happened to kinship?

Schneider is a key figure for a number of reasons. Although he was at one time part of the formalist tradition of kinship studies (see, for example, *Matrilineal Kinship* (1961), which he co-edited with Kathleen Gough), his later work was highly innovative. His *American Kinship: A Cultural Account*, which was first published in 1968 and reprinted in a second edition in 1980, was highly influential for later culturalist analyses of kinship – a point which I take up below. A crucial aspect of Schneider's influence is the role played in his writings by 'nature' or 'biology' and its separation from law, which is itself encompassed by 'culture'. The significance of biology in his writings is often highly contradictory (cf. J. A. Barnes 1973: 63–5), but these contradictions are at the heart of understandings of kinship and of wider knowledge practices in Euro-American cultures. The distinction between the biological and the social is also central to the analyses of local cultures of relatedness presented in this volume, and it is for this reason that I dwell on it at some length here.

Schneider's *A Critique of the Study of Kinship* (1984) can be read as a commentary on his earlier monograph *American Kinship: A Cultural Account* (1980). In the first book he outlined American kinship as a cultural system, explicating its symbolic logic. This was in many ways a path-breaking work, exemplifying a symbolic approach to culture. Schneider argued that sexual reproduction was a core symbol of kinship in a system which was defined by two dominant orders, that of nature, or substance, and that of law, or code. The sexual union of two unrelated partners in marriage provided the symbolic link between these two orders. It resulted in children connected to their parents through blood ties, or 'shared biogenetic substance', symbolising 'diffuse, enduring solidarity'. The idiom of nature was crucial to American kinship: 'The family is formed according to the laws of nature and it lives by rules which are regarded by Americans as self-evidently natural' (1980: 34). Here sexual intercourse had a critical symbolic role:

All of the significant symbols of American kinship are contained within the figure of sexual intercourse, itself a symbol of course. The figure is formulated in American culture as a biological entity and a natural act. Yet throughout, each element which is culturally defined as natural is at the same time augmented and elaborated, built upon and informed by the rule of human reason, embodied in law and in morality. (P. 40)

The role of the 'natural' or 'biological' here is telling. As Franklin comments, at least three different 'natures' emerge from Schneider's analysis of American kinship beliefs: biology, as in 'shared biogenetic substance'; nature, as in 'what animals do'; and human nature, as in 'man is a special part of nature' (1997: 54). The contradictions between these different 'natures', however, remain unexplored in Schneider's work. Franklin (1997: 54–5) demonstrates the tension in Schneider's analysis between 'nature' as a coherent symbolic idiom in American kinship, and 'nature' or 'biology' as a separate and distinct realm of scientific facts. As Schneider wrote in 1968:

These biological facts, the biological prerequisites for human existence, exist and remain. The child does not live without the milk of human kindness, both as nourishment and protection. Nor does the child come into being except by the fertilised egg which, except for those rare cases of artificial insemination, is the outcome of sexual intercourse. These are biological facts ... There is also a system of constructs in American culture about those biological facts. That system exists in an adjusted and adjustable relationship with these biological facts.
But these biological constructs which depict these biological facts have another quality. They have as one of their aspects a symbolic quality, which means they represent something other than what they are, over and above and in addition to their existence as biological facts and cultural constructs about biological facts. (1980: 116)

Franklin observes how such passages indicate that Schneider in fact preserved the same distinction he started with:

On the one hand, Schneider was arguing that there is no such thing as a biological fact *per se* in American kinship systems – there are only cultural interpretations of them. On the other hand, he was also arguing that there *are* 'natural facts' within science which are true and which are separate from the cultural constructions of them. (1997: 55; original italics)

A similar problem underlies Schneider's later work, *A Critique of the Study of Kinship* (1984; see Carsten 1995a). Here Schneider subjected the history of the study of kinship to the same kind of analytic scrutiny he had previously applied to American kinship, and demonstrated how sexual procreation was central to anthropological definitions of kinship – in this respect his argument reiterated one that had already been made by Needham (1971a).[4] Schneider showed that this was an indigenous assumption in Euro-American folk beliefs about kinship which had been imported into anthropological analysis. It was hardly news, however, that sexual procreation was not necessarily central to local idioms of relatedness – notably in the famous example of the Trobrianders, or in the case of the Yapese whom Schneider himself studied, where the link between coitus and procreation in humans was reportedly not made (see Malinowski 1929; Leach 1967; Spiro 1968; Schneider 1984; Delaney 1986; Franklin 1997). If 'kinship' was not the same thing in different cultures, then the comparative endeavour of anthropology failed, because like was quite simply not being compared with like. Schneider, like Needham before him, concluded that 'there is no such thing as kinship' (Needham 1971a: 5), and that the discrete domains into which anthropologists divided up the world – kinship, economics, politics, and religion – had to be abandoned. His argument thus had particular relevance for the comparative study of kinship.[5]

Although Schneider took the discussion about the role of biology in the anthropological study of kinship rather further than he had in *American Kinship*, he still seemed to hold back from abandoning the very separation which he was investigating – that between culture and biology:

[T]he point remains that culture, even were it to do no more than recognize biological facts, still adds something to those facts. The problem remains of just what the sociocultural aspects are, of what meaning is added, of where and how that meaning, as a meaning rather than as biological fact, articulates with other meanings. (1984: 199)

Schneider's *Critique* was very successful in demonstrating the Euro-centric assumptions at the heart of the anthropological study of kinship. This was undoubtedly one of the many nails in the coffin of kinship, and contributed to the shift away from the study of kinship in the 1970s. It was somewhat paradoxical therefore that his earlier work on American kinship, flawed as it was, provided a highly fertile model for later culturalist accounts of kinship, one to which Strathern (1992a: xviii) and others have made clear their debt. Schneider is a pivotal figure in the study of kinship precisely because of the link between these two projects – and this provides a crucial distinction from Needham's writings. Perhaps it is not surprising in retrospect that Schneider's stronger position, which focused on the 'meanings' of kinship rather than on formal properties, seems to have offered greater possibilities for the future study of kinship. By illuminating the role of nature or biology in American folk versions of kinship *and* in anthropological analyses of kinship, and by beginning to explore the connections between these two strands, Schneider left a particularly fruitful avenue for later scholars to pursue.

Marilyn Strathern claimed David Schneider as 'anthropological father' to *After Nature* (1992a: xviii), and this link is reiterated in Schneider's own comment on his *American Kinship* – one which might almost be taken as the epigraph for Strathern's book:

> Nor did I notice until almost after it was all done how much the Euro-American notion of knowledge depended on the proposition that knowledge is *discovered*, not invented, and that knowledge comes when the 'facts' of nature which are hidden from us mostly, are finally revealed. Thus, for example, kinship was thought to be the social recognition of the actual facts of biological relatedness ... The idea that culture, and knowledge, is mostly a direct reflection of nature is still very much with us, however inadequate that view is. (1995: 222; original italics).

The central point of Strathern's argument is that nature can no longer be taken for granted in late-twentieth-century English culture. In Thatcherite Britain, the effects of technological developments – particularly the new reproductive technologies – and the extension of consumer choice to domains in which such choice had not previously applied, have resulted in a destabilisation of nature.

> Nature, at once intrinsic characteristic and external environment, constituted both the given facts of the world and the world as context for facts ... Although it could be made into a metaphor or seen to be the object of human activity, it also had the status of a prior fact, a condition for existence. Nature was thus a condition for knowledge. It crucially controlled, we might say, a relational view between whatever was taken as internal (nature) and as external (nature). (1992a: 194)

What Strathern calls the 'modern cycle' involved a new conceptualisation of the ground for knowledge. In this new conceptualisation, nature does not disappear – in fact it becomes more evident – but its 'grounding function' is lost through being made explicit. If, for example, one considers the effects of the new reproductive technologies, which are often claimed to be merely 'assisting nature', then kin relationships, which in the past would have been seen as having their basis in nature, and could then be socially recognised – or not – may now be seen as either socially constructed or as natural relations which are assisted by technology. As Strathern (1992a: 195–6; 1992b) makes clear, the significant shift is that what was taken to be natural has become a matter for choice; nature has been, as she puts it, 'enterprised-up'. The more nature is assisted by technology, and the more the social recognition of parenthood is circumscribed by legislation, the more difficult it becomes to think of nature as independent of social intervention (1992b: 30). It follows from this that knowledge itself, which previously was seen as 'a direct reflection of nature', as Schneider put it, no longer has such a grounding in nature. It is not just nature, then, but knowledge itself which has been destabilised.

Kinship has a critical role in these shifts in knowledge practices precisely because, in the English view, kinship is defined as being the meeting place of nature and culture (Strathern 1992a: 87). Kinship facts can be seen as simultaneously part of nature and part of culture. Kinship performed a kind of dual function – it was based in a nature that was itself regarded as the grounding for culture, and it also provided an image of the relation between culture and nature (ibid. 198).

Strathern explores the cultural effects of 'the demise of the reproductive model of the modern epoch', where individuals can no longer be placed simultaneously in different contexts as social constructions and as biologically given (1992a: 193). Future technological developments, such as the mapping of the human genome, suggest that the shift from nature to choice will further destabilise the reproductive model. In the endless proliferation of a highly politicised discourse about consumer preference, new reproductive technologies, and gene therapies, it becomes possible to imagine 'a cultural future that will need no base in ideas about human reproduction' (p. 198).

Strathern's conclusion highlights once again the centrality of pre-given biological facts to Western knowledge practices and kinship relations. The cultural construction of a scientific realm of 'natural facts' has, of course, itself been made the subject of study by historians of science. Thus, for example, Haraway's (1989, 1991) work on primatology demonstrates how the boundaries between nature and culture are much more permeable than either biological or social scientists might suppose. The 'traffic between nature and culture' (1989: 15), which she illustrates through particular histories of the relationships between primates and those who studied them, puts into question the role of 'biological facts' as a domain separate from culture. Here scientific facts are shown not simply as 'pure truths', placidly awaiting discovery in a natural world, but as actively constructed by scientists whose work practices, gendered identities, and career paths situated them in particular historical and cultural milieus.

The view that scientific facts are as much made as they are discovered has radical implications because it runs directly counter to Western assumptions about the 'natural world'.[6] As Franklin observes, the fact that the science of biology itself admits no distinction between physical phenomena and the study of these phenomena marks a telling difference from social sciences such as anthropology.

The conflation of the object to be known with the discipline of its observation and description ... performs the collapsing of knowledge with its object distinctive of modern Western scientific ways of knowing. Indeed, that is the definitively scientific 'collapse': that objective knowledge in the sciences is so transparent it is isomorphic with the reality it describes (1997: 56).

Franklin argues that in the West the 'facts' of biology symbolise not just certain kinds of relationships called kinship ties, but the 'possession of a particular form of knowledge which offers a particular access to truth' (p. 208). There is a crucial link between a category of relations which is regarded as particularly powerful (and whose power is derived from biological reproduction) and the power of science to determine the facts of this reproduction. It is significant that Franklin situates her study of women's experience of IVF (in vitro fertilisation) treatment in two British infertility clinics in the late 1980s in the context of the debate around the 'social' construction of 'natural' facts in the anthropological literature, particularly the discussion of procreation beliefs. Hers is one among a number of recent works to explore the cultural implications of reproductive medicine and the new technologies of reproduction (see, for example, Edwards et al. 1993; Franklin and Ragoné 1998a; Ginsburg and Rapp 1991, 1995; Martin 1987, 1991; Ragoné 1994). At the centre of these studies is a project of 'defamiliarising' the natural basis of human procreation and reproduction (Franklin and Ragoné 1998b: 4), which, of course, has been closely linked to the emergence of a distinctive feminist anthropology. Schneider had already demonstrated that the status of the 'natural' in the anthropological literature on kinship was open to question. It could now be shown to be equally 'displaced' in English and American social life (see Franklin 1997: ch. 1).

Franklin illuminates the same kind of shifts in knowledge practices as those discussed by Strathern. The significant effect of the new reproductive technologies in terms of how knowledge is understood is that nature and technology become mutually substitutable. Technology is described in the literature provided to patients as giving nature a 'helping hand'; this capacity of technology is 'just like' nature (Franklin 1997: 209–10). Biology, in the sense of scientific knowledge, has its own generative power, and this is evidenced in the new technologies. Simultaneously, reproductive biology is denaturalised – it can be assisted by technology. Instead of a naturally given sequence of events, reproduction becomes an 'achievement' (Franklin 1998: 103). Science can no longer be viewed as extra-cultural; kinship is no longer defined against 'natural', 'biological' facts; it is no longer 'given' (Franklin 1997: 210–13).

Recent investigations of the articulation of biology and kinship in Euro-American contexts have not only focused on reproductive technologies. The place of biology and procreation has also been at the centre of studies of gay and lesbian kinship in America. Weston (1991, 1995) discusses coming-out stories which reveal that 'blood ties' are described as temporary and uncertain in the light of the disruptions to, and severance of, kinship ties experienced by gays who declare their homosexuality to their families. Meanwhile 'chosen families' of friends are invested with certainty, depth, and permanence, and spoken about in an idiom of kinship by those whose experience of biological kin has been thoroughly disrupted. This implies a view of kinship which, by displacing biology, turns the conventional understandings on their head – although Strathern underscores how the critique of gay kinship actually consists of making explicit 'the fact that there was always a choice as to whether or not biology is made the foundation of relationships' (1993: 196; cited in Hayden 1995: 45).

Investigating procreation in the context of lesbian relations, Hayden (1995) argues that, far from being displaced as a symbol, biology is here mobilised in myriad new ways. She outlines various strategies employed by lesbian co-mothers in order to equalise their claims and legitimate their relations to the child. These include giving the child the names of the co-parents in hyphenated form, emphasising the co-parents' joint decision to bring up the child, and the partner performing the insemination of the birth mother. Hayden discusses how lesbian co-mothers in these ways appropriate generative powers. She shows how other strategies suggest an abstraction of biogenetic substance from the identity of the donor, and a dispersal of biological connectedness. These strategies include both partners bearing a child through the use of the same donor, careful selection of the donor in order to produce a child who will physically resemble the co-mother, or the use of the brother of the non-biological parent as donor.[7] Hayden's exposition vividly conveys how, in her words, 'lesbian families' explicit mobilization of biological ties challenges the notion of biology as a *singular* category through which kin ties are reckoned' (1995: 45; original italics). Strathern claims that it is by rendering biology, or nature, explicit that its grounding function disappears. The disruptions which have occurred when biology is deployed to legitimate the claims of co-mothers seem to substantiate this thesis. For here biology no longer operates as a taken-for-granted or self-evident symbol. Instead, the meanings of blood ties, biogenetic substance, paternity, and generation, and their relation to each other, become contingent and variable (Hayden 1995: 56).

The writings I have discussed so far focus on how nature, or biology, and by implication kinship (which, in the indigenous view, could itself be read off from biology), are deployed in the West, and thus extend one part of Schneider's project. They are less directly concerned, however, with the questions raised in *A Critique of the Study of Kinship* about the future of the anthropological study of kinship and with specifically comparative studies. I have suggested that Schneider's work is crucial precisely because he demonstrated the links between these two sets of problems.

The 'denaturalisation' of kinship has been taken up by Yanagisako and Delaney (1995a), who explore the specificities of different natures and the implications of questioning 'nature' as a universal base. Most of the chapters in their collection focus on North America, and analyse how the discourses and practices of kinship, gender, ethnicity, and nationalism involve the naturalisation of identity and difference. In illuminating the naturalising force of Western kinship discourse, the authors of this volume once again explicitly acknowledge their debt to Schneider.[8] They take the symbolic analysis of kinship considerably further than Schneider in demonstrating how the plural meanings of kinship are themselves embedded in hierarchies of power, which these meanings also serve to naturalise. If kinship, after Schneider, could no longer be seen as the cultural elaboration of biological facts, and if the discrete domains of kinship, economics, politics, and religion no longer held, then what would kinship look like when shorn of its foundational assumptions (Yanagisako and Delaney 1995b: 11)? Once again they highlight the significance of Western hierarchies of knowledge which mark off science as a 'sacred domain' where truths residing in the natural world 'transcend agency' and are 'discovered by humans' (p. 13). The separation of science from culture serves to naturalise a particular hierarchy of knowledge and to prevent 'reading across domains' (ibid.).

A recognition that the boundaries that separate off domains, such as 'science', 'kinship', 'politics', 'economics', and 'religion', are cultural constructions offers the possibility of asking 'how culturally-specific domains have been dialectically formed and transformed in relation with other cultural domains, how meanings migrate across domain boundaries, and how specific actions are multiply constituted' (ibid.). These authors show that it is possible to abandon the foundational assumptions that have defined analytic domains, such as kinship, without abandoning 'the study of the meanings and relations previously confined to those domains' (Yanagisako and Delaney 1995b: 11). Indeed, the holistic project which anthropology has conventionally set for the study of 'other' cultures has involved just such a tracing of phenomena through the myriad contexts in which they occur – the most famous example being Mauss's (1966) argument that the gift constituted a 'total social phenomenon' which was at once political, religious, and economic.

In the remainder of this introduction I explore some of the interconnections among the chapters which follow, returning in the concluding sections to the implications of the work I have discussed so far for the study of relatedness in non-Western cultures. Although the chapters focus on different local contexts of relatedness, many of the themes which emerge are held in common. I highlight these as 'processual aspects of kinship', 'everyday practice', 'gender', 'substance', the 'social and the biological', and 'kinship as academic discourse'. The headings are intended as a means to explore the possibilities of a post-Schneiderian comparative study of relatedness.

The process of kinship

An increasing dissatisfaction with the formalism of much of the literature on kinship was one cause of the move away from kinship as a field of study from the 1970s onwards. Formalist approaches omitted not only some of the crucial experiential dimensions of kinship, including its emotional aspects but also its creative and dynamic potential. As Malinowski had famously put it,

The average anthropologist ... has his doubts whether the effort needed to master the bastard algebra of kinship is really worth while. He feels that, after all, kinship is a matter of flesh and blood, the result of sexual passion, and maternal affection, of long intimate daily life, and of a host of personal intimate interests. (1930: 19)

What is striking, however, is how taken for granted formalist assumptions have been (e.g. Needham 1971a, b). The authors in this collection reject a highly formal analysis, emphasising local practices and discourses of relatedness, and demonstrating how these impinge on and transform each other.

The accounts of Stafford, Lambert, and Hutchinson show how different the 'patrilineal' systems of Chinese, Rajasthani, and Nuer kinship are from the classical accounts. Stafford demonstrates how the division between lineage and family in classic studies of Chinese kinship,

and the exclusion of domestic ties from patrilineal kinship, has limited
an understanding of Chinese relatedness, particularly by obscuring the
importance of ties between women and their children. Instead, Stafford
discusses the importance of two cycles of reciprocity in the construction
of relatedness. The cycle of *yang* connotes the mutual obligation
between parents and children, and crucially includes not just birth
children but also foster children – in other words, *yang* is not just about
patrilineal descent, for this cycle can exist in the absence of descent,
while a failure of *yang* may terminate descent. As Stafford emphasises,
this cycle consists of small everyday interactions involving women, and
is essential to the lived experience of relatedness; it is comparable to
more obviously processual aspects of relatedness documented elsewhere
in this volume. The second cycle is the cycle of *laiwang*, which involves
reciprocal ceremonial transactions between those who do not consider
themselves genealogical kin. Here Stafford uses the term 'relatedness' to
include *any* kind of relation – including, for example, ties between
neighbours or co-villagers which would not normally be considered as
kinship. As Stafford points out, the justification for using relatedness in
this very broad sense is that the boundaries between different forms of
relatedness may in fact be more malleable than might be assumed, and
here he highlights parallels with the Nuer and Rajasthani cases considered by Hutchinson and Lambert. The inclusion of these two overlapping cycles of reciprocity, and a recognition of the importance of
'non-kinship' ties in an understanding of Chinese relatedness, modifies
the traditional restriction of Chinese kinship to a lineage paradigm. It
demonstrates that women are not just considered as non-persons, outsiders to the system, and allows a much more dynamic understanding of
Chinese relatedness.

Stafford also shows how the use of a broader concept of relatedness
may facilitate comparisons between supposedly more 'fixed', descent-
based kinship, such as the Chinese case, with examples of bilateral
kinship which have long been considered inherently 'fluid'. He rejects
the contrast between a 'fixed' unilineal model and a 'fluid' bilateral one,
which he shows to be more a product of a distinct type of kinship
analysis than of the actual dynamics of relatedness. The point that
restricting the analytic frame for kinship also restricts the scope of the
comparative endeavour is also made by Lambert in this volume.
Showing us that, in the Chinese case, very little is in fact 'given by birth'
illuminates similarities with 'non-unilineal kinship'. The contributions
of Bodenhorn and Edwards and Strathern make clear how 'bilateral
kinship' is amenable to a process of adding on or lopping off kinship
connections – indeed, both processes are a necessary part of this kind of

relatedness. Both Iñupiaq and English relatedness involve a continuous process of becoming connected to people, in the former case through naming, adoption, and marital relations, in the latter through a complex process of interweaving social and biological idioms of being related.

This dynamic quality is captured most vividly by Astuti in her description of Vezo relatedness. Here we are shown, through the eyes of an old Vezo man, how relatedness can only be understood as a dynamic process. As a young man, Dadilahy is part of a network of bilateral kin, a kindred, which can be imaged using the Iban metaphor of the concentric circles spreading out from a pebble thrown into water. The ripples gradually diminish until they merge with the background in the same way as one's recognition of kin gradually fades as kin become more distantly connected. As an old man, Dadilahy sees himself as the apex of a pyramid of ties to his children and grandchildren stretching through his daughters and sons and their spouses – and Astuti recalls another image from the Iban, that of a cone-shaped casting-net with Dadilahy at the top (cf. Freeman 1970: 68–9). Here Dadilahy sees himself as the source of numerous ties which he himself has created and which include men and women, affines and kin. In death, the image of relatedness changes again, for the Vezo are divided after death into *raza*, 'kinds', or patrilineal groups, which are buried together in the tomb. Astuti shows how the process of relatedness involves a transformation from 'kindred' to 'cognatic descent group' to 'patrilineal descent group' which accompanies the process of moving from youth to old age to death for particular Vezo women and men. Her account demonstrates the partialness of trying to understand Vezo kinship as either simply bilateral or simply unilineal. Indeed, it is the subtle transformation of one into the other, or the articulation of these different modes, which is not only particularly intriguing but also captures the essential dynamic of Vezo relatedness and its interconnections with personhood.

It is not accidental that a view of relatedness as essentially processual should also highlight the importance of children, who not only 'represent continuity' (in the classic formulation), but who may be said to embody processes of growth, regeneration, and transformation. Both Stafford and Astuti describe the importance of having children in Chinese and Vezo relatedness, while Bodenhorn discusses how Iñupiat continually 'add on' ties to children through adoption (which does not necessarily preclude maintaining ties between a child and her birth parents). As Bodenhorn emphasises, children are not merely passive recipients of these processes but themselves initiate them. What the Iñupiat see as crucial to the creation and viability of such ties is love – implying perhaps that parents who lose their children, because the children decide to move elsewhere or cease to recognise them as parents, have a limited capacity to love.

Constructing relatedness through everyday practice

There is a further dimension to the omission of women and children from the analytic frame, and this connects with Stafford's point about how the lack of participatory fieldwork in China has crucially affected the view we have of Chinese kinship. The formalisation of kinship as a field of study involved the separation of what Fortes termed the 'domestic domain' from the 'politico-jural domain' (1958, 1969). Both Malinowski and Fortes saw the nuclear family as a universal social institution which was necessary to fulfil the functions of producing and rearing children (see Malinowski 1930; Fortes 1949). They both had a keen interest in domestic family arrangements, which may in part be attributed to the influence of Freudian psychology (see Fortes 1974, 1977). Fortes also saw kinship as 'an irreducible principle', the souce of basic moral values (1949: 346; 1969). His study *The Web of Kinship among the Tallensi* (1949) devoted considerable space to relations between parents and children, sibling relations, and domestic family arrangements. The separation which he himself had introduced between two domains of kinship could, however, be taken to imply that the social context in which the nuclear family was set – in other words, wider kinship arrangements – carried greater analytic significance. The politico-jural domain of kinship – public roles or offices ordered by wider kinship relations, and the political and religious aspects of kinship – were described analytically as the source of cohesion in the societies anthropologists studied, and hence what rendered kinship of interest for anthropology (see e.g. Radcliffe-Brown 1950).

It is thus perhaps not surprising that the comparative study of kinship could devote relatively little attention to intimate domestic arrangements and the behaviour and emotions associated with them.[9] These were assumed to be to a large degree universally constant or a matter for psychological rather than anthropological study. If one considers Fortes's meticulous ethnography, it is quite paradoxical that the very data which documented in detail the small everyday acts of constructing relatedness between women, or between women and children, might be more or less excluded from the frame if his more general injunctions were taken seriously. Stafford makes a similar point with reference to scholars of China, who very early on noted the problems and omissions involved in operating with a descent-based paradigm for Chinese kinship.

However they are transmitted, these omissions may have important implications, as Stafford and Lambert both indicate, leading to a rather lopsided vew of what kinship is 'about' – lineages in the Chinese case, marriage and descent in the Indian one. For Iñupiat, as Bodenhorn emphasises, personal autonomy and the rejection of pre-given ties of dependence mean that relatedness is continuously 'under construction' through precisely these kinds of everyday acts. Here it is difficult to see what relatedness would be about at all without the everyday activities of women and men as they engage in the labour process. In a similar way, I have shown elsewhere (Carsten 1995a, 1997) how Malay relatedness is created both by ties of procreation and through everyday acts of feeding and living together in the house. Both procreative ties and shared feeding create shared substance or blood in a community largely made up of migrants. Here the small acts of hospitality and feeding, together with longer-term sharing of food and living space which fostering and marriage involve, create kinship where it did not previously exist. Women and houses may be said to be central both to the 'domestic' process of creating relatedness inside houses, and to the larger 'political' process of integrating newcomers and the establishment and repro-duction of whole communities.

Thus a focus on what I have called the 'everyday' – small, seemingly trivial, or taken-for-granted acts like sharing a meal, giving a dish of cooked food to a neighbour, dropping in to a nearby house for a quiet chat, a coffee, and a betel quid – has provoked a careful examination of the symbolic and social significance of the house (see Carsten and Hugh-Jones 1995) as well as a reappraisal of what constitutes 'the domestic' and the boundary between the domestic and the political (see also Moore 1988; Strathern 1984; Yanagisako 1979, 1987).

Gender and kinship

This volume was intended to address the question 'Where is the study of kinship at the end of the 1990s going?' rather than explicitly to focus on gender. There is a sense, however, in which all the contributors have implicitly or explicitly taken account of recent work on gender, and indeed would argue that the terms of studying kinship or relatedness are necessarily reformulated by that work (see Collier and Yanagisako 1987; Howell and Melhuus 1993; Yanagisako and Collier 1987).

The central concern of much recent work on the cross-cultural study of gender has been the extent to which gender identity is performative rather than biologically given (see Astuti 1998; Broch-Due et al. 1993; Butler 1990, 1993; Errington 1990; Moore 1988, 1993, 1994; Morris

1995; Strathern 1988). This discussion is highly relevant to an analysis of kinship partly because it in many ways replicates an analogous discussion on the nature of kinship which focuses on the articulation of social and biological aspects of kinship. And this only underlines the extent to which the anthropological study of gender in the 1970s and 80s in many respects encompassed the study of kinship (see Yanagisako and Collier 1987). The distinction between what is 'made' and what is 'given', and the degree to which kinship is necessarily predicated on the 'biological facts' of procreation, are discussed in the chapters by Bodenhorn, Bouquet, Edwards and Strathern, and Lambert in this volume. The starting point of Middleton's chapter on Karembola notions of relatedness makes clear the interconnections between these two strands of recent scholarship.

Middleton notes how the issue of maternity and the bond between mother and child have been neglected in anthropological studies of both gender and kinship. In part, this absence may be regarded as an effect of the explicit exclusion of the domestic, intimate world of women and children from the study of kinship which I discussed above. In part, as Middleton notes, it is linked to the way motherhood has been construed by anthropologists as having an apparently direct and obvious relation with the natural world (see J. A. Barnes 1973). For the Karembola, the image of motherhood is central to relatedness, and is also the key idiom of rank and power, but it is not restricted to women. This of course immediately problematises the status of motherhood as intrinsically 'biological' or 'domestic'. To be powerful, men imagine themselves as the mothers of other men. Middleton discusses what is meant when Karembola men describe themselves, or are described by others, as 'mothers' or 'mother people'. Noting in what ways such statements can be characterised as metaphorical, and what is left out by such a depiction, she asks how Karembola men are mothers – by what performative acts do they construct male motherhood? Paradoxically, however, men's performance of motherhood can only be made manifest by reference to the sexed bodies of livestock or women. Although male motherhood must be performed to become manifest, this performance aims to elicit what already lies hidden within men – here Middleton makes comparative use of Indonesian and Melanesian idioms of source and display. For the Karembola, she argues, men and women are really different kinds of people, and their difference is rooted in their bodies.

Middleton discusses how rank for the Karembola rests on the articulation of two kinds of marriage, asymmetric alliance and patrilateral parallel cousin marriage (another example of the way in which new anthropological descriptions simultaneously refigure and encapsulate

the old). Karembola notions of relatedness, like those of the other
Malagasy people described in this volume, can be described as both
cognatic and patrilineal, 'unkinded' and 'kinded'. In this case, however,
patrilineality is not banished to the world of the tomb but is part of the
experience of relatedness for the living. Patrilateral parallel cousin
marriage keeps together male and female agnates – people thought of as
of the same kind; asymmetric alliance divides people of the same kind.
Here wife-givers are thought of as superior to wife-receivers, and the
idiom of cross-cousin marriage is used to construct an image of a ranked
social order in which the image of mothering is central. Karembola
kindedness, although in their view intrinsic, has to be performed, and as
with male motherhood, the performance aims to elicit what lies within.
During confinement and after giving birth to a first child, a Karembola
woman is fed and nurtured in her father's house. In these and other
nurturant acts, fathers and brothers materially demonstrate their kindedness with sisters and daughters, just as they demonstrate that they are
the source and root of the child. For subsequent births, the child's father
rivals his wife's agnates' claims to be the source of the child by taking on
'women's work' in rituals of couvade which, likewise, have meaning only
in relation to the intermediate term of the mother's sexed body giving
birth. Thus the performance of male motherhood, Middleton argues,
focuses on the sexed body of women who give birth to children. It relies
on the consubstantiality *and* the sexed difference of brother and sister.
Men cannot substitute for women, because it is women who have to give
birth, just as, when a man gives gifts of cattle to his sister and her
children, the cattle must be female, because only cows give birth.

In her subtle exposition of Karembola ethnography, Middleton demonstrates how, for the Karembola, the performance of gender as well
as the construction of the imagined polity rests on what she calls 'the
natural capacities of the female body'. She also makes clear, however,
that fertility is not an intrinsic value of women *per se*; women are not
everywhere accorded this value. Rather, in the particular context of the
Karembola ritual economy, women's value is linked to work which only
female bodies can perform. For Karembola, properties of women and
men are rooted in their bodies rather than being the product of relations.
And this suggests a refinement to a rather crude division between the
social constructionist view of gender and a biological determinist position. This refinement allows for performance while also admitting a
place for material bodies; it reminds us of a not very surprising fact –
that the construction of gendered difference may invoke or rest on what
particular people take to be the intrinsic 'natural capacities' of male or
female bodies.[10]

Substance and relatedness

I suggested above that there are parallels between the discussion about the extent to which gender is either biologically given or socially constructed and the debate about whether kinship is necessarily rooted in the biological facts of procreation. The articulation of the 'social' and the 'biological' is central to the way both gender and kinship have been constructed as academic domains. While these terms may in themselves seem quite unproblematic, precisely what is meant by them is not always clear. The possibility that the boundaries between the social and the biological are more permeable in people's discourse than might be assumed emerges from some of the statements made about shared substance which are examined in this volume.

A simplistic opposition between social and biological ties is rendered problematic by the Rajasthani practices and discourse analysed by Lambert. Lambert demonstrates the importance of various types of relatedness which are not based on procreative links. First, she discusses ties of 'village kinship' between those who originate from the same village and who, after marriage, move to the same locality; and she discusses ties to the mother's natal village, which are maintained regardless of caste. Secondly, Lambert describes formal ties of adoption which provide a woman with a set of honorary agnates in her conjugal village. These relations are considered permanent, and they extend for at least one generation. Significantly, this kind of relatedness is actually described – at least in some contexts – as superior to and purer than reproductive kinship, because it does not originate in the pollution of sexual intercourse.[11] It is also significant that the adoptive household must be one from which the adopted daughter can drink water – commensality is an essential part of this relationship. The local view is that the impossibility of sharing substance with certain people limits the possibility of establishing relatedness with them. However, Lambert's argument also suggests an implicit inference – that the process of sharing substance may create relatedness. A third kind of non-procreative relatedness is constituted by a less formal, more individual, and voluntaristic form of adoption. Finally, Lambert notes the existence of another type of formal adoptive relation which is initiated in order to secure a male heir.

While birthing practices emphasise the tie between a child and its locality, and the link with the lineage of the child's father, children are also said to share substance with their mother and siblings through ingestion of the mother's blood before birth, and breast milk after birth. These bodily substances are themselves described as transformed food. 'Consanguinity' is described locally in various ways. In its broadest sense, it includes not just shared blood but shared qualities and affects transmitted through bodily substances and the local micro-environment. While the milk of a mother establishes future relatedness, the milk of livestock belonging to the household is important in establishing and maintaining ties to lineage ancestors. In the case of those who die young, offerings of 'housemilk' can create ancestral ties. In this sense, Lambert suggests, milk expresses the 'historical depth' of relatedness.

Although Indian kinship has often been seen largely in terms of affinal relations, it is significant here that the food-sharing which is so central to adoptive relations, and to the mother–child bond, is described as creating consanguineal rather than affinal ties. It is also significant that 'consanguinity' and affection are, in local terms, mutually constituted – feeding expresses degrees of relatedness and marks bonds of affection. Perhaps unsurprisingly, the affective component of affinal relations is here considerably devalued, in contrast to that of 'consanguineal' (including adoptive) ties.

What emerges from this analysis is that there is a combination of sentiment, substance, and nurturance as grounds for relatedness. Instead of attributing relatedness to a single indigenous, 'substantialist' model, Lambert shows how affection, shared substance, and nurturance underlie all forms of relatedness, whether genealogically based or not. The different forms of relatedness she discusses form a continuum based on the varying presence of these different elements. At various points, however, we can also perceive cleavages within this continuum. Thus 'affinal' ties can be contrasted to 'consanguineal' ones (here taken to include ties of substance and a shared local micro-environment) in terms of their affective content. But it is also possible to juxtapose 'procreative kinship', comprising a narrowly conceived consanguineal and affinal element, to a more broadly based 'consanguineal' relatedness. Here Lambert suggests that the explicitly superior valuation of non-genealogical ties should alert us to their creative potential.

This exposition thus goes beyond a simple opposition between substance and code, or an equally simple assertion of their inseparability in the Indian context. And this is where the omissions in previous accounts of lineage-based kinship, which Lambert and Stafford both allude to, become significant. It is not that the principles implicit in lineages or marriage are unimportant, but that they leave a lot out. Lambert demonstrates how oversimple oppositions, like 'substance' and 'code', 'real' and 'fictive' kinship, 'biological' and 'social', may constrain our understanding of indigenous practices, which in certain contexts allow convertibility from one form of relatedness into another, or the creation of new ties.

Hutchinson's rendering of Nuer relatedness bears some striking parallels to the Rajasthani case, but with different emphases in the area of convertibility or 'unboundedness'. She describes first the importance of blood to Nuer idioms of relatedness and vitality, and how not only milk, semen, and sweat are described as forms of blood, but so too is a newborn child. The birth of a child implies the fusion of parental blood. Blood is convertible to food (in the form of milk), and food is converted to blood in the human body. Food is nutritionally assessed in terms of its blood content – milk being the most perfect food in these terms. Blood relatedness is created through the sharing of food. Ultimately, food and blood are destined to meet and mix in the soil. Hutchinson goes on to show how cattle and blood are complementary – cattle are the 'symbolic counters' for human blood. The vitality of cattle is equated to that of humans, and cattle can be used as mediators in human relations and can create new relations. Cattle sacrifices and exchanges ensure flows of human blood, for example at marriages, funerals, difficult births, or various kinds of purificatory rites. It is the blood of cattle which ensures movement in Nuer society, taking away pollution and creating new relations. Both cattle and people are similarly capable of extending their reproductive vitality.

The analysis of how blood, food, and cattle are connected in Nuer idioms of relatedness is in many ways reminiscent of the emphasis on processual aspects of kinship in other cultures which is documented elsewhere in this volume. Hutchinson's departure is to expand the analytic frame to include other 'substantive vectors' which move between people and create or sever social relations – money, guns, and paper. By doing so, she is able to connect practices and discourses of relatedness to wider socioeconomic circumstances and to explore the effects of prolonged political upheaval on Nuer kinship. Hutchinson demonstrates how Nuer oppose money to blood as sterile and implying transitory ties. This makes it an ideal medium with which to sever ties and to break connections which are seen to be negative and polluting. In contrast to their attitudes to money, Nuer liken paper to blood and cattle. Like blood, paper is a substance linked to superhuman powers – in this case the state. Hutchinson describes how paper has become a fetishised object in the absence of schools or educational institutions, symbolising Nuer estrangement from the state, embodying a potential to tap government powers, and signifying political allegiance.

Hutchinson's discussion of the impact of the state on idioms of relatedness has, of course, a wider relevance, as does her observation that for Nuer not all 'enduring social bonds' are positive or desirable. Her depiction of the impact of violent deaths in feuding and warfare, and her inclusion of infant mortality, infertility, and adultery in a consideration of relatedness, are pointed reminders of the negative underside of kinship. Although anthropological analyses have tended to privilege its positive and harmonious aspects, kinship is also about disconnection and disjunction – a point taken up by Edwards and Srathern in this volume.

Perhaps the most challenging aspect of Hutchinson's analysis is the inclusion of guns in a discussion of relatedness. Here we are confronted with Nuer glorification and fetishisation of guns, which are linked to male potency, beauty, and strength, an aesthetic which she links to their lack of power *vis-à-vis* the state. She shows how the disconnections created by guns are contrasted to deaths by spear. While the power of a spear issues directly from the bone of the person throwing it, and is internal to the person, guns are seen as external and impersonal. Death by spear creates a blood link between slayer and slain, and there is no doubt about the responsibility of the slayer. The precise source of death from a gun is likely to be more uncertain, and this has consequences in terms of the pollution risks, and hence the bonds of moral obligation, involved. However, guns do not only sever human relations, for in a surprising twist which demonstrates an extraordinary capacity to turn weapons of destruction into ideological sources of regeneration, guns are now widely used instead of cattle in bridewealth payments. Hutchinson describes how guns which are collectively owned by groups of brothers may thus reinforce bonds of dependence between kin.

There could hardly be a more striking case than this of the unpredictability of idioms of relatedness. Nuer use of not only blood and other bodily substances but also food, soil, cattle, paper, money, and guns to invoke and to rupture bonds of relatedness vividly demonstrates the central thesis of this volume – that indigenous statements and practices of relatedness are infinitely more dynamic and creative (or destructive) than an analysis of kinship predicated on a straightforward division between biological and social domains would imply. The conversion and transformability of types of substance demonstrate the permeability of boundaries between objects, persons, and types of relations. They suggest that narrowly defined analytic spheres of 'biological' and 'social' aspects of kinship are inadequate to describe or analyse cultures of relatedness.

'Biological' and 'social' kinship

I have highlighted a single theme running through the chapters in this volume – the distinction between social and biological aspects of kinship, and the 'articulation' of these with each other. The discussion of how such a distinction might operate in any particular culture has forced us to consider what we as anthropologists might mean when we employ these terms. These issues are directly confronted by Bodenhorn in her discussion of Iñupiaq relatedness, by Edwards and Strathern on English relatedness in Alltown, and by Bouquet in her discussion of a particular kind of intellectual discourse in the academic and museum world in Europe. But as I have shown, there is a clear sense in which these themes underlie other chapters in this volume too. The cycles of *yang* and *laiwang*, and their articulation with patrilineal ideology, discussed by Stafford; the critique of a performative view of gender offered by Middleton; statements and practices relating blood, food, and bodily substance analysed by Lambert and Hutchinson; Astuti's depiction of the articulation of cognatic and patrilineal versions of relatedness among the Vezo – all of these can be understood as dealing to a greater or lesser extent with these same issues.

To understand why these issues seem so central to an understanding of local cultures of relatedness, it may be helpful to return to Schneider's *Critique of the Study of Kinship*. I have suggested that this marked a watershed in kinship studies. After its publication, it was impossible to take for granted the centrality of kinship to anthropology. Schneider had comprehensively undermined the analytic foundations on which kinship as a domain of academic theorising rested. He had done so by showing that kinship was quite simply not understood in all cultures to be the same thing. The comparative endeavour of anthropologists was therefore invalid. But in a curious way, Schneider's critique both rested on, and simultaneously took for granted, a division into the 'social' and the 'biological' aspects of kinship. He did not explicitly challenge the value or validity of this distinction.

Schneider's central point was that kinship did not everywhere arise from the so-called natural facts of procreation. In some cultures sexual procreation was not described as the basis of kinship. Such a proposition, however, only undermines the foundations of the study of kinship if a prior analytic distinction – between the 'social' and the 'biological' – is held in place. And this brings me to the central question of this introduction: What is kinship? Can we define it in such a way as to leave scope for the inclusion of a broad range of relations and behaviour while yet taking account of Schneider's critique? Anthropologists generally claimed that they studied the 'social aspects' of a domain that was in the last analysis defined by biology. Schneider demonstrated that if biology was removed from this definition, the whole edifice collapsed. Thus Strathern's suggestion that one might 'take nature out of the equation' immediately has the force of destabilising the meaning of kinship: 'think of the Baruya of Melanesia, and one is thinking instead of a system premised on the idea that kinship is the social construction of social relations' (Strathern 1992a: 87). The ethnographic evidence in this volume suggests some alternatives to the conclusions offered by Schneider.

In the Rajasthani case which Lambert describes, we can see a more fluid progression or continuum between different kinds of relatedness than a straightforward opposition between biological and social kinship would imply. Here it is sometimes difficult to ascribe the various forms of relatedness which are important in the local context to one or other of these categories. Instead, the different forms might be said to have more of some qualities, less of others. For the Iñupiat, by contrast, as Bodenhorn demonstrates, relatedness is both central to social life and does not have an immutable base derived from what we would term biology. The high value placed by Iñupiat on personal autonomy leads them to deny the possibility of birth creating particular obligations of reciprocity. What are immutable are claims based on particular contributions in the work process. Links created by birth to particular parents are not described as determinant in themselves; rather there is a value placed on 'adding on' relations through life. This is achieved through the conferral of multiple names on children which are associated with both personal qualities and kinship relations, through widespread adoption practices, and by marriage. All of these practices emphasise the negotiable qualities of relatedness. Bodenhorn shows how relatedness is central to social life but also crucially involves a denial of permanence, often thought to be an essential quality of kinship (see Bloch 1973; Fortes 1969).

Iñupiaq relatedness allows for the coexistence of a high degree of individual autonomy together with a sense of moral obligation. But as Bodenhorn emphasises, this kind of relatedness, which is permanently 'under construction', is both hard work and stressful for participants. And this point about the hard work of making and maintaining relations, often overlooked by anthropologists, is one that emerges from other contributions in this volume. Recalling Stafford's rejection of a strong inherent contrast between unilineal and bilateral kinship, it is not surprising to find 'hard work' at the core of the cycles of reciprocity which he discusses in the context of Chinese relatedness. More significant perhaps is the fact that Bodenhorn has no difficulty in describing

Iñupiaq relatedness in a context in which, as she makes clear, the connection between birth and permanence is constantly denied. It is the work process which creates immutable rights. But this does not appear to mean that ties of relatedness are either irrelevant or unimportant. On the contrary, the fact that Iñupiat are constantly adding them on suggests their high value.

It would seem that we have here a case in which birth or procreation cannot simply be conflated with biology in the sense of a given natural order, nor – according to Iñupiat statements and practices – do birth or procreation define 'kinship'; but this neither lessens the power of relatedness in indigenous terms, nor does it inhibit or invalidate comparison with other cases in this volume. Such comparison is possible if we hold in suspension the analytic terms 'biological' and 'social', allowing that for any particular case these terms may be irrelevant or unhelpful, or that their apparent indigenous equivalents might differ quite markedly from their use in either Western academic discourse or in the many Western folk discourses in which they occur.

This suggestion recalls an earlier argument made by MacCormack and Strathern (1980) about an equally pervasive contrasting pair of terms in anthropology and in Western folk discourse – 'nature' and 'culture' (see Descola and Palsson 1996). The overlapping domains of nature/biology and culture/society underline the point. While it may be easy to find resemblances between what anthropologists call social and biological aspects of kinship and certain indigenous notions, such resemblances may be misleading. In any one of the examples in this volume, it is clear we would have to be careful to specify what each of these terms might mean, where the division between them might lie, and their relative permeability or boundedness, as well as their relation to indigenous models of knowledge production.[12] Hutchinson's description of the conversions which Nuer make between paper and blood, or guns and cattle, vividly conveys the potential to move between what we might call the 'biological' and the 'social' – suggesting, in fact, unity rather than separation. What the terms 'biological' and 'social' would actually mean to particular Nuer or Iñupiat is very much open to question. What we can say quite definitely is that a contrast between the social and biological is central both to the anthropological analysis of kinship and to indigenous northern European discourses and practices of relatedness. And this brings us to the contributions of Edwards and Strathern and of Bouquet in this volume. These authors are concerned to tease out the articulation of these two terms in the experience of being related in England and in the development of anthropological analysis.

Edwards and Strathern begin with what they rightly perceive as 'the impasse set up by imagining kinship as divided between the "social" and "biological" manifestations of itself'. In order to avoid endlessly reproducing the terms of this debate, instead of focusing on the *content* of the terms social and biological in Alltowners' idioms of relatedness, they explore their intersection or 'interdigitation'.

One resident of Alltown recounts her concerns about losing touch with an adopted cousin. Her husband has a similar concern over his father's half-brother. Both the half-brother and the adopted cousin are understood to have an attenuated link with their families – connected by less 'concentrated' ties than full members of their families. Here the relationships are limited in terms of their apparently weaker biological content. This tenuousness is increased when the cousin and the half-brother move away, disappear, or lose touch – and here a social idiom is brought into play. In their daily lives Alltowners continually add on and truncate their interconnections by bringing into play different kinds of link – belonging to a family, or to a place, various kinds of ownership, names, biological ties, etc. This material provides an interesting contrast with Bodenhorn's, for while the Iñupiat are concerned simply to add on relations, Alltowners also need to limit them. Severance may be caused by simple lack of interest, losing touch, or a trivial or more deliberate act of forgetting, or it may come about through the competing claims of social and biological connection. And here once again Edwards and Strathern point to a significant contrast with the Iñupiat. For the Iñupiat, there is no particular tension between biological and social links between persons; biology does not extend or cut off connections. In English statements about relatedness, however, social and biological claims both link and truncate each other. For example, when a gestational surrogate (who did not contribute the ovum) gave up the child to the commissioning mother, the 'gift' both connected the two mothers and divided them. The commissioning mother spoke in terms of immense gratitude of 'the greatest gift of all'; the surrogate signalled that she was giving up all future claims (cf. Ragoné 1994).[13]

Edwards and Strathern discuss how inclusion and belonging carry positive overtones in English sociality, and these are reproduced in academic renditions of kinship. In these renditions we hear little about the negative aspects of kinship or community – connection is seen as intrinsically desirable, while exclusion is cast in negative terms. Although anthropologists long ago pointed out the potentially infinite connections in kinship of the English kind, they have tended to see its limiting aspects as somehow external to kinship – provided by factors like residence, land ownership, etc. 'Social' action was seen as constraining 'natural' ties. Both Astuti's and Edwards and Strathern's chapters in this volume make reference to a mid-century debate in kinship theory over the 'problem' of cognatic kinship – that it failed to provide a basis for the definition of discrete groups, and hence could not, on its own, provide the organisational base for society (see Freeman 1961). The significance of unilineal descent in this theory was its emergence from a kind of 'natural' undifferentiated background of cognatic kinship, which was, as Strathern (1992c: 88) put it, equivalent to the creation of 'society' out of 'nature'. Astuti shows how, for the Vezo, the unilineal and the cognatic images capture different aspects of the process of relatedness and the achievement of personhood. But it would be quite problematic to see one of these as more 'social' or more 'natural' than the other. Nor would it make sense to consider the depletion of relatedness, which is part of the process of death for the Vezo, apart from the context of relatedness and personhood. Edwards and Strathern argue that, far from being extraneous, the self-limiting aspects of English kinship are an intrinsic part of kinship reckoning.

According to Edwards and Strathern, the combination and division of the social and biological elements is paradigmatic of kinship, as opposed to other forms of association in the Euro-American context. Kinship here is inherently 'hybrid'. They also suggest that there may be a connection between the process of recombination of heterogeneous elements in Euro-American kinship and the contemporary interest in networks which focuses on the interdigitation of the human and non-human, the material and the immaterial. In the theories of Bruno Latour, which they refer to, and which I take up below, networks signify the passage between domains of a different order, and, significantly, he singles out the divide between nature and society. Edwards and Strathern suggest that the interest in networks of this kind may well have something to do with indigenous kinship thinking. Their analysis takes us further in understanding why the separation of these two aspects should have been so central to the development of an anthropological analysis of kinship; it also holds suggestive possibilities for future studies of relatedness.

Kinship as academic discourse

Schneider attributed the significance of procreation in anthropological definitions of kinship to its centrality in Western practices and idioms of relatedness. Taking our cue from him, we may go further and suggest that the analytic separation of social and biological aspects of kinship was attributable to the importance of separating them in indigenous

European relatedness. The creative and dynamic potential of these Euro-American cultures of relatedness resides in part in the endless possibilities offered by the separation and recombination of their constituent biological and social elements, and in the further impact of this mode of reckoning on models of knowledge in general. Analytically, however, one might say that the possibilities offered by a theory of kinship which presumed their separation and precluded the possibility of their recombination were considerably more sterile. The effects of this analytic separation were profound and, as Bouquet demonstrates, to a great extent obscured by academic practice.

Drawing her inspiration from the work of Bruno Latour (1993), Bouquet argues that the division between social and biological aspects of kinship was a replication of another division – between the social and the material in anthropology. Bouquet takes historical ethnographic collections, which are often reckoned to be part of the prehistory of the discipline, to represent the material, and the study of kinship to represent the social. Noting that the demise of anthropology in the museum collections of Europe coincided with the establishment of the discipline in academic institutions, Bouquet suggests that this split replicates the divide in the study of kinship between its biological and social manifestations. She presents us with an ethnography of anthropological practice in the form of two figures – the genealogical diagram and the museum display – using the particular example of the ethnographic collection in Oslo.

Bouquet traces the separation between the domains of kinship study in the academy and the ethnographic collection in the museum, but her argument is that there was an underlying connection. What she calls 'pedigree thinking' informed both the museum collection and the study of kinship (see also Bouquet 1993a, 1996a). Both were strongly influenced by nineteenth-century philology, an attempt to trace the connections and origins of languages and people. The collection of kin terminology by Morgan, Rivers, and others, like that of ethnographic artefacts, was premised on the genealogical connectedness of human groups, an idea derived from philology. Real or putative genealogical connections provided the rationale for displays in ethnographic museums and made it possible to systematise the display of peoples of the world, just as they did for the display of kinship information in genealogical diagrams. Rivers's transformation of pedigree into the genealogical method, and the visual representation of genealogy in diagrams, were critical steps. The diagrams, Bouquet argues, were timeless artefacts which, crucially, had a biological referent. They *enabled* the separation of the 'biological' from the 'social' in the study of kinship.

Genealogical diagrams allowed kinship to be appropriated at home, just as the museum display represented the appropriation of ethnographic artefacts. The connecting lines of the diagram are 'silent constructions' enabling us to take in kinship 'at a glance', a display of the collection of kinship in counterpart to the collection of objects presented to us in the museum.

Bouquet's excursus into our own intellectual history has implications for contemporary practice. Kinship diagrams, as she notes, remain part of the presentation of ethnography. They represent a kind of 'purified vision' of the people from whom they were collected. Tracing the historical connections between the collection of kinship systems and ethnographic collections enables us not just to reconnect the museum and the academy but also to understand how the separation of the social and the biological in kinship became apparently self-evident. And this point is one which is central to this volume as a whole. Hutchinson's presentation of Nuer relatedness, Stafford's demonstration of how the process of fieldwork crucially affects our view of Chinese kinship, Astuti's attempt to match Vezo relatedness to classical anthropological models of bilateral or patrilineal kinship, Lambert's discussion of Rajasthani ethnography in counterpoint to other renditions of Indian society, Edwards and Strathern's detailed examination of the interdigitation of social and biological elements in English kinship – all are premised on making explicit the effects of intellectual practice. They reveal what Bouquet terms the 'awkward layers' of ethnography, the points of contact between indigenous cultures of relatedness and particular anthropological practice.

Conclusion: non-modern kinship

The use Bouquet makes of Bruno Latour's work *We Have Never Been Modern* (1993) offers some suggestive possibilities for the future of the study of kinship which are worth pursuing further. Latour argues that two processes have shaped the modern trajectory. The first is the 'work of purification', that is, the separation of nature and society, whereby nature is seen as pre-existing social intervention, to be discovered by humans, and society is seen as constructed by humans. Here the non-humanity of nature and the humanity of the social sphere reinforce each other (Latour 1993: 30). The second process is that of 'translation', or 'mediation', which 'creates mixtures between entirely new types of beings, hybrids of nature and culture' (p. 10). It is essential to the modern project that these two processes are kept separate from each other – if we consider them together, then we cease to be modern.

However, translation and purification are linked. Nature is actually constructed in the laboratory, although scientists claim to discover it. The separation between the natural world, which is in fact constructed, and the social world, which is sustained by things, is reinforced by the separation of the work of purification from the work of translation (p. 31).

The paradox is that the modern constitution actually allows the proliferation of hybrids – in spite of denying the possibility of their existence:

Everything happens in the middle, everything passes between the two, every-thing happens by way of mediation, translation and networks, but this space does not exist, it has no place. It is unthinkable, the unconscious of the moderns. (P. 37)

It is in this sense that Latour argues that 'we have never actually been modern. Modernity has never begun' (p. 47). In contrast, those whom the moderns construed as 'pre-moderns' 'were accused of making a horrible mishmash of things and humans, of objects and signs, while their accusers finally separated them totally – to remix them at once on a scale unknown until now' (p. 39). While 'pre-moderns' endlessly connect nature and culture, the 'moderns' reject these connections, refusing to admit the existence of hybrids.

Latour's argument is, of course, highly relevant to the separation between the social and the biological on which the study of kinship has been based, and which I have discussed here. Just as we can understand the processes set in train by the new reproductive technologies as part of the 'proliferation of hybrids', which in the end highlight the contra-dictions of the modern constitution, we can also understand some of the analyses presented in this volume as dwelling on the 'connections between nature and culture'. But Latour also offers a way out of this impasse in suggesting that it is the very division between nature and society which is the problem. If we abandon this division, admitting that 'culture is an artefact created by bracketing nature off' (p. 104), then the field of a 'new comparative anthropology' opens up which 'compares nature-cultures' (p. 96) for their similarities and differences in their constructions of the world. Abandoning what he calls the Great Divide offers the possibility of a truly holistic anthropology which focuses on the process of mediation and the production of hybrids.

Latour does not deny the materiality of the physical world or the efficacy of scientific practice. However science 'works', it does so not in its own terms, that is, by being disengaged from society, but despite being thoroughly part of culture and politics. That science and its object – 'nature' – cannot be bracketed off from society or politics is precisely the point which emerges from Strathern's and others' studies of reproductive technologies which I discussed above. What Latour advocates is a kind of holism which enables us to trace the connections between domains which we have tended to keep analytically separated.[14]

Latour's language and project are undoubtedly visionary – not to say idealist. The solution he holds out to us is probably too neat to be entirely convincing. Strathern has noted that, for anthropologists, following 'networks', in Latour's sense, will not always lead to a critique of those pure forms which are of concern to Euro-Americans or appear relevant to a social analysis of science and technology. Indeed, they may lead in other directions – kinship being one (1996: 521). In their chapter in this volume, Edwards and Strathern go further in suggesting that Latour's interest in networks might itself be another manifestation of indigenous Euro-American kinship thinking.

Abandoning the divide between nature and society makes evident other problems for the comparative project – on what basis will we pursue such comparison? And this of course was the very problem which led Schneider to advocate abandoning kinship altogether. Our use of the term relatedness in this volume has effectively broadened the comparative frame, as Stafford makes clear in chapter 2, but it simultaneously begs the question of whether like is being compared with like (cf. Barnard and Good 1984: 188–9; Holy 1996: 167–70). Holding one set of assumptions in view, we necessarily obscure others. This may suggest that certain kinds of comparison will continue to demand more formalist methods even if we refuse some of the old definitions.

Lambek's (1998) reminder of the widespread occurrence of the kind of cultural dualisms discussed here is pertinent (see n. 12, this chapter). There are good reasons why, rather than abandoning biology, we need to subject its uses in different cultures to closer scrutiny. The cross-cultural comparison of relatedness is undoubtedly one promising area for doing so. But we can only carry out such a project by simultaneously grasping how biology is used in our own – analytic and everyday – statements and practices. It is in this spirit that it may prove fruitful to juxtapose accounts such as those which Bouquet and Edwards and Strathern provide here with, for example, those of Bodenhorn or Middleton for the Iñupiat or Karembola. And it is in this spirit that I take Latour's call for a 'symmetrical anthropology' as marking out an avenue for further investigation.

Bouquet's contribution here, and Strathern's (1996) exploration of Latour's concept of 'network' and how networks are limited by concepts of ownership, which she and Edwards pursue in this volume, may be regarded as first steps in a 'new comparative anthropology'. What they offer is the possibility of exploring in the same comparative frame English, Iñupiaq, Malay, Chinese, Indian, or Malagasy ways of being related without relying on a very specific analytic distinction between biology and culture, and without making strong presuppositions about what constitutes kinship. It is because this distinction has been so central to the analysis of kinship that we may claim, if nothing else, to have placed their similarities and differences in a fresh light.

This is of course not to reveal some finite truth, but to engage in an intellectual process (cf. Strathern and Lambek 1998: 24). Others will no doubt pursue the implications of this argument further – both by subjecting the division between biology and culture to further interrogation, and by suspending other sets of assumptions. There is no truly authentic anthropological modelling of local cultures of relatedness. Nevertheless, our attempt to privilege these cultures of relatedness over classical anthropological versions of what constitutes kinship may also offer new possibilities of understanding how relatedness may be composed of various components – substance, feeding, living together, procreation, emotion – elements which are themselves not necessarily bounded entities but may overflow or contain parts of each other or take new forms. None of these necessarily has priority or a predefined content beyond that given to it by particular people. The only necessary quality to the combination of these elements in particular cultures of relatedness is that they incorporate the capacity to generate new meanings and new experiences of being related.

Notes

1 In a vein similar to my argument here, Marshall argues forcefully for an approach to kinship which 'allows us to view *all* connections among persons in a single framework so that we might learn what they have in common and what differentiates them' (1977: 649; original italics). His analysis shows how 'created kinship' among the Trukese has the potential to be transformed into biogenetic links, and that what these various forms of kinship have in common is the concept of sharing. It is somewhat unclear at what level he accepts the separation entailed in his proposition that 'Two logical possibilities exist in the realm of kinship that can be developed and elaborated symbolically: *natural* (biogenetic) links among persons and *cultural* (created) ties among persons' (p. 650; original italics; footnote omitted).

2 In the introduction to their volume *Bodies and Persons: Comparative Perspectives from Africa and Melanesia*, A. Strathern and M. Lambek (1998) note an increasing tendency either to confine comparison to particular regions or to take a very broad selection; they suggest that there has been a decline in works which are devoted to comparison between specific regions (but see Carsten and Hugh-Jones 1995).

3 It is interesting to note that the chapter headings of two recent British introductory texts – that of Holy (1996) and Parkin (1997) – suggest a view of kinship for the most part unchanged from the way students learnt it in Britain in the 1970s. The subject can seemingly still be encompassed by headings such as 'the family', 'descent', 'lineage theory', 'marriage', 'relationship terminology', 'alliance'. But even here there are signs of change. Holy's final chapter is an extended discussion which focuses on the role of procreation, the meanings of kinship, and the relationship between biology and culture. The work of Schneider and Strathern is central to his discussion (see 1996: 143–73). Holy states, 'The most significant development in the study of kinship has been the growing awareness of the cultural specificity of what were previously taken to be the natural facts on which all kinship systems were built' (p. 165).

4 On the vexed relationship between 'physical' and 'social' kinship, see also J. A. Barnes (1961, 1973); Beattie (1964); Gellner (1957, 1960).

5 Although my argument here focuses on Schneider, it is worth noting that he was only one among a number of anthropologists who subjected the whole idea of kinship as an autonomous system to a sustained critique. Most famously, Needham demonstrated how kinship and its various components – marriage, descent, incest, and terminologies – were so variable as to be no more than 'odd-job words' (1971a: 5). However, whereas Schneider's analysis led him to an iconoclastic position which suggested that the study of kinship should be abandoned, Needham argued for a more moderate move away from empirical generalisations. Advocating a logical analysis employing formal criteria which would allow more rigorous comparison, he noted that such criteria would also make comparison more difficult (1971a: 10–13; 1971b). See also Leach (1961a, b); H. and C. Geertz (1975). Many of the participants in these debates nevertheless continued to write about kinship or teach it to their students.

6 On the relation between science and culture, and nature and culture, see also Rabinow (1996a, b). Rabinow argues that a future effect of the new biotechnologies (such as the mapping of the human genome) will be that instead of culture being modelled on nature, nature will be modelled on culture. 'Nature will be known and remade through technique and will finally become artificial, just as culture becomes natural.' This would then provide a basis for overcoming the divide between nature and culture and imply a dissolution of the category of the 'social' (1996a: 99). Similarly, in her more recent work, Haraway (1997) writes of an 'implosion' between nature and culture. This 'enterprised-up' or 'artifactual' nature 'still functions as a foundational resource but in an inverted way, that is, through its artifice' (p. 102). Here it is by being 'fully artifactual' that nature becomes a resource for naturalising technoscience (pp. 102–3). See also Hayden's analysis of the debates around the Human Genome Diversity Project and biodiversity prospecting, in which she pays close attention to the 'discursive ricochets' (1998: 197) between ideas of nature and culture.

7 On the fragmentation of motherhood involved in surrogacy arrangements, see Ragoné (1994, 1998).

8 Indeed, the volume derives from a session at the 1992 American Anthro-

pological Association meetings which was held in honour of David
Schneider and is dedicated to him.

9 J. Goody's edited collection *The Developmental Cycle in Domestic Groups*
(1958) is in some respects an obvious exception. Fortes's introduction,
however, underlined how the very separation between domestic and politico-jural domains implied an analytic hierarchy – the primary significance
of the domestic domain lay in its structural role of furnishing and replen-
ishing the politico-jural rather than in the comparative study of domestic life
per se.

10 See also Astuti (1998), who argues that a distinction between what is
acquired and what is innate is probably a universal cultural phenomenon.
She suggests that the Western categories of sex and gender come quite close
to the distinction made by the Vezo between aspects of the body which are
given (i.e. genitalia) and what is acquired – the appropriate behaviour for
men and women. Broch-Due and Rudie (1993: 32) also argue for the
retention of the distinction between sex and gender, not as 'transcendental
categories' but 'theoretical constructs' permitting specific comparisons of
the way bodies are interpreted and experienced in different cultural contexts
(see also Broch-Due 1993; Gay-y-Blasco 1997).

11 See also Marshall (1977: 649), who notes that Trukese 'created sibling
relationships' are perceived as 'an improvement on nature' in that they avoid
the tensions and rivalries that exist between consanguineal siblings.

12 Lambek's (1998) nuanced discussion of the mind/body distinction is relevant here. As he points out (p.122 n.12), there is a parallel between this and
the nature/culture opposition as well as that between sex and gender (see
Astuti 1998). Lambek suggests that such widespread dualisms should be
understood in terms of 'incommensurability'. They reveal 'a common
horizon of ideas' which may reflect universal aspects of human experience.
But he also accepts that local versions of these distinctions will fail to make
'complete contact' with their Western equivalents. Rather than sinking into
relativism, he advocates engaging in fruitful comparison of such 'alternative
formulations' (p. 111).

13 Ragoné demonstrates how invocation of the gift in the context of surrogacy
in America accomplishes a number of desired ends from the point of view of
the surrogate mother. It negates a perceived cultural image of the surrogate's
interests as primarily commercial, and substitutes motives of generosity and
altruism, which are more appropriate to the domain of kinship (1994: 41,
59–60, 71, 85). At the same time, the fact that this gift is described as
passing from the surrogate to the adoptive mother serves to draw attention
away from the relation between the surrogate and the genetic father, which
carries negative connotations of adultery and illegitimacy. Instead, what is
emphasised is a relationship of sharing and reciprocity, and even sisterhood,
between the two women (1994: 124, 128).

14 See Viveiros de Castro (1998) for a virtuoso attempt to subject the divide
between nature and culture to a rigorous critique by contrasting Western
categories with those which underlie Amazonian cosmologies.

2   Chinese patriliny and the cycles of *yang* and *laiwang*

Charles Stafford

As James Watson observes, anthropologists have tended to view Chinese society through a 'lineage paradigm' – in part mistakenly derived from the seminal work of Maurice Freedman, and thus, by extension, from the work of his Africanist colleagues – which assumes that in China 'the ideology of patrilineal descent takes precedence over all other principles of social organisation' (J. Watson 1986: 274). They have also often drawn, again following Freedman, a distinction between the study of Chinese 'kinship' (primarily meaning formal descent groups such as lineages) and the study of the Chinese 'family' (primarily meaning the informal business of everyday family life):

> We can show without much difficulty that kinship bound together large numbers of people in Chinese society and exerted an important effect on their political, economic, and religious conduct at large. Family is another matter. Essentially, its realm is that of domestic life, a realm of co-residence and the constant involvement in affairs of the hearth, children and marriage. Kinship is something different. (Freedman 1979: 240–1)

In short, while the 'lineage paradigm' assumes that the ideals and realities of descent-based kinship are paramount in Chinese social organisation, family life and the 'affairs of the hearth' have generally been, as a matter of definition, explicitly *excluded from kinship* and thus from this central organising role.

   Whatever its analytical strengths and weaknesses – and Freedman's contribution to the study of Chinese kinship is beyond question – this formalist approach is liable, I think, to obscure in anthropological accounts the lived experience of Chinese kinship, and to misconstrue the relationship of 'affairs of the hearth' both to formal kinship and to other kinds of relatedness in China. I should stress that the term relatedness, as I use it in this paper, refers to literally *any* kind of relation between persons – including those seemingly 'given' by biology and/or 'produced' via social interactions – and is thus obviously intended to encompass formal and informal relations of kinship and much else besides. The justification for using such a decidedly general term is the fact, illustrated in most of the contributions to this volume, that the boundaries between various categories of human social relations (including those defined as 'formal kinship', 'informal kinship', 'fictive kinship', and 'friendship') are often very malleable indeed. This is why it is useful to question these categories *together*, and in particular to examine the boundaries between them, under the encompassing category of relatedness. When this is done in the Chinese case, we discover, not surprisingly, a wide range of indigenous or popular notions of relatedness. Two of these will be set out below. These are not the ones classically associated with China, and they therefore help challenge some of our preconceptualisations about Chinese kinship (e.g. about the status of women within it).

I would suggest that the 'lineage paradigm' of Chinese anthropology, when placed in comparative perspective, has helped sustain the impression that Chinese kinship is, *in essence*, an extreme and non-fluid version of patriliny: a male-dominated system of rigidly defined agnatic groups, of kinship given by birth, of immutable connections, of exclusion, and of women who have power only as disruptive outsiders. (This impression is the product of a particular definition of kinship, and of what this definition excludes.) The implicit and potentially misleading comparison is with seemingly less rigid, less exclusive systems of kinship: those portrayed as fluid, negotiable, incorporative, and processual, and in which the roles of women are seen in a positive light. Here I have in mind recent discussions of 'fluid' Austronesian kinship and identity (e.g. Carsten 1995a, 1997; Astuti 1995; and the contributions to this volume by Astuti and Middleton). The mutability of kin relations portrayed in these accounts – their creative production and transformation over time – seems almost directly at odds with the supposedly 'given' nature of Chinese patrilineal descent.

In this chapter, however, I want to stress precisely the processual and creative aspects of Chinese kinship and relatedness. I will suggest that alongside patriliny, which undoubtedly does carry a great force in China, and alongside affinity, which in recent years has received greater attention in sinological anthropology, we find two other *equally* forceful, and relatively incorporative, systems of Chinese relatedness. In an attempt to remain close to informants' models, I'll tentatively gloss these as 'the cycle of *yang*' (which centres mostly on parent–child relationships) and 'the cycle of *laiwang*' (which centres mostly on relationships between friends, neighbours, and acquaintances). In both cycles, the *production* of relatedness (often through rather everyday or domestic transactions) is clearly seen; and I will argue that in China 'rigid' patrilineal descent is crucially articulated with these distinctly fluid, creative, and incorporative systems.

The contributions by Lambert and Hutchinson to this volume, which draw on Rajasthani and Nuer material, similarly stress the articulation of patriliny with other bases of relatedness. Lambert, for her part, discusses the significance of 'fictive' Rajasthani kinship – ties based on co-residence and commensality – in a strongly patrilineal and virilocal setting. Hutchinson discusses 'substances' (money, guns, paper) which have become, in recent decades, increasingly salient in Nuer social life. She argues that these have become new 'media of relatedness' for the Nuer – thus transforming, and being transformed by, long-standing conceptions of 'blood' and kinship. In all three cases – Nuer, Rajasthani, and Chinese – patrilineal ties of blood and descent, however defined, must be seen in the context of other notions of relatedness, notions which themselves change in the flow of history.

In what follows, I will first describe a wedding in rural north China in order to illustrate what is meant by the cycles of *yang* and *laiwang*, and in order to show how they coexist and partly merge with patriliny and affinity.[1] Then I will turn to the literature on Chinese kinship in order to ask why the patrilineal image remains dominant in our understandings. Finally, by way of conclusion, I will return to the more general question of Chinese relatedness in comparative perspective. I should perhaps stress at the outset that the paradigmatic examples of Chinese patriliny have been drawn from the powerful lineages of South China, whereas my material comes from communities in north-eastern China and south-eastern Taiwan where lineages, as such, are not elaborated. I would however suggest that these two cycles of relatedness are certainly found within even the most 'exclusive' Chinese descent groups, and that my argument is supported by existing ethnography from all regions of China.

The wedding

The setting is the courtyard of a brick farmhouse at the end of a dirt path in Dragon-head, a small farming village in north-eastern China. Here a crowd of local people (about fifty of them) have gathered to watch over and to participate in various preparations for a wedding which will take place tomorrow. Noisily joking amongst themselves, women squat in a makeshift tent outside and prepare food for what they say will be a forty-table (i.e. about 300-guest) wedding banquet. The mother of the groom seems very agitated, and the father looks distinctly ill, as if he may shortly have a heart attack. A large pig has been slaughtered and its carcass dragged, on the back of a cart, into the middle of the courtyard. Now an elderly man and his wife carve up big chunks of pork and weigh and sell this meat to a circle of standers-by, mostly women. Young men loiter around the edges, smoking cigarettes and talking, while children race in and out of the house and the courtyard.

In the midst of this preparatory activity, a friend suggests that I should be introduced to the groom. I'm taken up to the house and led into the 'new room' (*xinfang*), i.e. the newly prepared bridal chamber. Here I'm left alone with a young man who sits in splendid isolation, smoking nervously, not allowed to help with the preparations for his own wedding. Through the window we observe the activity outside. The room itself is in striking contrast to the rest of the austere farmhouse. The floor is newly painted a shiny red, and guests are expected to remove their shoes on entering. The *kang* (i.e. the fire-heated brick platform bed) on which he sits is surrounded with new lace curtains and piled high with pink and red quilts. (I'm reminded of Emperor Pu Yi's observation about his own wedding chamber: 'It all looked like a melted red wax candle.') A 'cute' (*ke'ai*) poster of a baby boy and girl adorns the wall. The room is equipped with a series of new appliances: an electric fan and a small washing machine from the bride's family; and a colour television, stereo, and VCR from the groom's family.

The young man explains that his parents have spent about 20,000 *renminbi*, i.e. over £1,600, on this event, including the preparation of the *xinfang*. This amount – now an average sum for the 'groom's side' (*nanfang*) to spend on a wedding – represents (very roughly) from two to ten years' income for a rural family.[2] Getting married in this way, he says, is of course a lot of trouble (*mafan*), but (as has often been explained to me) it is almost impossible to get by in rural China with a simple, inexpensive wedding. This is partly because, for rural families with sons, wedding-related expenses are unavoidable in a market which favours the 'bride's side' (*nufang*). In order to attract a bride, as one man put it, 'even a poor groom's side still has to spend a lot of money – and if they're rich, they must spend even more!' By contrast, these days 'the ones raising daughters strike it rich' (*yang guniang de dou facai*).

The groom tells me that he and his fiancée, a young woman from a village about two and a half hours away by bus, were 'introduced' (*jieshao*) by an intermediary, and now they know each other fairly well. Tomorrow morning he will collect her from her parents' home, and before leaving she will eat pork, literally 'departing-mother-meat' (*li-niangrou*), 'so that she will not miss her mother' (*weile ta buhui xiang mama*). Then bride and groom will be transported, along with some forty of her relatives, by taxi and bus back to this very room. Various wedding-day activities – including *yakang* ('pressing the *kang*' with a baby boy), and *naofang* (in which the bride and groom are roughly teased about sex while sitting on the *kang*) – will then highlight the hope that this outsider woman will quickly provide her husband's family with a new descendant, and the hope that her first or second child will be a son.[3]

Although this is a wedding – and by definition a moment for celebrating affinity – the expense, the bother, and the symbolism of the event also seem fairly clear manifestations of an elaborated Chinese concern with patriliny and descent. Of course, the new affinal link to the bride's family is acknowledged and celebrated. The respected guests at the wedding banquet will be *her* parents and elder kinsmen, all of whom will eat in the place of honour (the *kang* room of the groom's parents), while the groom's parents will themselves eat outside. In the coming years, the newlyweds will continue to have important ties to the bride's natal home. But the centrepiece of the wedding is precisely her separation from this home and her installation in her new family's bridal chamber, the purpose of which – producing children to continue a patriline – is made very clear. The woman is 'marrying out' (*chujia*), the residence is virilocal, her children will belong to her husband's family and take his name, and she will respectfully serve (*fengyang*) her husband's parents now and in their old age. From the perspective of the groom's parents, the expense of the marriage, however inflated, is necessary: it is essential to attract a good daughter-in-law, because a daughter-in-law is a crucial element in their hoped-for future.

Childhood and the cycle of *yang*

In any case, the emphasis in the wedding on descent and on affinity is made explicit. But there are at least two other systems of relatedness which impinge on this wedding, the first of which I have discussed elsewhere, and have glossed as 'the cycle of *yang*' (Stafford 1995: 79–111). *Yang* is a very common Chinese expression meaning 'to raise' or 'to care for', e.g. in 'raise flowers' (*yang hua*), 'raise pigs' (*yang zhu*), or 'raise children' (*yang haizi*). In the case of children, the provision of *yang* – a kind of all-encompassing nurturance – is, of course, very complex. It is also productive of an almost inescapable obligation: once they have grown up, children are heavily obliged to *yang*, 'care for', or *fengyang*, 'respectfully care for', their parents in old age. More specifically, the receipt of *yang* from one's parents during childhood obliges *sons* to return *yang* to their parents later in life. But while old-age provision for parents is often discussed as if it were only a son's business, most daughters effectively transfer *their* 'debt of *yang*' to their parents-in-law upon marriage while in many cases still providing some care to their own mothers and fathers. Indeed, contrary to popular perceptions, the cycle may have as many implications for daughters as for sons, and it arguably has *more* practical implications for women than for men. This is because it is women who normally shoulder (often 'on behalf of' their husbands) the actual process of providing *yang*: in many cases for their parents-in-law, their parents, their children, and their grandchildren.

But what is the detail of this provision? People often mention that parents provide their children with housing, clothing, education, money, and food, but on examination none of these categories is very straightforward. For example, in my account of Angang (in Taiwan) I described how the category of food could arguably include the popular remedies and traditional medicinal foods which parents provide for their children. It could also include the expensive magical charms (*fu*) – slips of paper on which possessed spirit mediums write divine script – which children swallow for protection against evil spirits. Through providing food, medicines, magical charms, etc., parents 'protect and strengthen the bodies/persons' (*hushen, bushen*) of their children (Stafford 1995: 97–100). And the expense and bother involved in providing this kind of 'protection and strengthening' to children – which goes on for many years – is not thought to be a waste, because, as I have said, it is these very children who will be relied upon in the future. Their eventual 'respectful nurturance' (*fengyang*) of their parents may include the provision of material assistance – primarily money, food, and housing (cf. Hsieh 1985) – but also emotional support, e.g. affection.

The 'cycle of *yang*' is, then, a very involving system of mutual obligations between parents and children which centrally entails the transfer of money and the sharing of food. This cycle is also closely linked to the provision of care for ancestors, who similarly receive food and money from their (heavily obligated) descendants. For this and other reasons, the idea of a 'cycle of *yang*' may appear to effectively overlap with the notion of patriliny, and with the Chinese emphasis on descent and on *xiao*, 'filial obedience'. But I would suggest that it does not entirely do so, for three reasons. First, it is possible to produce, through *yang*, relatedness with children who are not one's own 'natural' descendants. Children raised by foster parents (called *yang* mothers and *yang* fathers) are obliged, *because* they have received *yang* from them, to care for their foster parents in old age. This might simply be seen as a way of imitating descent: adults without children 'produce' them through *yang*. But I think it is wrong to assume that descent, as such, is the point, or to assume that *yang* cannot have a force – or a desirability – of its own (as I have tried to show). Second, it is possible to have a 'cycle of *yang*' where descent, in the normal sense, is not a consideration. For example, in Dragon-head I know a woman who, after the death of her mother, raised and cared for her younger brothers; they now provide her with *yang* in the form of money and food as if they had been her descendants. But they are *not* her descendants, and she has her own husband and children. Her brothers say that they support her because she raised them (*yang*); and many other examples suggest that *yang* may produce its own return (i.e. 'without descent'). Third, there are many cases in which a failure in the 'cycle of *yang*' is what provokes the termination of relations of descent. Sons who fail to provide their parents with *yang* may be dropped from family estates, ties of blood notwithstanding. In sum, *yang* may produce kinship where there is no 'natural' tie of descent, and the absence of *yang* may end kinship where a 'natural' descent tie exists.

Here I have provided only a cursory outline of this cycle, but there are two further observations I would like to make. First, I would suggest that in informal Chinese kinship – i.e. the kind of kinship one observes in everyday life in a Chinese community – idioms related to the cycle of *yang* are as salient as idioms related to patrilineal descent as such, and perhaps even more so. In other words, the lived experience of Chinese kinship is closely connected to the cycle of *yang*. And this cycle – through its emphasis on feeding, nurturance, and care – is comparable (as I have mentioned above) to the processual, fluid, and transformative forms of kinship which anthropologists do *not* generally associate with China. Second, I would suggest that if we paid as much attention to the cycle of *yang* as has been paid to patrilineal descent, our view of the role of women in Chinese kinship and society might be considerably trans-formed. It may be true that from the perspective of formal kinship ideologies Chinese women are 'dangerous' and sometimes even 'pol-luting' outsiders. But women are at the centre of the most important processes in the cycle of *yang*, and it is through their everyday engage-ment with this cycle that they play, *and are seen to play*, a highly valued role in Chinese kinship.

Now, what has this cycle to do with the wedding I have been describing? Forget for a moment the idea that the wedding shows how interested people are in honouring ties of affinity, or in generating descendants for a patriline. Instead, note that a wedding is one of the key elements in the parent–child cycle of *yang*. The last great, and often very expensive, obligation of Chinese parents to their children – having provided them with food, clothing, housing, education, etc. throughout childhood – is to arrange for them to be properly married off. Until this has happened, the work of parents is not done. As much as the son, sitting in the 'new room', is obliged to marry for the sake of his parents, his parents, rushing about making final arrangements, are obliged to provide him with a wedding. They do this knowing that their son, along with his wife and their children, will eventually provide them with support and care (*yang*). The bride, coming into this new family, effectively transfers her obligations to her parents-in-law: they are the ones she will live with and *yang*. And the marriage itself partly compensates her own parents for the expense and trouble of having raised her, while an incoming daughter-in-law (assuming that they have a son) will hopefully provide *them* with the *yang* they are due in old age.

Notice however, and this is an important point, that the bride and groom are also involved in providing themselves with a wedding. Once young people (both sons and daughters) are old enough to work and earn money, they usually hand over most of their income to their parents. But this is not yet 'support for parents'. A good proportion of this money is usually spent to cover future wedding expenses, including the preparation of the 'new room' (in the case of the groom) or the provision of a dowry for the bride (cf. Chen 1985). The fact that children in this way effectively subsidise their own weddings may seem to diminish what I have been saying: that the wedding manifests a parental obligation which is part of the cycle of *yang*. But in fact this flowing back and forth of support (my assistance makes it easier for you to assist me) is at the very core of Chinese notions of parent–child reciprocity.

Neighbours and the cycle of *laiwang*

A somewhat similar notion of mutual support is at the core of the other cycle I have mentioned, the cycle of *laiwang*. In certain ways – not least because it involves many similar processes and idioms, especially transfers of money and food – this cycle could be characterised as the extension of *yang* to the outside world. In the anthropological literature on China it has most often been discussed in relation to the question of social 'connections' or *guanxi* (see especially Yang 1994 and Yan 1996). I will briefly illustrate this cycle by again returning to the wedding in Dragon-head village, and by presenting a different, and rather cynical, view of the proceedings.

On the night before the wedding I visit the home of an elderly friend, Mr Zhang, who really cannot understand why I should be so interested in attending tomorrow's celebration and banquet. He warns that they will expect money from me, and is very concerned that I'll try to give more than necessary. When attending wedding banquets, he notes, most neighbours (assuming they are farmers of average income) normally give 20 renminbi (£2.50), and Mr Zhang repeatedly stresses that I should not give more than this amount. (His own annual income is only about 2,000 rmb.) Relatives and friends often give 50 to 100 rmb for wedding banquets, and the well-to-do are expected to give even more. Mr Zhang notes that he does not himself intend to go, because of the expense and also because the kinship connection is 'distant' (*yuan*): the groom's family are merely the relatives of his wife's sister-in-law. Beyond this, he disapproves of the practice (much expanded in recent years) of having very elaborate banquets for weddings and other occasions. According to him, cadres with 'advanced thinking' (*sixiang jinbu*) set a good example by not being wasteful in this way. He points out that in the case of this wedding the groom's family are quite poor, and they have gone heavily into debt in order to have a celebration which will 'look good for the guests' (*dui keren haokan*). They have borrowed 14,000 rmb, a sum he says they will never manage to repay.

Late the next morning I go to the house where the wedding is to take place. The groom has long since departed to collect his bride, and it is raining on and off – a potential disaster, given that they are hoping to feed some three hundred people outside. Most of the activity centres on food preparation (inside the house and under a small tent). But a small crowd has also gathered on the porch where the village head (*cunzhang*) and an assistant are collecting money. Arriving guests hand over cash, and their names and the amount given are written in a book; in return they receive six pieces of candy wrapped in auspicious red paper. Some women point out to me that this is a good thing: you give money, it is registered, and then if you later have some 'matter' or 'business' (*shi*) of your own, this family will come and help you (cf. Potter & Potter 1990: 210; Pasternak 1972: 64).

Then I am spotted by my friend Mr Zhang, who after all has decided to attend. He immediately drags me off to the furthest corner of the courtyard where he and a group of *laotou* (old men, literally 'old heads') have staked a claim to the place of *least* honour. Around a wooden table set close to the ground, we squat on bricks which are sinking in the mud. We fiddle with bowls and chopsticks, chatting about the weather and the wedding, and impatiently wait for the food to be served. Meanwhile the number of tables around us and in the neighbouring courtyard has expanded to fifty. Because nothing can happen, and no one can eat, until the bride arrives, there is much discussion of the bad arrangements which have been made for her transportation (she might, after all, have been lodged close by last night). After a while this conversation focuses on the possibility that she might not arrive at all, in which case, as everyone agrees, we would certainly still need to eat. One old man knows of just such a case in which the bride-bringing bus had broken down, and the guests at that wedding had definitely eaten.

Then, belatedly, the bride and groom and her family arrive in cars and minibuses, which move slowly through the muddy village lanes. The guests step out, and the bride and groom approach the house, making their way through a volley of firecrackers. In front of the assembled hungry crowd, they bow to their elders and then to each other before walking into the house. As far as the guests outside are concerned, that is the end of the ritual, and now the food should be served. But there is further delay, and people keep coming out from the house and looking anxiously up the village lanes. A rumour goes around that the bride's mother has not yet arrived, and one of the old men at my table says to forget the mother; the banquet should begin (*kaixi*). But it is not the mother who is missing, and after a few more moments the banquet does begin – sixteen dishes are served, and we get down to the serious business of eating and drinking. I am told that the meal probably cost about 3,000 rmb – for Mr Zhang one and a half year's income – but that this expense is more or less offset by the cash gifts collected in the morning. The consensus is that the food is only very average (*yibande*). At the weddings of rich people, I am told, the food does not include vegetables (*cai*) and is instead all meat dishes (*rou*): chicken, pork, beef, and very big fish.

From Mr Zhang's perspective, it may seem that this particular wedding is a waste of time, an unwelcome economic burden. He is indifferent to the fate of the groom's patriline and to its affinal network. As I noted, he measures this kinship connection as a distant one. Furthermore, much of the ceremonial associated with weddings is private (i.e. not displayed to the crowd), so in effect Mr Zhang is only there for the meal, which he concludes is nothing special. So what, in the end, is the reason for going? Later he reiterates that contributing to these ceremonies of various kinds is expensive and burdensome, especially in communities such as Dragon-head where everyone is an acquaintance, friend, or relative. But he also quickly stresses that 'attending ceremonials' (*ganli*) is important because it is part of *laiwang*, literally 'come and go'. The expression *laiwang* describes the reciprocal movement back and forth between people who have a relationship of mutual assistance. (Thus the expression *wo gen ta you laiwang*: 'I have *laiwang* with him', meaning 'to have relations'.) As Mr Zhang puts it, 'When you have some business, I'll come to you; when I have some business, you'll come to me' (*ni you shi wo lai, wo you shi ni lai*). In our discussion, Mr Zhang also refers to the Chinese idiom *li shang wang lai* – 'courtesy demands reciprocity' which could be translated as 'ceremonial generates back-and-forth', i.e. *laiwang*. The point is that the cycle of *laiwang*, which often consists of seemingly minor or 'ceremonial' transactions, is a crucial element in the building up of relatedness between those who are *not* related (or not closely related) by kinship.

The example Mr Zhang spontaneously gives is this. He had recently been forced to build a new home – for him an almost unimaginably expensive undertaking – because his old one was literally collapsing. At that time, many relatives, friends, and neighbours had offered assistance (in the form of both gifts and loans). The father of the groom at today's wedding had given Mr Zhang some help, albeit small, and it was only right that Mr Zhang should therefore 'attend the ceremonial' (*ganli*) for the man's son, thus helping to pay for a banquet which would 'look good' for the affines: 'courtesy demands reciprocity'. For the bride and groom, and for their families, the wedding banquet is important not least because it manifests a community of support. As with the cycle of *yang*, the cycle of *laiwang* is built up through small actions and interactions, and it often similarly involves commensality, transfers of money, and the sharing of responsibilities. And although *laiwang*, like *yang*, is sometimes conceived of as a transaction between men, this view is once again very misleading; the actual burden of producing everyday *laiwang* – and even that of special occasions – is often undertaken by women.

The source of the lineage paradigm

In sum, the cycles of *yang* and *laiwang* – these two idioms of relatedness – carry great force in China, and any Chinese 'family history' inevitably includes them, as surely as it includes a history of descent and intermarriage. They stand alongside patriliny and affinity, but are not reducible to them. However, as I said at the outset, Chinese kinship seems almost inevitably to stand, in the context of anthropology, for a strong version of patriliny. One reason for this is undoubtedly the influence in sinological anthropology of a Freedman-inspired lineage paradigm. (Freedman's on-going influence is highlighted in a volume on 'the Chinese family' published in 1985 in which, as Arthur Wolf notes, fully thirteen of the fifteen articles address Freedman directly (A. Wolf 1985: 3–4).) Freedman's work, in turn, must be seen in the context of the central themes of British social anthropology, and the development in the 1940s and 50s of an Africanist 'lineage theory' which stressed the overriding significance of lineage and descent in certain kinds of societies, and especially in non-state 'homogeneous' societies (Kuper 1988: 190–209).

Freedman was clearly influenced by this literature and addressed it directly in his own work (e.g. 1958: 126–40), while always trying to stress the unique characteristics of Chinese society and history (for example, by rather drily pointing out that 'however we define the category 'homogeneous societies' we can scarcely say that China falls within its scope' (p. 136)). Indeed, Watson notes that Freedman himself had serious misgivings about an overly lineage-oriented view of China, and also notes that the lineage paradigm has been subject, over the years, to many critical studies. But he suggests that even these critiques (focusing on e.g. affinity, ethnicity, class, and gender) have tended to be structured around the lineage paradigm (J. Watson 1982, 1986: 274–5). Thus, as recently as 1995, David Faure and Helen Siu were again commenting – in a work which relates South China lineages to land and ethnicity – that 'Maurice Freedman's seminal works on Chinese kinship and descent are so influential that many scholars have long taken for granted the lineage paradigm for understanding Chinese social life' (1995: 210).

But this comment seems to me slightly misleading. What is striking is not that scholars have taken for granted the lineage paradigm (and I would guess that most of them have *not* done so), but rather that in spite of their best critical efforts, including those of Freedman, we often still sum up Chinese kinship and social life with reference to patrilineal descent. The impression still lingers that patrilineal descent (i.e. the 'essence' of Chinese kinship) *does* take precedence over all other principles of social organisation in China. Why should this be the case? I propose four interlinked explanations in the history of the anthropology of China: the use of a formalist definition of kinship (which excludes 'family life' and informality); an emphasis on regional analysis (which tends to emphasise the role of formal descent groups and the 'public' roles of men, while overlooking the significance of local processes of kinship and relatedness, and the 'private' roles of women); an emphasis on historical sources (which often take a male-dominated view of kinship, and therefore tend to reinforce the 'lineage paradigm' view of China); and an underemphasis on participant-observation fieldwork. That is, the emphasis on regional and historical analysis has tended to devalue, in sinological anthropology, the role of village-based participant-observation fieldwork, and this has perhaps been further compounded by the practical difficulties of conducting village-based research in the PRC. One result is that Chinese ethnography is sometimes difficult to compare with ethnography from settings where 'intimate' fieldwork is more common. I would suggest we have partly missed the 'fluid' nature of Chinese kinship because we have not always done the kind of fieldwork in which the production of relatedness is there to be seen.

Perhaps a more prosaic reason for the on-going influence of the lineage paradigm is simply that much of the best work in sinological anthropology has focused on descent groups, often based on ethnography in South China, where such groups were very strong. This material (which after all originates in the concerns of Chinese informants) is sometimes very striking. For example, James Watson notes (in a review article which stresses precisely that Chinese kinship is *not* all about descent) that a Chinese lineage can be 'a remarkably closed corporation' in which absorbing outsiders is a messy business (1982: 598–9). He points out that 'one of the commonest forms of slander among the Cantonese is to assert publicly that one's rivals have sunk to such depths that they have had to recruit outsiders' (p. 599).[4] A similar principle is arguably shown again in the images, equally striking, of the incorporation of 'dangerous outsider women' into the patrilineal system. As Watson observes, 'viewed strictly in formal terms, Chinese women stand outside the male-dominated kinship system altogether' (1982: 615). Based on research in Taiwan, Emily Martin Ahern (1975) suggests this may help to explain, at least in part, Chinese religious ideologies of women's spiritual pollution. For example, in giving birth (something obviously *necessary* to the continuation of patrilines) women are contaminated with their own pollutedness, and this follows them to their graves. Ahern suggests it is partly the ambiguous status of women – as outsiders who produce insiders – which makes them simultaneously powerful and polluting (1975; cf. Seaman 1981). Rubie Watson notes that in Ha Tsuen (New Territories), a community where 'patrilineal values dominate social life', married-in women are 'suspect' (R. Watson 1986: 620). This is partly reflected in naming practices, which implicitly devalue (or, more accurately, ignore) their status. While men during the life-course acquire various names which mark important social transitions and roles, and which are often linked to the classical scholarly tradition, women progressively become nameless. In the end they are simply called 'old woman', and this implies that they 'do not, indeed cannot, attain full personhood' (p. 619). Selective readings of these kinds might (however wrongly) give the impression of a kinship system in which outsiders are almost impossible to absorb, and in which women (defined as outsiders) are polluters and non-persons. More generally, the image has perhaps been given of a society dominated by kinship[5] and dominated specifically by the ideology of patrilineal descent.

Towards a new paradigm of Chinese relatedness

But consider some of the work which might be said to show otherwise. Anthropologists have increasingly shown the importance attached in China to relationships which are *not* based on kinship. Some recent examples include DeGlopper's work on voluntary association among the residents of Lukang in Taiwan (1995), the discussions by Mayfair Yang (1994) and Yan Yunxiang (1996) of personal *guanxi* networks in post-Mao mainland China, and my own work on the relationship between teachers and pupils in Taiwan (Stafford 1995: 56–68). Without question, in many Chinese contexts ties based on mutual assistance, co-residence, friendship, and discipleship may be more significant than ties of kinship.

Historians and anthropologists have also shown that Chinese patriliny only ever operates in a wider politico-economic context (see e.g. Gates 1996). That is, they have problematised the notion of pan-Chinese timeless principles of kinship, and shown that descent, as such, never 'stands alone'. The volume edited by Faure and Siu (1995) addresses, among other things, the mutual impact of ethnicity, state-building, and lineage development in a single Chinese region, suggesting that the political economy of land control, and considerations of ethnic differentiation, may be as significant in lineage development as considerations of kinship in the narrow sense. Rubie Watson (1985) examines the interrelation of patrilineal ideology and class, and shows how patriliny may underpin class exploitation within lineages. The volume edited by Davis and Harrell (1993) analyses the (often paradoxical) impact of state intervention and official ideology on kinship practice in post-Mao China. In short, in terms of Chinese history, and even within the history of Chinese kinship, ethnicity, class, and state intervention must be viewed as equal players with 'patriliny'.

Anthropologists have of course also stressed the significance in Chinese kinship of marriage and of affinal links (e.g. Pasternak 1972: 60–94; R. Watson 1985: 117–36; J. Goody 1990: 21–51; R. Watson and Ebrey 1991). James Watson observes that for most Chinese people, agnates have probably been 'no more significant than affines, matrilateral kin, and neighbours' (1982: 606). Freedman himself stressed, for instance, the significant and on-going involvement of 'married-out' sisters and daughters with their natal families (1979: 295), while Bernard and Rita Gallin (1985) have argued that matrilateral and affinal ties are often characterised by informants in positive (and utilitarian) terms, and should therefore not be analysed as if they were simply negative. This work on marriage and affinity coincides with a re-examination of Chinese gender relations, which has also transformed the anthropological view of Chinese patriliny and kinship. Not surprisingly, ideologies of female subordination are often contradicted by fieldwork observations, and several writers have tried to address the ensuing paradoxes (e.g. M. Wolf 1974; Ahern 1975; Martin 1988).

From this perspective came the model which, in my view, came closest to genuinely challenging the dominance of the lineage paradigm: Margery Wolf's notion of the 'uterine family' (1972). It is interesting that Wolf's original fieldwork focused precisely on informal kinship and on an intimate understanding of everyday life in several rural Taiwanese households (i.e. it was initially based on intensive participant observation in one community). She came to the conclusion that, from a woman's perspective, work on behalf of a uterine family (comprising a woman and her children) was more important than work on behalf of her husband's patriline. Through developing strong emotional ties with sons in particular, a woman could solidify her current position and protect her future security. So the uterine family stood both inside and alongside the male-dominated patrilineal family, potentially as a powerful competitor for loyalties.

The processes Wolf describes (e.g. those relating to child development) are very much part of what I have described as the cycle of *yang*, but the uterine family model clearly has some weaknesses. One is that it characterises the position of Chinese women in largely negative terms: women, as marrying-in outsiders, had to develop ties because otherwise they were without power. The power they developed was a threat to the unity of patrilines – and seen to be so.[6] These views undoubtedly come from the statements of informants and from situations Wolf observed during fieldwork, but I think they under-represent the positive evaluations of women, and are thus potentially misleading. Another weakness of the uterine family model is that it implies a distinctive 'female consciousness' and distinctive 'women's strategies', useful notions which may nevertheless be problematic in the Chinese context, as elsewhere (cf. the discussion by Martin 1988).

In any case, Wolf has tended to withdraw the 'uterine family' model from serious consideration, in part perhaps because she accepts Freedman's formal definition of kinship, which excludes informal family life, and thus excludes the processes she herself has described (M. Wolf 1985: 204). She suggests that 'China was – and still is – a patriarchy', and has suggested that the uterine family was only ever a coping strategy:

Women, in their struggle for some security in their day-to-day existence with the all-powerful male-oriented family and its larger organisation, the lineage, worked like termites hollowing out from within places for themselves and their descendants ... Uterine families were in fact only a way of accommodating to the patriarchal family. (p. 11)

Furthermore, she suggests that in mainland China the uterine family has now disappeared ('because the need for it has disappeared'),[7] although reciprocal parent–child obligations have not (pp. 207–8).

I am certain, however, that Margery Wolf had (and has) something right. What she is pointing out is the profound significance in China of relatedness constituted through the small interactions of daily life (e.g. between mothers and children), and the significance of this kind of relatedness for our understanding of formal Chinese kinship. In this chapter I have proposed the cycle of *yang* as a more inclusive and positive way of viewing this processual relatedness, one in which the idiom of *yang* is raised to the significance of 'descent'. I have also suggested that another, somewhat overlapping, process, the cycle of *laiwang*, is equally important, and helps us to understand Chinese ties which are not based on kinship. These two cycles, in combination, help to place Chinese patriliny and affinity in perspective. They (the cycles) are also already documented in the ethnography of China[8] – our difficulty is in grasping what this ethnography has been trying to tell us.

Conclusion

In comparative perspective, as I said at the outset, Chinese kinship has often been assumed to be of the rigid and non-incorporative kind. I have suggested that such a view is, however, partly the product of a particular definition of kinship, and of particular ways of doing anthropological research. Not surprisingly, the reality is that in China, as elsewhere, people *make* kinship – it is, of course, never simply 'given' to them by birth – and patrilineal ideologies, however powerful, are forced to compete in a crowded field of ideas about the ways in which relatedness is produced. This is not to say that people in China ignore or devalue what are seen to be 'natural' connections between kin. It is rather to stress the social malleability of such connections: the ways in which they are both reinforced and cut (e.g. through successes or failures in the cycle of *yang*), and also extended (e.g. through adoption, or the extension of *yang*-like reciprocity to the outside world).

By comparison with the 'lineage paradigm', the cycles of *yang* and *laiwang* are rather homely folk models of Chinese relatedness, and ones in which kinship and friendship are seen to be hard work, the product of everyday human interactions. But this perspective has at least three advantages. First, it allows us to see Chinese relatedness as a continuum

– comprising everything from the most formal relations of descent to the least formal relations of, say, secret friendship – and to see how certain idioms of reciprocity effectively link the elements in this continuum. Second, it helps us unravel the complex roles of Chinese women in a system of relatedness which often seems, at least formally, to devalue their contributions. Finally, it has the virtue of making Chinese kinship – or more precisely Chinese relatedness – seem less strange, less distant from the kind of 'fluid' or processual relatedness anthropologists encounter elsewhere, e.g. among the Vezo of Madagascar or in Malaysian fishing villages. Of course, Chinese patriliny has been, and remains, a remarkable sociocultural institution. And when seen against the background of the two cycles discussed in this chapter, it is, in my view, *more* rather than less remarkable.

Notes

1 My fieldwork and research in Taiwan and China has been supported by the Wenner-Gren Foundation, the Taiwan Field History Project (Luce Foundation), the Institute of Ethnology (Academia Sinica, Taipei), and the Chiang Ching-kuo Foundation. I am also deeply indebted to the people of Angang (in Taiwan) and Dragon-head (in north-eastern China) for many kindnesses shown. Michael Lambek, Janet Carsten, and many other colleagues (including participants in the Edinburgh conference) provided useful comments on an earlier draft of this paper, and I am grateful for their help.

2 Household incomes now vary quite dramatically in this community. Well-to-do families make as much as 10,000 rmb per year (some even more); average families (and workers in the city) make about half that amount, while others make do with 2,000 rmb or less per year. School-teachers make about 2,400 rmb per year.

3 Under birth-control regulations, a rural woman who first gives birth to a daughter is allowed a second child (i.e. given an opportunity to have a son), but if her first child is a boy she must stop. Ideally, most couples would prefer to have two children, i.e. 'one of each', and so are quite happy to have a daughter first. But ending up with two daughters is considered by most people to be a misfortune.

4 In another article he discusses in detail the adoption rules for one lineage: 'any adopting father who attempts to bring an outsider into the village must submit to an initiation ceremony [nominally for the son] during which he is humiliated by his peers'. This involves an expensive banquet for village elders and leaders, who, unusually, do not bring gifts of cash to the event. Instead they eat and drink, and then insist on borrowing money from the host, all the while shouting insults at him for failing to produce a son. Finally he *pays* them to sign a banner which confirms his son's position in the lineage (J. Watson 1975: 293–306). The point of Watson's article is that many people actually *prefer* to go through this ritual humiliation rather than adopt an 'insider' son

(who may be more difficult to control if segmentary rivalries get out of control).

5 So it is perhaps surprising to read the following comments by anthropologists of China. Maurice Freedman: 'The Western literature ... is full of variations on the theme that the family was the basic unit of Chinese society ... But this is not significantly truer of China than of most other societies' (1979: 240). Donald DeGlopper: 'To be sure, most people belonged to families and family membership was a very significant aspect of every person's identity, but I fail to see what is so distinctively Chinese about this' (1995: 24). Fei Xiaotong: 'I do not think that [in China] kinship possesses any force of extension by itself and is valued as such' (1946: 6).

6 In another article, Wolf discusses the power of women's gossip – again a negative formulation of women's power (M. Wolf 1974; cf. Ahern 1975: 199–200).

7 In this she is contradicted by Hill Gates, who suggests that women in mainland China 'still marry principally to establish uterine families' (1996: 202). To my mind this is an extremely odd characterisation of why Chinese women marry. I would suggest that they generally *must* marry in order not to be left out of the cycle of *yang*.

8 On the cycle of *yang* (to cite only a few examples), see discussions of the on-going relationship of *yang* between the living and dead (J. Watson 1988; Thompson 1988), and discussions of 'meal rotation' as a way of providing *yang* to one's parents (Hsieh 1985). See also M. Cohen on the process for sons of *becoming* (as opposed to being born as) co-parceners in estates (1976: 70–85), and Chen on the contributions of daughters to their own dowries (1985). On the cycle of *laiwang*, see e.g. Pasternak's discussion of the on-going system of reciprocal obligations between non-agnates (1972: 64; cf. Yang 1994; Yan 1996; and Potter and Potter 1990: 210).

3   Identity and substance: the broadening bases of relatedness among the Nuer of southern Sudan

Sharon Elaine Hutchinson

Questions of boundaries, identities, and connections lie at the molten core of the encounter between local forms of power and understanding on the one hand and increasingly globalised forces of social and economic transformation on the other. The impact of these broader historical forces is often experienced at the local level in conjunction with the introduction of 'new' objects, substances, and vectors of social exchange. All over the world, people are experimenting with everything from bullets to computers in an effort to define and actualise their evolving sense of relatedness to diverse others. What's more, much of this 'experimentation' is carried out, I suspect, in blissful ignorance of the social/biological divide so prominent in anthropological analyses of human interpersonal relations. Grappling with these themes in a war-torn stretch of southern Sudan, I have sought – in other contexts – to identify the specific conditions and practices that have led contemporary Nuer men and women to problematise fundamental aspects of who they are and how they relate to one another (Hutchinson 1996). I have been especially intrigued by the ways they have been critically re-examining the socially binding force of three key exchange media – 'blood' (*riɛm*), 'cattle'(*ghok*), and 'food' (*mieth*) – in their efforts to comprehend and cope with the massive social and economic changes wrought by more than twenty-five years of colonial rule (1929–55), by eleven years of 'southern regional autonomy' (1972–83), and by two extended civil wars (1955–72 and 1983–present). This chapter focuses on how Nuer concepts of 'blood', in particular, have both shaped and been shaped by intensifying Nuer engagements over the past half-century with powerful 'new' media of relatedness emanating from outside their immediate social world – and, specifically, those of 'money' (*yiou*), 'guns' (*maac*), and 'paper' (*waragak*).

By framing this chapter in terms of the 'substantive vectors' that move between people rather than of people's interactions themselves, I am

resorting unabashedly to a form of 'methodological fetishism' (à la
Appadurai 1986: 5) which inevitably obscures how contemporary Nuer
concepts and practices of 'relatedness' (*maar*) are the historical product
of specific value controversies and power struggles. I will nevertheless
adopt this analytical short cut here on the assumption that 'imagined
communities' of whatever scale or complexity may be approached, at
least in part, as a set of mediated relations that combine complex
symbolic and material concerns. I further assume that the subjectively
experienced boundaries and connections that uphold all such communities are both reinforced and blurred by the circulation of key 'substances' and 'objects' between persons and groups. With respect to
'human blood', I shall argue that Nuer experience the dialectic between
social boundaries and connections more directly as a physically embodied tension between human vitality and human vulnerability. And it is
this experiential 'reality' that has continued to shape their evolving
interpretations of the socially binding and divisive potentials of 'food',
'cattle', 'money', 'guns', and 'paper' as well.

In advocating a more 'vectorial' approach to the study of relatedness
that encompasses the social circulation of imported objects like 'guns',
'money', and 'paper', this essay cuts across some of the central theoretical assumptions guiding Evans-Pritchard's earlier accounts of Nuer
'kinship' and 'social structure' during the 1930s (1940, 1945, 1951).
Whereas Evans-Pritchard, like many of his contemporaries, was pre-
occupied during the 1930s and 40s with issues of 'unity', 'equilibrium',
and 'order', viewing culture as something shared and ethnography as the
compilation of those shared elements, my own research has concentrated on evolving points of confusion and disagreement among Nuer,
particularly with regard to the historical fluidity of their relations
amongst themselves and with the world at large. Evans-Pritchard, for
instance, tends to separate his analyses of Nuer 'social structure' –
defined as 'relations between groups of persons within a system of
groups' (1940: 262) – from his discussion of more individualised
'kinship' networks. He characterises the former as governed by a
'segmentary lineage system' and the latter by the unchallenged supre-
macy of the 'agnatic principle' (1951: 28). Evans-Pritchard's conclusions in these respects have been extensively reworked by a wide range
of scholars undertaking secondary re-analyses of his Nuer ethnographic
corpus. Some have stressed the complicating presence of countervailing
social values and principles in what must be viewed as a historically
dynamic and internally differentiated society (Gough 1971; Holy
1979a, b; Kelly 1985). Others have rejected various aspects of Evans-
Pritchard's 'Nuer model' on the ground that it is inconsistent with the

empirical evidence provided (Southall 1986; Kuper 1982, 1988). Here I am less interested in extending academic debates over whether or not Nuer 'lineages' exist than in showing how their systems of relatedness are constituted through the flow of multiple substances. I assume from the start that the dynamic social and cultural systems in which Nuer men and women live and work are inherently unbounded, unfinished, and riddled with uncertainties. Far from being determined by an inherited set of 'value principles', Nuer concepts, patterns, and practices of relatedness are continually being reworked as people struggle – often under extremely difficult and bewildering circumstances – to live valid and meaningful human lives.

Blood: the vital weakness

Contemporary Nuer concepts and patterns of 'relatedness' float on a sea of human blood. For 'blood', or *rïɛm* (pl. *rïmni*), is both the most powerful and most mysterious 'substance' capable of uniting – and thus dividing – human beings. Intimately associated with the powers of divinity (*kuoth nhial*) as well as with the energies and ambitions of ordinary folk, Nuer concepts of blood meander along the experiential boundary line separating what lies within and beyond human control and influence. Although not equated with life (*tëk*) itself, blood is the substance out of which each and every human life begins. Conception is understood as a mysterious merger of male and female 'blood' flows, forged by the life-creating powers of *kuoth* (divinity). Without the direct participation and continual support of divinity, no child would ever be born or survive long enough to bring forth another generation. This dependence on the life-creating and life-sustaining powers of *kuoth* is a reality that cannot be ignored in a war-blighted world where many couples experience long periods of infertility and where at least half of the children born alive die before reaching adulthood. Procreation, moreover, is the paramount goal of life and the only form of immortality valued. Every adult fears 'the true death', 'the complete death': the death without children to extend one's name and revitalise one's influence in the world. For men, the immortality sought is motivated in part by strong collective interests: without heirs, a man acquires no permanent position in the patrilineal chain of descendants from which he emerged. For women, childbirth is the threshold to adulthood, security, and independence. In fact, the comprehensive term for adult woman/wife (*ciek*, pl. *män*) is conferred only on women who have experienced childbirth. From this perspective, blood (*rïɛm*) may be seen as that which unites the greatest of human desires with the profound sense of humility with which Nuer contemplate the transcendent powers of divinity. In fact, a newborn child *is* 'blood' and is often referred to as such during the first month or two of existence. Milk, semen, sweat – these, too, *are* blood. It is as though *riɛm*, blood, were the mutable source of all human – and hence all social – energy.

Moreover, unlike breath (*yiegh*) and awareness (*tiiy/tiei*), two other cardinal principles of life, blood passes from person to person and from generation to generation, endowing social relations with a certain substance and fluidity. It is the gift of blood bestowed from parent to child on which the authority and respect of the older generation ultimately depend. Similarly, the perpetual expansion, fusion, and dissipation of kin groups is conceptualised in terms of blood's creation, transferral, and loss. The coming of both manhood and womanhood is also marked by emissions of blood. For a girl, the blood that flows during her first childbirth (not at puberty) ushers her into adulthood. For a boy, it is that shed during the ordeal of the knife at initiation, when six (and sometimes seven) horizontal cuts are drawn across his forehead from ear to ear. The shedding of blood at initiation also forges a brotherhood (*ric*) among age-mates and ensures continuity of the patriline as well as supports a broader sense of community among Nuer as 'the people of the people', the 'true human beings', the *nɛi ti naadh*.

Though imbued with connotations of vital force, blood is not equated with 'physical strength', *buom puany*. Human strength is never a matter of blood or 'flesh' (*ring*) but derives, rather, from the inherent 'hardness' (*buom*) of a person's 'bones' (sing. *coaa*, pl. *cou*). Indeed, considerable evidence suggests that blood is viewed as the weakest point in the human constitution. Illness, for example, is generally thought to harbour in a person's blood, and thus Nuer practice an elaborate art of medicinal bleeding. Consider also associations between human blood and human vulnerability implicit in Nuer images of *pɛth* (sing. *pɛath*), or 'possessors of the "red" eye'. These evil beings, who masquerade as true human beings, are said to relish secretly wrenching out the hearts of others, draining their blood and milk, festering their wounds, and snatching the blood/foetus (*riɛm*) from one woman only to hurl it into the womb of another. More to the point: one's blood linkages with others are the open portals through which potentially lethal forms of pollution associated with acts of homicide (*nueer*), incest (*ruaal*), adultery (*koor*), and other transgressions may enter and spread to endanger the wider community. In the words of one eloquent Lou Nuer man, 'Blood is like a medicine (*wal*) in that it carries all the indirect consequences of other people's actions.'

Food: blood's twin force

Like blood, food, or *mieth*, is essential for human life. Its social circulation is thus equally bound up with human experiences of sexuality and procreation, of illness and death – as well as with the life-generating and life-sustaining powers of divinity. Fundamental distinctions of age, gender, descent, and community are likewise inseparable from the daily gathering, giving, and/or withholding of food. More important for my purposes, Nuer regard 'blood' as being generated from 'food' and 'food' from 'blood'. The nutritional qualities of different food types are, in fact, assessed in terms of their relative 'blood' contents. Some foods, such as *koang in boor* (white beer) and *bɛɛl* (sorghum), are considered far richer in 'blood' than are *koang in caar* (black beer) and *maintap* (maize). Milk (*caak*), of course, is the perfect food – the food that can support human life unassisted. One need only trace the swollen veins running along the underbelly of a cow towards its udder to conclude, together with Nuer, that 'milk is blood'. Even agricultural products are considered blood-based in this sense. A man who has sweated day after day tilling the soil may refer to his crops, once harvested, as 'my blood'.

From this perspective, the perpetuation of human social life depends on the continual transformation of 'blood' into 'food' and 'food' into 'blood'. Nuer concepts of *maar* (kinship or relatedness) are, in fact, founded on this idea: ideally, 'relatives' (*nɛi ti maar*) celebrate their 'oneness of blood' through the constant sharing of 'food'. It is only after a child matures and begins to develop the unique 'blood' bonds acquired at birth with counter-gifts of 'food' that he or she achieves the status of a true relative among relatives. In contrast, newly created affines (including husband and wife) normally avoid one another completely in matters of food and drink until some time after the birth of a child solidifies the union. Whereas the social bond created through bridewealth cattle is potentially reversible, the birth of a living, healthy child is taken as indisputable evidence of a successful fusion of different types of 'blood'. Restrictions on commensality between the families concerned are thereafter gradually relaxed. Until then, there is no socially recognised blood bond between the families and hence nothing to be solidified and affirmed, as it were, through the sharing of food. But as long as a child of the union survives, a relationship of *maar* exists between the families of the husband and wife – even in situations where the marriage itself later falters and ends in divorce and in the return of bridewealth cattle.

The 'blood brotherhood' forged between age-mates at initiation, *maar ricä*, also carries with it expectations of uninhibited commensality. In fact, the 'blood' men gain from the common bowl is explicitly equated with that later spent in acts of mutual defence and in communal work projects. One eastern Gaajok youth went so far as to suggest that food-sharing, in itself, creates a quasi–blood bond between people: 'If I have a little food and I share it with you, that means we are brothers. Once we have eaten together, we should not marry each other's daughters or kill one another.' *Maar* thus combines an ideology of shared substance, shared vitality – shared food and blood – with expectations of exogamy and communal peace.

Although there is nothing shameful about eating or drinking in the company of relatives, to be caught in the act of satisfying one's hunger or thirst before a stranger is everyone's nightmare. For to do so is to admit lack of self-control and physical dependence in a situation requiring, instead, firm displays of inner strength and outward dignity. Rules of exogamy are, in fact, stamped with this principle: unrelated men and women 'respect' each other completely in matters of eating and drinking. Moreover, any act of commensality – even indirect forms conveyed through a neutral third party – is considered lethal for persons related through a 'bone' or 'blood' feud (*tɛr*). The buried bones of the slain – which remain firm and whole beneath the earth long after all remnants of blood and flesh have disappeared – are thought to create a social rift so deep, so strong, that relations of commensality, sexuality, and intermarriage between the extended families concerned are prohibited, in principle, 'forever'. Active states of intercommunity feuding may be tempered by a transfer of bloodwealth cattle and by the completion of special sacrifices of atonement performed by an 'earth priest' (*kuäär muon*, also known in the literature as a 'leopard-skin chief'). But 'relationships of the bone' (*maar coakä*) endure, like those of agnation (*böth*), for as long as they are remembered. The hereditary powers of the 'earth priest' are capable of nullifying the pollution dangers associated with blood feuds as well as those originating from incestuous contacts, unwitting acts of cannibalism, and other potentially lethal fusions of either blood or food. Indeed, their powers in this regard appear to be based on the implicit premise that, ultimately, all cycles of 'blood' and 'food' meet and mingle in the earth, from which they re-emerge, as it were, afresh. Consequently, the most effective means of voiding 'dangerous' passages of human blood and food is to rechannel them – symbolically, if not also physically – through the earth (*mun*, gen. *muon*). In sum, Nuer experiences of food-sharing, like those of blood-sharing, reinforce the cultural tenet that human vitality and human vulnerability are 'one'.

Cattle as symbolic counters for human blood

Because contemporary Nuer equate so many of their aspirations and fears with delicate states and flows of *riɛm*, they often attempt to manipulate blood in ways that they hope will promote their wellbeing. Acts of blood vengeance, male initiation rites, and various forms of medicinal bleeding are all motivated in part by the desire to promote specific blood flows. Direct physical attempts at manipulation such as these, however, are rare compared with the abundance of cattle rites and exchanges thought capable of achieving these objectives indirectly. Indeed, the vast majority of cattle sacrificed are offered in the hope of eliciting divine support for either the confirmation, facilitation, extension, or negation of specific states and passages of blood. Among the many types of sacrifices I would include in this category are those performed at marriages, funerals, difficult births, initiations, adoptions, bloodwealth transfers and purification rites associated with homicide, in addition to others intended to promote conception and to rid people of the polluting effects of homicide, incest, adultery, and other dangerous 'blood states'.

Moreover, because the inner state of one's blood connections with others is never immediately apparent, Nuer use cattle as symbolic counters for human blood in numerous contexts of exchange and sacrifice. Otherwise expressed: Nuer concepts of 'relatedness' (*maar*) are founded on the continual equation of the 'vitality' and 'fertility' of cattle with those of human beings. And it is this equation that enables people to extend the potency of human action in tempering the numerous vulnerabilities associated with human blood. Specifically, it enables people to transcend, as individuals and families, experiences of infertility, illness, and death. For example, if a man dies without heirs, his relatives are able – indeed obliged – to collect cattle and marry a 'ghost wife' in his name in order to give children to him. Similarly, should a woman prove infertile, she is 'free' to become a social man, gather cattle, and marry a woman to bear children for her. And were it not for rites of cattle sacrifice, people would stand condemned to a passive forbearance of outbreaks of pollution sickness (*nueer*), severe droughts, and other collective hardships. One highly respected Lou Nuer man summed up this continuing dependence on the mediating role of cattle as follows:

Without the blood of the cow, there would be nothing moving in Nuer society. It is the blood of the cow [shed in sacrifice] that brings in the good and takes away the evil. If I were alone without the cow, I could not build new relationships. What this means is that, without the cow, I am not worth very much.

But what is striking about Nuer concepts of relatedness is the extent to which shared human blood and shared cattle are complementary means of defining the same relationships, the same categories of related-ness. Although the primacy of human 'blood' is often stressed, kinship ties are invariably reinforced and specified through some form of shared cattle rights or bridewealth claims. Consider, for example, the trans-generational reach of cognatic linkages among Nuer. These connections are generally conceived as generating themselves out of an apical brother/sister pair whose postmarital relations extend across the genera-tions through 'the daughters of daughters', or *nyier nyiët*. However, the exogamic limits of these and many other forms of enduring social bonds are more easily traced through shared bridewealth claims – the principle being that no man may marry a woman upon whose marriage he may claim a portion of her bridewealth. And thus, just as the transgenera-tional limits of cognation may be conceptualised either in terms of blood passing and thinning out through chains of women or in terms of bridewealth claims honoured across the generations, so, too, the *maar* binding close affines is rooted in the social circulation of both blood and cattle. In this case, the union of 'blood' binding close affines is realised through the birth of children into the families of both parents. Similarly, the bonds between a genitor and his offspring are both blood- and cattle-based: a genitor has the right to claim the 'cow of begetting' upon the marriage of his natural daughter or, in some cases, upon the maturity of his natural son. So, too, a woman who has suckled and raised another's daughter may claim the 'cow of nurturing' (*yang romä*) upon the girl's marriage. It is thus only with respect to bonds of distant agnation that the overlapping blood/cattle bonds of *maar* wither with time into those of 'shared [sacrificial meat]', or *both* – into those of the 'blood of the cow' consumed, as it were. In brief, cattle are the primary medium through which Nuer render the mysterious powers of human blood socially significant and stable. Or as contemporary Nuer men and women more commonly express this idea: 'Cattle, like people, have blood' – which is to say that both cattle and people are capable of a parallel extension of procreative vitality across the generations.

Money is bloodless

This 'blood'-based interpretation of the unique ties binding Nuer to their herds appears, if anything, to have become more pronounced following the introduction of currency and the concomitant develop-ment of regional cattle and labour markets during the colonial and post-independence eras. 'Money', as Nuer put it, 'has no blood' (*yiou thilɛ riɛm*) – which is to say money has no potential for transgenerational 'growth'. The concept of monetary interest, I should stress, is entirely unknown to all but a few highly urbanised Nuer. If anything, Sudanese currency appears condemned in people's eyes to a continual loss of force, to a perpetual withering in the face of mounting inflation. And for this reason, most contemporary Nuer men and women reason that money is an 'inappropriate' medium for certain exchange contexts because it cannot bind people together like 'blood' – whether such blood be thought of as human, bovine, or both with regard to particular social bonds. Money's ascendancy is thus associated with a world of transitory ties, a world that has neither a centre nor boundaries.

For these reasons, cattle's roles as sacrificial surrogate and indispensable exchange object in times of initiation, feud settlement, and, to a lesser extent, marriage have scarcely been affected by the increasing circulation of money through Nuer hands over the past half-century. This is not to say that Nuer attitudes towards these rites have remained unchanged. On the contrary, cattle's sacrificial importance, in particular, has been seriously undercut in recent decades by mounting waves of Christian conversion among Nuer. But money has still not developed into a generalised medium of exchange among Nuer. Rather, Nuer have incorporated currency into a weighted exchange system in which cattle remain the dominant metaphor of value.

Although contemporary Nuer men and women have rejected the idea that cattle and money are wholly interchangeable, they have actively sought out and used money in other contexts to temper perceived instabilities and inequalities within their cattle economy itself. As a result of the massive dislocations and deprivations experienced during the first and second civil war eras (1955–72 and 1983–present), many men and women have come to regard cattle wealth as far too fleeting to be dependable. It is thus considered essential for a person to marry or remarry as soon as the size of the family's herd makes this possible. Were a man to delay, his relatives, I was told, would pressure him into marriage with the argument that his cattle might otherwise be lost 'for nothing': *Bi thul kɛ jiek* ('A stormy wind might engulf them'). When an immediate investment of cattle wealth in marriage and children is not possible, money can serve as an important, if temporary, store of cattle wealth in times of severe hardship. In fact, there is a well-known expression that runs *Baa ghok tolkä koam* ('The cows will be broken up into small pieces and stored in the light wooden carrying case'). This expression was allegedly coined by a man named Kolang Toat who recognised long before many others that the forthcoming floods of 1961 were likely to devastate the local cattle population. He thus sold his herd and stowed the money in his ambatch carrying case until the floods finally receded eleven years later, whereupon he used the money to purchase other cattle in the marketplace. Since that time other people confronted with spreading cattle plagues or other natural or political disasters have attempted to follow Kolang Toat's example. The potential benefits of this protective strategy, however, have been steadily eroded by the post-1983 collapse of the cattle market coupled with skyrocketing inflation generated by the continuing second Sudanese civil war.

When times were better and markets more operative, 'money' could also 'protect cattle on the ground' in the sense that a person with money could keep his cattle with him longer. In fact, in exchange for grain, cloth, guns, and medicines, as well as in the payment of taxes, court fines, and school fees, most people gladly substituted money for cattle whenever they could. Ideally, cattle are to be reserved for more important occasions, such as for the creation and affirmation of 'enduring social bonds' (*maar*).

But then again, not all 'enduring social bonds' are 'positive' or 'desirable' in Nuer eyes. Feuding ties, or 'relationships of the bone' (*maar coakä*), as Nuer refer to these, are certainly 'enduring' in the sense that they are recognised across the generations. However, they are also defined as inherently 'dangerous', even in situations where open hostilities have been tempered by a successful transfer of bloodwealth cattle from the slayer's family to that of the slain. With respect to relationships such as these, Nuer can sometimes use the bloodless currency of money in an attempt to rupture, symbolically and materially, human blood linkages and/or cattle connections perceived to be 'socially negative', 'death-ridden', and 'potentially polluting'. Some contemporary Nuer men and women argue, for example, that the divinely sanctioned prohibition on the return of cattle earlier offered in bloodwealth compensation to the slayer's family (via third-party bridewealth transfers or any other type of exchange) can be eluded by immediately selling the cattle received and purchasing market substitutes. By passing briefly through a monetary phase, the potentially lethal form of pollution (*nueer*) normally provoked within the slayer's family by a direct or indirect return of bloodwealth cattle could be avoided, these people reason, because 'money has no blood'. Similarly, I was told that the tainted status of cattle received as adultery compensation – cattle that never sit well in the cuckolded husband's byre – may be removed by swiftly channelling them through the marketplace. The symbolic logic of these – albeit socially contested – assertions is especially intriguing because it suggests an implicit analogy between 'money' and 'the earth' as terminal points at which the social circuitry of human and cattle blood may begin afresh.

Over this same half-century period, Nuer men and women have also developed a unique system of hybrid categories of cattle and monetary wealth that facilitates movements of money and cattle between 'blood' and 'non-blood' spheres of exchange while simultaneously maintaining a value distinction between these spheres. It is now generally accepted, for example, that cattle purchased in the marketplace ('the cattle of money') with money earned through wage labour ('the money of work') may be owned by individuals. In contrast, cattle received through bride-wealth and/or inheritance ('the cattle of girls') as well as any money acquired through the sale of such cattle ('the money of cattle') are collectively owned by groups of relatives. Whereas the two former categories have given wage-earning younger brothers and sons a bit of turf to begin negotiating for a greater share of status and autonomy within the family fold, the two latter categories have continued to support more 'traditional' age-, gender- and descent-based differentials of power and wealth within and between Nuer families. Nevertheless, as issues of power have become increasingly fused with those of definition – fused, that is, with potential disputes over who has the right to define the 'type' of money or cattle in question – cattle ownership rights have, in general, become less clear-cut, less collective, and less age-stratified. Whereas the sense of self people cultivated through their relations with cattle before the introduction of currency invariably implied the support and participation of a wider collectivity of persons (including ancestors and divinities as well as many contemporaries), cattle's role in creating this socially expanded sense has been seriously weakened in recent years by emerging opportunities for the individual acquisition of cattle. As a result, it is increasingly difficult for senior Nuer men to monopolise power through the manipulation of cattle wealth.

Blood and guns

Significantly, Nuer men and women perceive a fundamental difference between the force of a rifle and that of a spear: whereas the power of a spear is said to issue directly from the bones and sinews of the person who hurls it, that of a gun is eerily internal to it. Outside of the minimal guiding effort required to hoist and fire it, a rifle's power is seen to be completely independent of its human bearer – 'all a person does is aim it'. Hence the force of a gun, they reason, demonstrates nothing definitive about the human being behind it. The contrast Nuer perceive between the power of guns and that of spears has not only shielded their warrior ethos from occasional crushing defeats by government troops but, more important, has provoked broader reassessments of the meaning of violent deaths as well as of the ethics and tactics of local forms of intercommunity fighting and feuding. As firearms have burned deeper and deeper into regional patterns of warfare, many people have begun to wonder whether the spiritual and social consequences of inter-Nuer gun slayings are identical to those realised by spears. Whereas everyone seems to agree, at present, that to kill someone with a spear is to accept full responsibility for that death, matters are less clear in the case of inter-Nuer gun slayings. Not only are bullets (*dei mac*, lit. 'a gun's calves') more prone to unintentional release, but, once having been fired, their trajectories – and hence fatal consequences – are often difficult if not impossible to trace accurately in the context of major intercommunity confrontations. Unlike an individually crafted spear, the source of a bullet lodged deep in someone's body is not easily identified. Relationships of 'the bone' have thus become far more ambiguous and impersonal, since the exact scope and intensity of the pollution risks associated with them are impossible to specify without clear knowledge of the slayer's identity.

In order to understand the historical significance of this difficulty, it is important to realise that, prior to the widespread dissemination of firearms during the first civil war era (1955–1972), Nuer conceptualised relationships of the 'bone' or 'feud' as emanating outwards from a mysterious 'blood' bond forged between slayer and slain at the moment of death. Specifically, they believed that some of the blood of the victim passed at death into the body of the slayer, being driven forth, as it were, by a mission of vengeance (*Bi riεmdε lony kε jε*). Were the slayer to eat or drink anything prior to having this 'embittered' blood released through a small incision (*bier*) made on the upper arm by a *kuäär muon*, or 'earth priest', he was sure to die from a highly contagious and lethal form of pollution known as *nueer*. However, as a direct consequence of the brutal realities experienced during the first and second civil wars, many people have begun to wonder whether the dangers of *nueer* are equally grave in all cases of inter-Nuer homicide. Some people, particularly eastern Jikany Nuer, now maintain that the blood curse of the slain is only operative in situations where assailant and victim are known or related to one another. Nor are people in complete consensus today about the specific rites required for the removal of such pollution. While it is still widely accepted that inter-Nuer spear killings necessitate the ritual intervention of an 'earth priest', many eastern Jikany Nuer consider the blood-letting rite of *bier* insufficient to eliminate the dangers of pollution when the victim (whether related or not to the killer) has died of bullet wounds – though some people argue that it might be carried out as a secondary precaution. The principal rite, however, is called *piu thorä*, or 'the water of the cartridge shell': the slayer, I was told, must pour some water (preferably mixed with a few grains of salt, if available) into an empty cartridge shell and drink it. It is noteworthy that the word for rifle or gun in Nuer means *mac*, 'fire' – an image that suggests that a cross-flow of 'heat' is established between victim and slayer (either in addition to or in place of 'blood') which must then be 'cooled' by drinking the 'water of the cartridge shell'. This association between 'cooling' and curing is also apparent in the blood-letting ceremony of *bier*: the drawing of 'blood' in this context is explicitly directed towards restoring the 'bodily coolness' – *koac puany* – or 'health' of the slayer. Indeed, all curative operations involving the extraction or transfer of bodily fluids are spoken about in terms of the removal of 'heat' (sickness or pollution) from the body of the afflicted. From this perspective, a shift from 'blood' to 'temperature' as the dominant metaphor of purification rites for homicide is not as radical as it might appear. Rather, the central prohibition on the drinking of water at the heart of this pollution state has been incorporated into the curative rite of *piu thorä* along lines similar to preventative inoculations in Western medical practices. Moreover, fighters who are in doubt as to whether or not they have killed someone can easily take the precaution of sipping some water of the cartridge shell and thus avoid the immediate danger of pollution. From a historical perspective, it is, perhaps, not surprising that a purificatory rite that could be performed by anyone, anywhere, at any time, without disclosing the identity of the slayer would have been 'discovered' during the late 1960s in the region most heavily devastated during the first civil war (1955–72) and thereafter avidly adopted by the eastern Jikany Nuer.

Contemporary Nuer living west of the White Nile, in contrast, have continued to rely on the purifying powers of 'earth priests' in all cases of inter-Nuer homicide through the outbreak of the second Sudanese civil war in 1983 – regardless of the type of weapon used. Since that time, however, they have begun to develop an elaborate analogy between gunfire and lightning – the deceased victims of both being thought to create a uniquely direct spiritual linkage with divinity (*col wic*) which can be actively cultivated through cattle sacrifice and, thereafter, effectively called upon in times of danger by surviving kin. And thus, like their eastern cousins, contemporary Westerners have also turned to metaphors of temperature (as opposed to those of blood) in their efforts to comprehend the mysterious inner force and ambiguous impact of guns. In both regions, moreover, feelings of increasing vulnerability to gun warfare have been symbolically transformed into assertions of greater individual control over the social and spiritual consequences of homicide. However, the fact that these spiritual developments have occurred at a time when the frequency of violent deaths has been rising and the size of local cattle stocks diminishing has significantly reduced the ability of families to ensure the procreative immortality of kinsmen slain in battle through the provision of 'ghost wives'.

Beginning in the mid 1980s, moreover, leading Nuer members of the Sudanese People's Liberation Army (and its subsequent spin-offs) have sought to persuade local citizens that violent deaths resulting from the current civil war should be completely dissociated from the pollution forms and spiritual consequences of homicides generated by more local forms of intercommunity feuding and fighting. In essence, the southern military elite is arguing that the overarching political context of the present war – which it defines as a 'government war' (*koor kume*) – should take precedence over the personal identities and interrelations of the combatants concerned in assessing the social and spiritual ramifications of homicide. These developments have further undermined the procreative and moral obligations binding together communities of kin – and, in particular, fellow-agnates.

Above and beyond their increasing use as weapons of intra- and intertribal warfare, guns have also become key value referents in the definition of many contemporary social relationships and distinctions. Rifles now being commonly used as an element of bridewealth payments, an offer of a rifle sometimes confers a competitive advantage over full cattle transfers. With the cattle exchange values for most models having doubled during the years of relative peace (1972–83) separating the first and second civil wars, Nuer now consider guns sound economic as well as sound security investments. More important, guns are not considered individual possessions but rather are owned collectively by families – or, more commonly, by groups of brothers. And thus, unlike the 'money of work' or 'the cattle of money', guns continue to reinforce strong bonds of mutual dependence among close kinsmen. More uniquely, the eastern Jikany Nuer have also adopted guns as fresh focus for a culturally creative aesthetic deeply entwined with local concepts of male potency, beauty, and strength. Their phallic forms are scarified on women's bellies, their golden bullets are girded to the right arms of men – indeed, gun displays had even replaced the imitation of cattle in male dance forms throughout the East. Rifles are also an increasingly indispensable item in courtship display, often being fired off as celebratory acts of self-affirmation during rites of engagement, marriage, and sacrifice.

And yet this ideological glorification of the relationship between men and guns would appear to be in large part defensive. Eastern Nuer men, it would seem, have latched onto guns as a fresh rallying point for their otherwise flagging sense of self-esteem. For the fact remains that the weapons and ammunition to which they currently have access are profoundly inadequate for the protective challenges they now face with respect to their families and herds. In brief, no amount of ideological bravado can cover up the fact that the material gap separating their own military capacities from those of successive state regimes has widened considerably during the colonial and post-independence eras.

Paper and blood

Because the vast majority of contemporary Nuer men and women remain as yet totally uninitiated into the mysteries of 'writing', 'paper' is becoming an increasingly powerful – if not 'fetishised' – symbol of their simultaneous dependence on and estrangement from the powers of 'the government' (*kume*). Movements of 'paper' now mark the conclusion of each new court case and the passing of each taxation season. Indeed, when attempting to enlist the support of higher-ranking administrative officials affiliated with the Sudanese People's Liberation Army or the national state government in Khartoum, most Nuer men and women, whether literate or not, operate under the assumption that the written word is far more potent than the spoken. 'It is better to talk to the *Turuok* (persons wielding 'foreign' powers) in their own language', one woman explained, 'which means you must speak to them through paper.' Touring government agents and their SPLA counterparts are thus normally pursued wherever they go by a steady swarm of little white 'papers', each carrying a personal plea for attention and assistance. Court clerks and other literate members of the community are constantly being asked by their non-literate associates to inscribe their requests for assistance on 'paper'. Through their mastery of 'paper', the literate elite is capable not only of speaking to the *Turuok* in their own language but of helping people, more generally, to transcend their 'second-class' status within the profoundly 'racialised' structure of the contemporary Sudanese state. Everyone recognises the pressing urgency of developing a large Nuer-speaking literate elite for these purposes. Indeed, of all the hardships caused by the current second Sudanese civil war (1983–present), it is the total collapse of local educational opportunities – the absence of schools, teachers, books, paper, and pens – that most distresses many of the rural Nuer villagers. For without access to the hidden powers of 'paper', Nuer women and men remain profoundly vulnerable to arbitrary interventions by national, regional, and rebel governments. As a young man named Machar explained:

You could be presenting your case before the District Commissioner, when, all of a sudden, he reaches into his breast pocket and pulls out a piece of paper, saying: 'It says here you are lying!' What can you do? You didn't see the paper written. How can you argue with a piece of paper? Your case is finished!

In brief, 'paper' is the principal medium through which contemporary Nuer men and women seek to tap the powers of 'the government' (*kume*).

More interestingly, where one sends one's tax papers – that is, to which chiefs and which courts – is increasingly viewed by many Nuer as a political commitment as to where one's loyalties will lie in the event of an eruption of intercommunity fighting. This is partly because membership in any particular administrative 'community' is defined on a voluntary social basis rather than a territorially circumscribed one. In fact, I witnessed several cases among the western Nuer in which local government chiefs arrested and publicly reprimanded individuals who had 'crossed over' community lines (*caa ro wel/caa kai kuic*) in order to support relatives on the opposing side during major intercommunity battles. As far as the arresting chiefs were concerned, the key question was 'Where does he send his papers?' (*Waragaanikε, baa kε jak nika?*).

In many ways the emerging symbolism of 'paper' mirrors that of 'blood'. For people experience both these social media as 'substances' that bind their individual and communal welfare to distant – and largely inscrutable – suprahuman powers. Like 'blood', 'paper' is a deceptive medium in that it conveys hidden inner distinctions despite its outward uniformity. Indeed, many contemporary men and women have begun developing this analogy explicitly. I recall, for instance, a situation in which a young non-literate western Nuer man attempted to explain to me how a man could have many 'loves' while still favouring one above all the rest. 'Why, it's like paper', he remarked: 'A person can have many pieces of paper and still have one piece that s/he likes very much.' On another occasion, I was discussing the relationship between menstrual blood and the human foetus with a non-literate Gaajok mother, who firmly maintained that 'the woman's blood is the child'. When I then asked about what role 'sperm' (*dieth*) played, she laughed and said: 'Oh, it's like [that of] paper'. I interpreted her enigmatic comment to mean that sperm, like 'paper', is *pualε*, or 'light' – which is to say that it is insignificant in comparison with the mother's contribution of blood to the child. On yet another occasion, an elder eastern Gaajok man invoked a 'paper' metaphor to explain to me how so many thousands of Dinka men could have been absorbed by the Nuer as 'Nuer' during the nineteenth century. 'It's like this, Nyarial', he began: 'If you take a piece of paper and it is a "real person" (*raam mi raan*) and you place it down here on the ground. Tomorrow, when you come back you would find a whole stack of papers and the top piece would look exactly like the bottom one.' I found the implicit 'reproductive' imagery of these metaphors fascinating. For though Nuer have defined money as 'blood-less' and thus as lacking the procreative capabilities of both cattle and people, their images of 'paper' and the mysterious powers of literacy it embodies appear more ambiguous.

Significantly, some people have begun to develop metaphorical linkages between 'paper' and 'cattle'. For example, a person who has succeeded in acquiring cattle as a direct result of his or her literacy skills will sometimes refer to such cattle as *ghok waragak* (the cattle of paper) – this being a subcategory, as it were, of the more general category 'cattle of money'. Furthermore, when significant numbers of such cattle are used by their owner to marry a wife, it is not uncommon among the western Nuer for the first child born to the union to be named *Waragak* if a boy, or *Nyawaragak* if a girl. This is done in recognition of the fact that, had it not been for the father's knowledge of 'paper', that child might never have been born. Clearly, *waragak*, or 'paper', holds the promise of becoming an increasingly important symbol of interpersonal relations for Nuer in the years ahead. For like 'blood', 'paper', too, is capable of spanning, whether as metaphor or medium, the experiential extremes of social intimacy and social distance and of human vitality and human vulnerability. Its ascendancy, however, is inextricably linked to distant political forces which, as one non-literate man lamented, 'have come to know people in ways that we cannot know'.

Conclusions

Nuer images of 'blood' revolve, as we have seen, around an experientially embodied tension between human vitality and human vulnerability that, potentially, runs through all forms of enduring social bonds. This tension reverberates through people's attitudes towards and daily interactions with 'food' and 'cattle' as well – these being the two primary media Nuer use to render the mysterious powers of human blood bonds socially significant and stable. By helping to ground more abstract social distinctions and connections in the immediacies of bodily experience, evolving Nuer concepts of 'blood' lend greater substance and flexibility to contemporary processes of 'identity' formation. More important, the profound aspirations and vulnerabilities that people associate with specific states and passages of 'blood' have also coloured their attempts to understand the socially binding and divisive potential of 'money', 'guns', and 'paper'. As part of their more general efforts to intervene, consciously and actively, in the broader historical forces shaping their immediate life circumstances, contemporary Nuer men and women have selectively incorporated these three media, as we have seen, in ways that attempt both to enhance the 'vitality' and to reduce the 'vulnerabilities' inherent in their changing interpretations and experiences of human blood connections as well as of their evolving engagements with the world at large.

Note

A highly simplified system of spelling Nuer has been used in the text to facilitate easy publication. For those interested in more accurate transcriptions of the terms used, please see Hutchinson 1996.

4   Sentiment and substance in North Indian forms of relatedness

Helen Lambert

Indian kinship as described by anthropologists has usually been taken to comprise only those relationships produced by marriage (affinity) and birth (descent), and in northern India kinship thus described appears as a bounded sphere which is closely structured by certain well-known characteristics: patrilineality and patrilocality, the centrality of alliance in the perpetuation of patrilineal descent groups, status distinctions between wife-takers and wife-givers, and village exogamy. I first began to think about alternative forms and understandings of relatedness through some observations about the salience of locality and gender in the formation of cross-caste relationships in Rajasthan that suggested there are ways of being related other than through birth or marriage (Lambert 1996). In this chapter I attempt to offer a wider consideration of relatedness and to ask what this suggests about conventional views of kinship.

Such conventional views, as Carsten (this volume and 1995a) has indicated, rest on a narrow definition of biology to circumscribe what kinship entails, and in the Indian context, this has produced particular difficulties in thinking comparatively about Indian kinship because of the existence of caste. The endogamous character of caste groups has produced a very limited treatment of kinship as necessarily confined to the relationships that exist within castes (Mayer 1960), since most studies in the region have implicitly presumed that a (putative) heredi-tary principle – that is, subcaste membership – is coterminous with the outermost limits of kinship. The resultant separation between 'caste' and 'kinship' in Indian sociology bears comparison with Stafford's description in this volume of the conventional segregation of 'kinship' and 'family' in Chinese studies. As another society characterised by patrilineal descent, kinship in northern India too has generally been treated as entirely discrete from 'family', with the latter given far less importance in studies of social organisation; but 'kinship' has in turn been taken as subordinate to, and discrete from, caste (witness the number of volumes entitled *Caste and Kinship in . . .*).

Although castes are endogamous and their hereditary character is generally considered one of their defining features, caste – rather than lineage as in China – has been analysed primarily as the distinct form of social stratification which is central to Indian society (cf. Burghart 1996: 92–4). Louis Dumont, whose work following Lévi-Strauss emphasised the importance of marriage alliance in the study of Indian kinship, regarded caste as an 'extraneous factor' to kinship and in discussing the case of North India (as compared with the South, where marriage rules are encoded in the kinship terminology) wrote of how '... status, i.e. caste, *invades* the sphere of kinship ...' (1994: 101; my emphasis). In other words, caste as an encompassing feature is not generally considered to have anything to do with kinship as conventionally defined, and most studies of kinship have indeed taken these two domains to be quite discrete – with the exception of Östör, Fruzzetti, and Barnett, who have asserted that formal analyses of kinship obscure 'the significance of indigenous categories that crosscut the boundaries of kinship and caste' (1992: 6).

Experiences of local views of caste, however, suggest an alternative understanding of what caste stands for. Starting fieldwork in a relatively traditional, largely Hindu area of Rajasthan,[1] I had awaited inquiries about my caste identity with some trepidation. Steeped in an anthropological literature on caste as a system of hierarchical inequality based on gradations of purity, I feared reactions of either distaste or disbelief at my claim to castelessness. Instead, my first reluctant admission that in my country there are no castes provoked the response 'Then how do you know who to marry?' This question revealed a quite different view of caste as an essential consideration in the selection of marriage partners – that is, in the formation of kinship.

In this chapter I suggest that the domain of intracaste affinal and agnatic relations, which has conventionally been taken to comprise the whole domain of kinship in northern India, does not encompass all the forms of relatedness that are locally recognised and valued. Since most other forms of relatedness have been little described, except incompletely and misleadingly under the catch-all designation of 'fictive kinship', the bulk of this chapter concerns these. Locally recognised forms of relatedness are not confined to connections of shared bodily substance based on birth/ancestry, but extend beyond these to ties based on shared locality, adoption (of children and of in-marrying women), and nurturance, including feeding. In my discussion of these various forms I try in particular to tease out the roles of affective values and 'substance' in constructions of relatedness, and to ask what the local emphasis on non-procreative cognation as an ideal form of relatedness suggests about the relative importance of sentiments and substances in indigenous views.

That a variety of grounds for becoming related and ways of being related exist does not mean that these are considered to be equivalent or interchangeable. Forms of relatedness which cannot be classified under the rubric of agnatic or affinal kinship are locally recognised to be different in kind from these, and for this reason it is appropriate to maintain a distinction between (necessarily caste-specific) 'kinship' and other forms of relatedness. Relationships of consanguinity within household and lineage are regarded as connections of substance arising naturally from biological processes, and in this respect my account suggests that the assumption of a 'biological' and immutable component to kinship is not exclusively Euro-American. However, in the Rajasthani context affections flow along with substance as forms of natural connection and constitute the model for other, optative forms of relatedness. These two forms – consanguineal and optative – are sharply contrasted with affinal relations, which are assumed to lack the natural affective qualities commensurate with consanguineal ties. Hence 'relatedness', those social connections between persons that are collectively recognised and regarded as enduring, as extending beyond individual interpersonal relationships, and as carrying rights and responsibilities associated with being related, is broader than the domain of 'kinship' as the latter is both locally and analytically understood.

This approach to relatedness qualifies our understanding of what goes into being and, especially, becoming related in this particular cultural context. Here, for example, 'relatedness' extends only uneasily to include relationships of affinity, although affines are unequivocally kin. This is arguably because the creation of relatedness in any form is, ultimately, premised on differentiating between essentially similar persons; in Wagner's view (discussed by Williams 1995: 209ff), such differentiation is achieved through restricting flows of similarity. In India this patently applies to the restrictions on flows of substance, especially through limitations on commensality and marriage, which famously constrain relations between members of different subcastes (*jati*), each *jati* (also 'genus') being conceptualised as fundamentally different in nature. My account describes the forms of relatedness which can nonetheless be created between members of such differentiated groups. The case of affines offers a Rajasthani example of the difficulties in establishing relatedness between persons who are similar. For marriage to be possible within a North Indian subcaste, affines can only be those who, despite their subcaste identity, are classifiable as 'unrelated' at the time of marriage alliance. This may explain their problematic status in terms of local understandings of what constitutes 'relatedness', despite their unequivocal status as 'relatives' within the formal kinship system.[2]

In my account I take the conventional facts about such North Indian kinship systems to be common knowledge and start by describing two forms of what in the ethnographic literature on North India has previously been described as 'fictive kinship'. My account goes on to consider other indigenously recognised forms of relatedness and their characteristics and meanings, before returning to the question of how kinship is related to caste and concluding with a discussion of the implications of this material for understanding the meanings of 'kinship' and 'relatedness' in this highly socially stratified context.

Locally created relatedness

The general characteristics of social and kinship relations that I found to be present in the area of Rajasthan where I did fieldwork are common to the region more generally. As elsewhere in the northern part of India, co-residents of a village consider themselves to be 'village relations' and use kin terms of reference and address to one another (cf., on 'village kin', Mayer 1960: 144–6, Marriott 1969: 177–8; Mandelbaum 1970: 151–2, Vatuk 1975: 157); in keeping with this, villages are conventionally exogamous. Women move to the husband's home upon marriage, and in Rajasthan they veil their faces and maintain silence in front of all men in their marital village who are older than their husbands or equivalent in age, as well as their senior affines of both sexes within the conjugal household. They do not, however, veil in front of natal relatives and can interact freely with their natal village relatives. Away from their parents' village, people who come from the same natal place are explicitly acknowledged by each other, through terms of address and behaviour and forms of ritual, as agnates, regardless of their caste. For example, on the occasion of a child's marriage, the mother's brother arrives bringing gifts not only for his sister, sister's child, and affines but also for any other married women who come from the same natal village as he and his sister; and these women – regardless of their caste – are invited to participate in the pre-wedding feast. The *nanihal* – mother's natal place – also remains a significant location for both men and women; some children are even raised there by their maternal grand-parents, thus tempering the putative exclusivity of agnatic links in what is ideologically a strongly patrilineal milieu.

Such locality-based links produce networks of relatedness beyond those of the geographically limited place of residence and the socially restricted membership of a particular subcaste and lineage. Networks created through shared locality of origin can be important politically and economically for men and for women, and they can provide valuable sources of social and personal support, particularly in the early years of marriage when young brides have little status in their affinal homes and few opportunities apart from these networks to signal distress, make requests, or simply communicate news. Another means of tempering the alien character of a woman's conjugal village is to make use of any genealogical links that already exist between the woman's natal village and persons in her conjugal village. The cases documented by Raheja for Uttar Pradesh villages (Raheja and Gold 1994: 106–20) and by Vatuk (1992: 68–70) show that where such alternatives exist, closeness of consanguineal connection and matrilateral links from the natal village are generally favoured in determining modes of address and behaviour over what in literal terms are often more direct linkages traced through affinal kin (the woman's husband).

In addition to these locality-based forms of relatedness – that is, natal village relations and their extension into women's conjugal villages – there are several types of adoptive relation. I first became aware of one of these when, on arriving at a Gujar compound one day, I found the wife of the household head having a meal with a senior Rajput woman from another village household. I had never before seen this Rajput woman outside her house, since women of this high caste keep strict *parda* (seclusion) in their conjugal homes; seeing my astonishment, she explained, with a gesture towards her older Gujar companion, that she was visiting her 'mother'. As a result of this encounter I came to learn that, on marriage, a Rajasthani woman may be provided with a set of honorary agnates in a household other than her affinal one, often of a different caste. Although women emphasise the importance of the mother–daughter tie so created, these relationships are not confined to a dyadic relationship between two women but entail the establishment of ties between the adoptive daughter and all the other members of the adopting group of kin. As a consanguine, in her adoptive household a woman can dispense with the necessity for veiling and avoidance practices that must be maintained in the presence of all affinal kin (including village relations). For a woman whose natal village is distant and who thus can receive visits and return home rarely, such ties are particularly valued. Moreover, in circumstances where male natal kin are unable to fulfil affinal obligations or are deceased, *dharm* or *jholi* kin perform the ritually indispensable legitimating roles of father or brother on the occasion of life-cycle rituals in the woman's affinal household.

This form of relatedness, known locally as *jholi*, is formally established through a vow given by the adoptive father at the time of the marriage of the adoptive daughter, when he takes the bride on his lap and under-takes to treat her as his own. Adopting a daughter as *jholi* entails for the adoptive household the taking on of all the customary ritual obligations and costs entailed by natal kin, including the provision of appropriate gifts on all life-cycle occasions. Such formal adoptive relationships are permanent, extending at least to the next generation and being recognised in ritual transactions and festive occasions that concern other members of both families.

The initial selection of the adoptive household is made by the bride's affines. Selected households are usually, of course, those with whom there already exist both affective ties and relations of reciprocity (*vya-vahar*). Informants identified only one restriction on the choice of a household for establishing *jholi* with a daughter-in-law; that it should be of a caste from which they can drink water. From the local point of view this is straightforwardly because commensality between the adoptive family and daughter is obviously essential; certainly all the cases of *jholi* which I recorded were between housholds of the 'clean' castes, who formed a disproportionate number of my informants (I have no evidence regarding such relationships between 'low' or 'untouchable' households of the same or different castes). Here in effect caste boundaries are selectively maintained through restrictions that are placed on estab-lishing new relations according to the limits of commensality. In local views it is simply the self-evident fact that it is impossible to accept sustenance from certain kinds of person (for higher castes, those of low caste) that limits the range of practical possibilities for becoming related; but conversely, commensality could be regarded as a means of creating kinship, as discussed in the section on substantive relations below. Thus the state of 'non-relatedness' between the 'clean' and 'unclean' castes is not only acknowledged but actually maintained by restrictions of this type on sharing of sustenance (cf. Williams's 1995: 209ff discussion of Wagner's view, discussed above, that relatedness is about differentiation between the essentially similar nature of all persons, achieved by actively restricting flows of similarity).

Adoptive *jholi* relationships can also be referred to as *dharam (ki)*, as in *dharam ki ma*, 'honorary mother', or *dharam bahin*, 'honorary sister'. The prefix *dharam* (Hindi *dharma*) is used also to designate adoptive relations that are created in a less formal and more individually voluntar-istic manner than that of *jholi*. Hence siblingship between a man and a woman (*dharam bhai/dharam bahin*) who decide to formalise their friendship on a permanent basis may be established by the ritual tying of a thread (*rakhi*) by the woman on the man's wrist and receiving a small gift from him on the annual festival when birth sisters and brothers are expected to do this. Henceforth these individuals maintain relations as between birth siblings, including the giving of gifts to the woman on appropriate life-cycle occasions. The term *dharam (dharma)*, right action in a religious sense, refers to the implicit local assumption that it is meritorious to take on such obligations. It may, moreover, be consistent with broader moral evaluations of such 'honorary' forms of relatedness. When I returned to the village in 1995 where I had done the bulk of my fieldwork and started inquiring about *jholi* relations, a couple of young Rajput sisters-in-law in the household where I had previously lived argued that relatedness of this kind is actually superior to kinship created by birth, because one's relationship with one's birth parents is derived 'from sin' (*pap syu*). These women both expressed regret that (unlike the wife of their husbands' father's brother who lived in the same extended household) neither of them had been provided with such an adoptive family upon marriage into the village. Their comments suggested that relatedness not originating in sexual intercourse (understood as a polluting act) is considered purer than kinship produced through procreation. This view is reminiscent of Marshall's assertion regarding the Trukese notion that 'created' sibling relationships are better than natural ones in that they compose the 'purest expression of "brotherly love"' (1977: 649; cited in Williams 1995: 208). The underlying notion is that relatedness based solely on voluntarily created ties of affection is closer to an ideal of kinship than that based on biological reproduction.

A more 'conventional' type of adoption also exists which is undertaken to ensure a male heir in the case of childlessness. In such cases the adoptive son is usually an agnatic relation (brother's son or equivalent) and is drawn from the same local subcaste. The adoption is formalised by ritually pronouncing the adoptive child (often already a young man) as the legitimate heir of the adoptive father at a 'living-death feast' (*jivat mausa*). Death feasts are customarily held twelve days after the death of a male householder in this region and are the occasion on which a turban is tied on the head of the main mourner – usually the son of the deceased or a younger brother – in recognition of his new status as the head of household. Such a feast, and the associated ceremony, can however be held before death, in order to avoid the necessity of surviving relatives' bearing the considerable costs, and in the case of adoption in order to legitimise inheritance by the adoptive son. In such cases, although the adoptive son moves formally from one household to another only once the ritual is performed, as members of the same local clan segment they already consider one another to be close kin. It is not uncommon for such adoption to be the formal culmination of a fostering situation in which the child in question has already been living partly or exclusively with the adoptive couple for some years. Within local agnatic kin groups there is no contradiction between recognising both biological parenthood and other, nurturant ties of kinship.

Nurturing relatedness

This type of adoption between related lineages introduces a consideration of some aspects of reproduction and lineage-based kinship that will illustrate how both place or territory and notions of shared substance enter into the formation of relatedness. Sexual intercourse is referred to in only the most allusive terms but is clearly understood to be essential for the production of offspring, which in turn is the primary purpose of marriage. Both men and women are considered to have seminal fluids, which mix together for conception to occur. Among Rajasthanis, women usually give birth to their first child in their conjugal home; after each birth the placenta and umbilical cord are buried in the earthen floor of the delivery room (or, in *pakka* houses, in the courtyard). After the birth of a first son, this burial is symbolically performed by the husband's younger brother, who breaks the ground with a plough spike (the cord is actually buried by the mother-in-law or, if present, a midwife). Aijmer argues that disposal practices of this sort 'anchor' the individual to a particular territory (1992: 6), and in the Rajasthani context the existence of forms of relatedness based on locality, such as the village relations described above, testify to the presumption of an enduring tie between a person and his or her place of birth. In this patrilocal context children are understood as belonging unequivocally to their father's lineage and they remain in his house if their parents divorce (as may occur among all except the Brahman, Bania, and Rajput castes) and their mother leaves, even in the case of very young children.

An infant's tie to local territory in this respect is simultaneously a link with its patriline, which is retained throughout life, albeit in very different ways for men and women (see my discussion above regarding a woman's enduring ties to her natal home). During pregnancy, however, the foetus is thought to be nourished by its mother's blood. Blood, breastmilk, and semen, according to indigenous physiology and medicine, are all formed through the digestive cooking and subsequent progressive refinement of ingested foodstuffs. The ingestion of breastmilk thus continues the process of maternal nourishment, and a child hence comes to share the bodily substance of its mother as well as of its siblings, who have also shared the uterine environment and ingested the mother's milk (cf. Fruzzetti, Östör, and Barnett 1992: 13 for similar notions in Tamil Nadu, and Busby 1997b: 262–3 for Kerala, where, however, male and female substance is more explicitly distinguished). Breastmilk is, moreover, an especially effective medium for the transmission of qualities and affects. Since the kinds of food a woman eats are transmitted through breastmilk to her child, a mother must be very careful of her diet when breastfeeding. Negative conditions and qualities such as illness, spirit or witch affliction, and moral deficiency can also be passed on through breastmilk, and a woman's mental or emotional state similarly affects the quality of her milk (cf. Reissland and Burghart 1988: 465–6). Although these nurturant relations cannot supersede children's primary identification with their father's house and lineage, what a child is like as an individual is considered to be more significantly shaped by its mother, owing to what are considered to be natural connections produced through gestation and breastfeeding (cf. Das 1976: 4–5). The symbolic as well as substantive significance of breastmilk and breastfeeding is illustrated by the ritual performance enacted by Rajasthani Rajput males immediately prior to marriage. The very last act that a bridegroom performs, already seated on his horse, before he leaves his house in the wedding party is literally to 'suckle' from his mother's breast. This act reaffirms the enduring character of his milk tie (tie of substance) to his natal kin – and in particular his mother – in the face of the impending establishment of affinal relations.

Breastmilk both is a paradigmatic symbol of nurturance and is itself constitutive of relatedness. In this Hindu semi-pastoralist milieu, all milk is considered both pure and strength-giving, but within the household, milk from livestock seems to have special symbolic resonance in relation to a household's and lineage's kinship identity through time. It has a place in all contexts relating to the veneration of deceased members of a household. Following a death, on the third day relatives go and place a clay cup of unboiled (kacca, lit. 'raw') milk on the place of cremation. During the collective ancestral shraddha rituals performed annually by the Gujar, Mina, and Balai castes, an offering of khir (milk rice) is offered by all male lineage members to their collective ancestors. Characteristic ploys of the troublesome undeparted spirit of a deceased relative (ut) are to make the household's milk go sour or to cause the milch animals of the household to become dry. In order to satisfy such a spirit, it can be provided with a permanent place of its choosing – on a shelf in the home, in a stone tablet in the family fields, or, most commonly, in a silver icon around the neck of a family member. At the ritual to establish the spirit in its place, it is worshipped by the family members and is offered khir, after which it is referred to as an 'ancestor' (patar or ut-patar; Hindi pitr). On Amavas, the moonless day of special observance to ancestors in Hinduism, the spirit of a deceased relative who has been established in this way as an 'ancestor' is worshipped. Such an ancestor may also be venerated by members of that extended lineage (the local segment of a clan group) residing in other households. Its representation is bathed in milk and water, and on that day all milk from the household's milch animals is cooked to make *khir*, which is eaten by the household members instead of being sold or made into butter.

Clearly, the use of milk produced by household livestock in the veneration of that lineage's deceased members is a recurrent theme. I suggest that all these uses of household milk are expressive of the historical depth of kinship. In relation to ancestors, it is through the milk of the house that the residents as kinship unit nurture their lineage antecedents and maintain a link backwards in time. Moreover an analogy exists with the mother–child relationship, in which nurturance of the subsequent generation, and thus the projection of kinship into the future, is through (breast)milk. As a form and vehicle of nurturance, milk in this way provides a connection between two modes of related-ness: that of women, coming from outside to sustain the future, and that of the ancestors, as agnatic forebears.[3] The continuity between new members of the household (created through the incorporation of women from outside the lineage and clan) and its ancestors is empha-sised by the custom of ceasing to observe calendrical festivals on which a member of the household died until a new member of that household is born on the same day.

A particularly interesting feature of the 'ancestral' nurturance that I have described is that spirits which trouble the household and are then 'seated' there and fed regularly, are not always genealogical ancestors. Rather they are usually children or young men who have died untimely deaths before marrying and having children themselves (and whose bones have not been 'made to arrive', *pahumchano*, in the realm of the ancestors by the ritual of immersion in the Ganges in the twelve days following cremation). Through the rituals I have outlined, such indi-viduals who stay around the household and make their presence felt are nonetheless transformed into 'ancestors'. It seems, then, that the rituals characterised by the use of 'house milk' (cf. Moller n.d.) do not just express the remembrance and nurturance of ancestral links but actually help to create them. Indeed, occasionally the deified deceased are not household, clan group, or even caste members at all. One Kumhar (potter caste) lineage in the village where fieldwork was conducted collectively venerated as 'ancestors' two men, described as 'brothers', who had been killed while working together on building a dam as part of a local drought-relief scheme. While one of these men had been a member of the Kumhar lineage who venerated the pair, his 'brother' had actually been a Nai (barber caste). This example shows how, in ritual nurturance and local recognition, a deceased man could be incorporated by the lineage of a different subcaste as an ancestral relative; and it concords with other evidence relating to the role of nurturance as symbolised by milk-feeding, and more generally of commensality, in the constitution of relatedness.

Substantive relations

Among ethnosociologists of South Asia much emphasis has been placed on the concept of 'substance-code' as an illuminating characterisation of Hindu ideology. The ethnosociological approach, which proposes for the Indian context a non-dualistic inseparability of Schneider's 'substance' (nature) and 'code of conduct' (law), or, in effect, of actor and action, originated in the study of caste systems (see Marriott 1976; Marriott and Inden 1977), with their identification of ethnic identity and appropriate conduct or 'right action' (*dharma*). Subsequent transactional analyses of social relations have mainly focused either on food exchanges between castes or on gift exchanges between kin within castes. Despite the originating connection between the transactionalist approach and the study of American kinship, the well-known facts concerning the ways in which flows of substance and sustenance are regulated in India have not influenced understandings of Indian kinship.

This may be owing to the tendency, discussed at the beginning of this chapter, to subordinate kinship analytically to caste as a marker of social identity (Lambert 1996), together with an overriding focus in Indian anthropology on the notion of religious impurity as a fundamental determinant of social relations. Hence food exchanges and relations of commensality have been examined primarily by reference to the overarching logic of purity and pollution. Water and certain types of food are said to be more permeable to pollution than other types and thus cannot be shared between those of widely differing statuses in the social hierarchy. This approach implicitly takes the social categories of caste to be primary and interprets restrictions on commensality by reference to them. Following the logic that associates being related with flows of substance (which create similarity and connection), it is, however, possible to invert this approach and to argue in 'substantialist' (cf. Vasavi 1994: 287) terms, as I have done with reference to the role of caste in the selection of *jholi* kin, that restrictions on food exchange not only express but *create* degrees of social distance – that is, 'non-relatedness'. The household constitutes an intimate micro-environment within which persons are related through the sharing of food, as well as bodily substance in the forms of blood and milk and, in the case of married couples, seminal fluids. Despite the continuing relevance of caste in determining marriage eligibility (see Fuller 1996), the oft-observed apparent breakdown of caste as a salient social category in urban environments, as restrictions on commensality disappear, would suggest that there may be some 'substance' in this way of understanding the construction of relatedness.

Ayurvedic doctrine (Zimmerman 1988) and Indian philosophical traditions (Sax 1990: 494) both invoke an ecological conception of relations and flows of substance between person and place, and the idea of a locality-specific social identity is concordant with substance shared through a common local environment. The identification with a specific place as expressed both in rituals which recognise the legitimacy of village siblingship and in postpartum practices can be linked to such an ecological understanding. Indian villagers generally attribute impor- tance to the micro-environment that they share, persons being held to be affected by the qualities of the water and soil of their particular locality (Daniel 1984; Vasavi 1994). In Rajasthan, notions of ecological compatibility in relation to personal health were very important, par- ticularly with respect to an assumed compatibility between the drinking water of 'one's own place' and the maintenance of bodily wellbeing. In general terms, a minimal degree of relatedness, which could be said to exist between persons as the 'natural' consequence of sharing a micro- environment, can be further enhanced in direct correspondence to the extent to which substances – in the forms of water, food, and milk as well as breastmilk and blood – are actively shared between persons. I have suggested how this operates at the level of the household and clan segment through time and have discussed relatedness across caste boundaries associated with shared environments at the level of the village.

Examining my ethnographic material in this light, it would seem that who eats and drinks with whom – a form of sharing substance – not only reflects and expresses differences in purity between persons of different social categories, but also operates as an idiom for expressing degrees of relatedness between persons; and this, in turn, is because feeding serves to mark bonds of affection. Even with respect to the deceased, when I asked why some spirits but not others hang around the family after death, I was told by several informants that those who stay (and who are then nurtured) are the ones whom surviving relatives shed tears for. In other words, those whom one feeds are those one cares for and who thus are – or can be – relatives. As Trawick remarked of 'her' Tamil family with respect to their non-exclusive eating practices, 'In this household, the defiance of rules of purity ... was a way of teaching children and onlookers where love was' (1992: 105). Flows of sustenance parallel flows of affection, and the paradigm for emotional and substantive nurturance is, of course, the mother–child relationship, in which actual bodily substance is shared.

The findings that relatedness is conceived in terms of shared substance and affection, and that these are mutually constitutive, are consistent with the ethnosociological proposition that 'substance' and 'code for conduct' are immanent in one another. However, consanguineal kinship constitutes the ideal model of relatedness, and optative forms of relation invoke this model, rather than being entirely identified with it. Relatedness produced by feeding does not create consubstantiality to the same extent as that produced by procreative ties. It is possible to see 'substantialism' in the creation of relatedness between persons simply as an idiom – of especial importance to women – that facilitates the development and maintenance of affectionate and binding ties, especially those which are not acknowledged within the dominant ideologies (Shimizu's 'ideological kinship' – 1991: 397) of patriliny and caste. Similarly, although I have shown how milk-feeding of deceased relatives transforms these spirits into 'ancestors', such rituals of nurturance could reasonably be interpreted as a symbolic reaffirmation of the affective and substantive ties that have been abruptly severed by premature death rather than as an example of action based on 'substantialist' thinking. The precise articulations between sentiments and shared substances in the formation of relatedness may be interpreted according to their utilisation in the various contexts I have described, rather than taken as evidence of a single underlying model.

Qualities of kinship

In my descriptions of relatedness based on shared locality, of adoptive practices, of kinship between mother and child, and of relatedness created by feeding, I have intimated that the sharing of substance and sustenance are locally assumed to entail, automatically, positive affective ties. All these forms of relatedness are expressed in cognatic terms. In a context in which alliance has been so strongly emphasised by anthropologists, it is notable that both adoptive (*jholi* or *dharam*) and locality-based ties always take the form of putative consanguinity in terms of reference and address (cf. Vatuk 1969). The particular characteristic inherent in consanguinity – as contrasted with affinity – that the construction of new relations symbolically invokes (or, rather, strives to invoke) is permanent affection, or 'diffuse enduring solidarity' in Schneider's (1968) terms. The kinship systems proposed in conventional anthropological analyses posit cognatic and affinal relations together as constitutive of kinship and exclude what have been described as 'fictive' kin relations, these being considered metaphorical extensions of such systems. By contrast, indigenous reckoning implies that only 'consanguinity' constitutes kinship, the distinctive feature of which is that it invokes moral qualities – the *feelings* of being related (permanent affection, love, or 'diffuse enduring solidarity'). Here, however, by 'consanguinity' is meant not strictly the sharing of blood but of substance as indigenously conceived, including qualities and positive affects transmitted through bodily fluids. In this local understanding, relatedness is further created and sustained not only among those of the same lineage and household whose consanguineal kinship is acknowledged in the terms of the formal kinship system, but also – and more ideally – through sustenance and the media of a local environment shared between those who are not so related by birth.

Those who are eligible for marriage, by contrast, must not be related in this way. For while castes are endogamous, in North India alliances between close kin are prohibited, and in the area where I conducted fieldwork, most castes conformed to the 'four-clan exclusion rule' whereby a man cannot marry a woman who belongs to his own clan (*gotra*), his mother's clan, or his paternal or maternal grandmother's clan. Persons of the same subcaste are, at the level of contrast with other castes, assumed to be related in some vague ultimate sense (for example through a common origin myth and often through the operation of judicial caste councils). Within the subcaste, however, there exist for each family and lineage both kin who are related through shared blood (bodily substance) and non-kin. By definition, affines cannot, prior to being brought into relationship by virtue of the conjugal tie, be kin, and the local understanding of relatedness as essentially consanguineal is congruent with this requirement.

After marriage, sets of affines obviously become relatives (*rishtadar*) by virtue of the marital tie, but this type of relatedness is understood to be different from other forms. At the level of the household, Das has suggested that the archetypal tensions which exist in North Indian families between mothers-in-law and daughters-in-law are expressive of a conflict between the ties of sexuality (between husband and wife) and those of procreation (between mother and child). My observations of the social practices in Rajasthani joint families concord with Das's

(1976: 9–16) and Vatuk's (1992: 93–4) accounts, which argue that the affective bonds both between spouses and between them and their children, which are assumed to exist naturally, are severely restricted in the presence of other members of the household, in favour of an emphasis on the affective ties between these children and their other close kin. The 'base relation of sexuality' (Das 1976: 10) between husband and wife is socially disvalued by comparison with relations of procreation (between parents – especially mother – and child), over which in turn are valued non-procreative relations of consanguinity. The latter, as we have seen, can include not only kin relations such as brother and sister, mother's brother and sister's son and daughter, but also adoptive relations, which, as we have seen, are regarded as superior to the ties between parents and their birth children that are assumed to exist as a natural consequence of procreation.

Conclusion

I have indicated that the components of sentiment, substance, and nurturance which are indigenously regarded as constituting the grounds for relatedness are themselves common to different forms of relatedness, and thus all these forms of relatedness can be viewed as a continuum based on a series of characteristics that are present in varying degrees. Local evaluations of adoptive parenting as, at least in some respects, superior to parent–child kinship based in procreation suggest that optative forms of relatedness arising primarily from shared affections and sharing of sustenance may be valued over those forms deriving involuntarily primarily from consubstantiality. Indigenous understandings nonetheless recognise there to be a difference between such optative ties and those produced by both birth and marriage, while being modelled on the former, that is, on relations of consanguinity arising from procreation. These procreatively based relations have the character of taken-for-granted forms of relatedness which are regarded as both natural and immutable and which can from one perspective be distinguished as kinship, together with the affinal relations that are the product of the marital relation which is assumed to be equally essential to reproduction. Kinship, in this sense, comprises a subset of ways of being related that are encompassed by a broader concept of relatedness. Forms of relatedness which do not comprise kinship in this sense are actively desired and constructed against the backdrop of caste-specific relations, which are taken for granted as being genealogically essential. It is, perhaps, precisely the opportunity which such optative forms present for actively creating relatedness that results in their superior valuation over those which are seen as resulting inevitably from social and biological necessity.

In this chapter I have argued that ties based on locality as well as on biology can be bases of relatedness and that a continuum exists between adoptive and procreative forms which is articulated in an idiom of affection. This has resonances with Edwards and Strathern's character-isation of Alltowners' views of kinship as being based in relations of locality as well as of blood. Not all forms of relatedness in Rajasthan form a continuum, however; marriage and the kinship ties it brings constitute a problematic break point in this milieu, since although alliance generates a whole range of 'relatives', affinal relations do not naturally entail flows of affection, as does consanguineal kinship. It is for this reason that people tend, where possible, to 'convert' affinal relations into consanguineal ones. A second point of cleavage that crosscuts the continuum of relatedness based in affection is the largely implicit but salient distinction between kinship ties that are seen as 'given' and undeniable, and those that are seen as produced voluntarily.[4] This distinction bears comparison with Bodenhorn's description of a distinc-tion between 'optative' and 'non-optative' categories of kin. However, whereas the 'non-optative' category appears similar in its taken-for-granted character in both societies, among Iñupiat this category is far narrower than in Rajasthan, where a tie, however distant, produced through relations of birth, marriage, or locality is unequivocally ac-cepted as one of relatedness regardless of actions which demonstrate this. For example, it is not uncommon to find complete strangers attempting to establish, by virtue of a long discussion of mutually known bilateral links of kinship and locality, that they are somehow 'related'. Conversely, whereas among Iñupiat 'optative' kin are defined as such because of the way they act, in Rajasthan they are defined on the basis of sentiment, considered to be the underlying and automatic ground for acting the way those who are related consanguineally should. In terms of my earlier characterisation of relatedness, following Wagner, as con-cerned with differentiation brought about by restricting flows of simi-larity, consubstantiality (consanguinity) is revealed as entailing unrestricted flows of affection, while marriage, in contrast, entails highly restricted flows of affection and sustenance commensurate with the process of bringing into relation substantially differentiated persons.

The limit that conventional definitions of kinship have placed on situating the North Indian case comparatively is that, as long as kinship is seen as biologically defined and hence as existing only within localised caste (descent) groups while being distinct from caste itself, it can only characterise a very confined sphere of social relations while excluding most of everyday life that occurs beyond these groups. My account, in contrast, by examining other forms of relatedness, has tried to demonstrate some of the more processual ways in which people can modify and extend the more limited set of relations that they generally regard as immutable. This has allowed me to discuss adoptive forms of relatedness based on affection and on shared locality and to identify where points of cleavage other than caste boundaries arise. I have limited this account to a reading of local understandings of 'being related', but, following Stafford's more generous definition of relatedness, it could fruitfully be broadened to include kinds of relationship which do not entail being relatives but certainly do entail having relations, such as the relations (*vyavahar*) of reciprocity (*len-den*, lit. 'give-and-take') that are maintained between sets of neighbours and friends as well as subgroups of relatives.

Notes

1 The data on which this paper draws derive from fieldwork undertaken in 1984–6, for which the Economic and Social Research Council provided indispensable support as part of my D.Phil. research. I made shorter follow-up visits in 1993 and 1995 to the village in which I conducted the bulk of my initial research.
2 This reading bears comparison with Busby's (1997a, b) analysis of gendered relatedness in Dravidian kinship systems. She demonstrates that in South India, cross-cousin marriage is preferred, as it entails alliance between individuals who are related but not identical, owing to having different bodily substance; males pass to their sons male substance, and females pass female substance to their daughters. By contrast, parallel-cousin marriage is prohibited, because children of two sisters or of two brothers inherit the same substance and hence are as similar as full siblings. My account suggests the beginnings of a parallel argument regarding the role of clan and subcaste in North Indian presumptions regarding bodily identity (consubstantiality) and difference.
3 Complementary to this point is Strathern's suggestion, in a discussion of the gendering of persons through initiation rituals (1993: 51), that at marriage the 'male' lineage expels a 'female' it has produced, just as at birth a 'female' body expels a 'male' (agnatically speaking) child.
4 While from an analytic point of view marriage alliance would seem to fall into the category of kinship relations that are produced 'voluntarily', this is not how it is seen locally. Marriage is regarded as essential, at least for women, and the relations it produces are regarded as unmodifiable. Among lower castes in which divorce is permitted at an early stage, the dissolution of a marriage also dissolves the other kinship relations that are contingent on the alliance, only to be replaced in due course by a different set of affines (since women cannot remain unmarried).

5   Kindreds and descent groups: new perspectives from Madagascar

Rita Astuti

Introduction

When I first met Dadilahy back in 1989 during my first period of fieldwork among the Vezo of Madagascar, he was very old and, like most old people, had plenty of time to spare. He liked to tell me stories about his past adventures at sea, about sea-turtle–hunting, about the first Europeans he had met. He soon realised, however, that we also shared an interest in the process through which Vezo people come to be related to one another, and so we also spent a great deal of time talking about *filongoa* (relatedness). Dadilahy knew a lot about *filongoa*, because his great age meant that he had been able to follow its creation and expansion over many generations. Most of the time, he made me look at *filongoa* through his eyes, from his particular point of view; in doing so, he conveyed his strong feeling of self-admiration and satisfaction at seeing how many descendants he had accumulated during his life.

Dadilahy's view of *filongoa* was oriented in one particular direction. He no longer had parents or grandparents above him, and he had very few surviving siblings around him; but he had a vast number of descendants below him. His sight, therefore, always moved *downwards* at his children (*anaky*), at the children of his children (*zafy*), at the children of the children of his children (*kitro*), and so on. In fact, Dadilahy liked to impress me by reciting the whole list of Vezo terms used to designate one's descendants down to the sixth generation (*anaky, zafy, kitro, zafiafy, zafindohaliky, miny*), despite admitting that no one will ever live long enough to see the birth of all of them.

This, however, was not such a big problem, since Dadilahy could boast a vast number of descendants just by looking at the two or three existing generations below him. The reason why he had so much to show for himself was that in claiming his descendants he drew no distinctions between male and female lines of filiation and therefore included in his sight not only his own children but also all of his brothers' as well as all of his sisters' children; both his sons' and his daughters' children; both his grandsons' and his granddaughters' children; and so on. All of these were *his* descendants because either himself, or someone he was related to, had contributed to their generation.

When I returned to the field five years later, Dadilahy was dead. His funeral, I was told, had been a happy event which did not mourn his death but celebrated his long life, the success of which was embodied in his many children, grandchildren, and great-grandchildren who accompanied him, dancing and singing, to his tomb.

From inside the walls of his tomb, Dadilahy has a very different vision of relatedness from the one he shared with me. This is because he has now become part of 'one kind of people' (*raza raiky*): inside his tomb, he is with the children on his father's but not those on his mother's side; he is with his brothers' but not his sisters' children; with his sons' but not his daughters' children. Since I last saw him, Dadilahy's expansive and inclusive view of *filongoa*, which used to please him so much, has been dissolved by death.[1]

This chapter is an exploration of Dadilahy's different views of human relatedness during his life and after his death. Following his past and present gaze, I will reconstruct three different perspectives: one held by Dadilahy's descendants (a perspective Dadilahy once had when he was a young man); one which Dadilahy enjoyed as an old man; and one which is what Dadilahy is left with now that he is dead. One could economically label what one sees from each of these perspectives as kindreds, cognatic descent groups, and unilineal descent groups. But the problem with such formalisation is that kindreds and cognatic and unilineal descent groups have often been treated in kinship theory as forms of social organisation that are fixed in time and place – the Iban have kindreds, the Maori have cognatic descent groups, the Tallensi have unilineal descent groups. My contribution aims to show instead that they are three transformative stages in the process of making human relatedness, all of them coexisting among the same people: the Vezo of Madagascar. This discussion will offer a new perspective on debates which flared among kinship theorists in the 1950s and 60s, and which most recently have been revisited by Marilyn Strathern (1992c), showing the close connection between the process that goes into making social persons and the process of creating, multiplying, and curtailing human relatedness.

Kindreds and cognatic descent groups

Dadilahy's view of the relatedness which was being produced all around him when he was still alive is well captured by an analogy drawn by

Unggat, one of Freeman's Iban informants. To illustrate the amazing extension of a person's kindred, Unggat likened bilateral kinship to the making of a casting-net, which when finished is conical in shape. At the start, the net is a very small cone, but as the knotting proceeds and one circle of mesh loops is succeeded by the next, it increases in size until its final circumference is measured not in inches but in fathoms. In the same way, kinsfolk whose forebears were once closely related grow further and further apart until in the end they do not even know that they are related (Freeman 1970: 68).

While Unggat, who was at the time a young man, regarded himself as one of the many people positioned along the widest and most peripheral circle of mesh loops, ignorant of many of his actual relations, Dadilahy, following the same analogy, used to position himself at the very apex of the small cone out of which the casting-net had grown, and he regarded all the people reached by his net, no matter how far away they stood from the original cone, as *his* descendants. In this sense, the Iban image of the casting-net seems particularly appropriate in conveying Dadilahy's desire to 'catch' as many descendants as he possibly can. Also, the image usefully underscores the structural equivalence of all the knots and mesh loops that make up the final conical net, and thus the fact that Dadilahy's vision of the relatedness he has created grows and expands bilaterally and inclusively, drawing no distinctions between the different (male or female) lines of filiation.[2]

Yet Freeman's interpretation of Unggat's analogy was different from my own as I try to imagine how the same casting-net would look from Dadilahy's perspective.[3] Freeman used Unggat's net to the same effect as the other famous Iban image of the cognatic kindred: the concentric ripples made by a stone flung into a pool, which eventually become indistinguishable from the surrounding water (Freeman 1970: 69). The point here is that although bilateral relations theoretically extend indefinitely outwards, in practice the ties of relationship become gradually but inevitably attenuated, since people are unable to follow up the infinite ramifications of their relations, as this would involve remembering ever more distant forebears.[4] Thus, when the ripples reach far out and are no longer perceptible on the surface of the pool, people become strangers to one another. The image of the ripples vanishing into the surrounding water is conveying the same ignorance of existing (but no longer traceable) relations which was expressed in Unggat's image of the casting-net. There is however a significant difference, left unexplored by Freeman but crucial to my analysis, between the expansion of the concentric ripples and the widening of the circumference of the casting-net. And this is that one image is *flat* and expands outwards from its centre, while the other is *vertical* and expands downwards from its apex. In kinship terms, this means that the first image is ego-centred and refers to the kindred as defined by Freeman, while the other is ancestor-focused and refers to a cognatic descent group (by definition[5] *not* a corporate group, whose membership is *not* exclusive; see below).

The distinction between tracing relations from ego, as opposed to tracing them from a common ancestor, was crucial to Freeman's understanding of the kindred as a cognatic *category* (the category of people whose shared characteristic is that they are all related cognatically to the same individual), which he emphatically contrasted to the kind of corporate group created by tracing unilineal descent from an apical ancestor. The implication of Freeman's analysis is that kindreds and unilineal descent groups cannot be found in the same society;[6] but what about cognatic descent groups, which, like their unilineal counterparts, are ancestor-focused?[7] Can they coexist with kindreds; and if so, how?

I already suggested the answer to this question when I pointed out the different perspectives taken by a young man like Unggat and a very old man like Dadilahy with regard to the same casting-net. From the point of view of Unggat, placed as he is on one of the widest circles of mesh loops, the net has grown so big that its conical shape seems almost irrelevant. Unggat's point is that people like him can have only a partial view of the net; what matters to them is the flat expanse of relations (their personal kindreds) which they did not themselves generate, but at whose centre they now stand. By contrast, from the point of view of Dadilahy, who regards himself as the first and generative loop, the net can be admired in its entirety, and from this perspective its conical shape becomes its most salient feature: as far as Dadilahy is concerned, what matters is that he is at its apex, and that he regards himself as the original generative source of all the people caught in it.

The existence of either kindreds or cognatic descent groups is therefore a matter of perspective. Which perspective one takes depends on the kind of person one is. Crucially, it will depend on whether one has lived long enough to see oneself reproduced in one's children, in one's grandchildren, in one's great-grandchildren ..., so as to be able to imagine oneself as a generative (ancestor-like) source of relatedness. In this respect, perspectives can change gradually and according to context: on acquiring children, parents will begin to imagine themselves as the generative source of their small group of descendants; but in other contexts they will themselves be subsumed as descendants of a larger cognatic descent group which originates further back in time. Also, when still active, mobile, and enterprising, a young or middle-aged person is likely to privilege the flat, expansive, and ego-centred view of relatedness, reaching out for cooperation and support to its ascendants, its siblings, and its descendants alike (i.e. to its personal kindred), rather than focusing on the latter alone as Dadilahy does.

There is therefore a great degree of continuity between Unggat's and Dadilahy's perspectives – between cognatic kindreds and cognatic descent groups. There is nonetheless one moment when the interests of those who hold one perspective appear to clash with the interests of those who hold the other. And this takes me back to Unggat.

As mentioned earlier, Unggat used the image of the casting-net to emphasise that in the Iban system people who are distantly related will eventually cease to know that they are in fact related, and will consider themselves strangers – further away from the original cone, people grow further apart from each other until they do not even know that they are all part of the same net. To this, Dadilahy would have responded that so long as the original cone holds, all the other knots will also hold together. In other words, so long as someone as old as Dadilahy is alive, he will be able to tell his many descendants that they *are* part of the same net. Thus, while Unggat emphasised the inevitable loss of potential relatives through ignorance, Dadilahy made the point that the number of relations a person has depends upon the memory of older men and women who know how people were related in the past, and how these past relations extended and grew into the present. Not surprisingly, Dadilahy took great pleasure in telling stories to his children, grand-children, and great-grandchildren of how certain people come to be related to one another ('what makes them related', *mahalongo an-drozy*). For his children, grandchildren, and great-grandchildren, Dadilahy's good memory meant a far greater number of relatives around them; for Dadilahy, his good memory meant an even greater number of descendants below him – an even greater 'catch' in his net.

In most cases, both of these outcomes were highly appreciated by Dadilahy and his descendants alike. My informants never tired of priding themselves on the very large number of relatives the Vezo have – in other words, on the extension of their personal kindreds. Anywhere they go, they can always find people who are their grandparents, parents, siblings, children, or grandchildren, as the case may be, and they will always find somebody who will host them and feed them as relatives do (did I realise how convenient it is to have relatives in all the villages along the coast when one travels by sea?).[8] There is nonetheless one significant exception to the general enthusiasm for one's many relations, and this is when one is trying to find a marriageable partner.

Unlike the Iban, who prefer marrying their close kin, marriage for the Vezo should occur only among people who are unrelated, called 'different people' (*olo hafa*). This means that the web of ego-centred relations grows even faster and extends even further than among the Iban, and this is precisely why the Vezo generally prefer absolute exogamy – in their view, it does not make sense (*tsy misy dikany*) to marry someone who is *already* related (*fa longo*), for this would waste the opportunity for one's offspring of doubling their number of relatives by turning previously unrelated people into kin (see below). The Vezo, however, are also aware that having so many relatives makes it very difficult to find 'different people' to marry (*maro mare longonteña, tsy misy olo hafa*: one's kin are far too many, there are no different people left).[9]

It is on this point that Dadilahy's good stories of how people come to be related to one another become problematic for his descendants; it is on this issue that Dadilahy's perspective clashes with theirs. This is because while Dadilahy's desire is to 'catch' as many descendants as possible in his net, that of his descendants is to find people who are left out of it whom they can marry. The clash of interests is resolved only with Dadilahy's death, when some of his stories will be forgotten, so that, as Unggat had it, some of Dadilahy's descendants will never even know that they are related. In some ways, this periodic loss of knowledge is a good thing (*raha soa*), for, as people point out, it makes it possible to marry a relative without even knowing it.

In fact, this is what would happen anyway, even if all of Dadilahy's stories were remembered, for even his knowledge was necessarily incomplete. On one occasion, after lecturing me once more about the vast number of kin that the Vezo have, Dadilahy offered his general view on the pervasiveness of human relatedness: 'people are really just one people, but it is marriage that separates them' (*olo raiky avao, fa fanambalia ro mampisaraky*). Although Dadilahy felt he could not explain this statement any further,[10] I am inclined to interpret it in this sense: his knowledge of how people are related to one another was so broad that he could see (or was able to imagine by extension) that everyone is in fact related to everyone else; people are just one vast related family. If this is so, marriage can *never* occur among 'different people', and in fact it is marriage itself which separates people, by *creating* the 'difference' that is necessary for an exogamous marriage to occur.

Let me explain this with one example. Lefo and Sary are related (*ampilongo*), as they are both descendants of Dadilahy.[11] Nonetheless, they live together and have had a child together. Despite her fondness for Lefo, Sary acknowledges that her marriage is not good (*fanambalia ty raty, tsy soa*), because she has no in-laws: 'I don't have a father-in-law, because my father-in-law is already my father, my sister-in-law is already my sister' (*tsy mana rafoza zaho, ka rafozako mbo babako, velahiko mbo rahavaviko*). Yet when I told Sary's father that his daughter had no in-laws through her marriage with Lefo, he replied that this was mistaken (*diso io*), because Lefo's father *is* now Sary's father-in-law and Lefo's sister *is* now her sister-in-law. Thanks to the marriage, Lefo's father, who was previously Sary's father, is transformed into her father-in-law (*babany manjary rafozany*). In this case, it is the act of marrying that makes Sary and Lefo and their respective kin – *who were related* – unrelated, 'different' from each other. In the same way, according to Dadilahy's view, all Vezo people, who are really just one people, *become* 'different' through the act of marriage. And yet this difference is established only to be retransformed into relatedness at the next generation.

The Vezo emphasise that marriage does not erase the 'difference' between oneself, one's partner, and the partner's kin. Hence, one's in-laws do not become one's kin. On the other hand, if 'different people' generate children, they establish new relatedness. Since both parents are related to their offspring, all those who are 'different people' with respect to the parents become related with respect to the children: parents-in-law become grandparents, sisters- and brothers-in-law become mothers and fathers (*laha latsaky anaky teña, rafozanteña manjary longon' anakinteña*, 'if one has children, one's parents-in-law become one's children's kin').[12] This transformation of 'difference' into relatedness explains why 'people's kin increase all the time' (*longon'olombelo mihamaro isanandro isanandro*), for each new generation of children is bound to have more kin than their parents' generation.

Vezo marriage can thus be said to oscillate between the creation of 'difference' and the creation of relatedness. In the first instance, marriage is the artifice whereby 'difference' is created within the universe of relatedness; in the second instance, marriage transforms the 'difference' created at one point in time into new relatedness for the generation at the next remove. This recursive feedback allows one to emphasise one of the two elements while ignoring the other, for each of the two poles (relatedness and 'difference') logically includes the other. It is for this reason that Dadilahy was able to place so much emphasis on the *creative* aspect of marriage, for it was this that allowed him to claim an even larger 'catch' of descendants.

It was noticeable that Dadilahy tended to disregard the 'difference' that existed between himself and the people who had generated his descendants through marriage; he disregarded the fact that his children's, grandchildren's, great-grandchildren's spouses were *not* his descendants, and included them in his sight as if they were his own people.

Thus, when he talked to them and about them, he insisted that they were *not* his children-in-law, but rather his children (*tsy vinantoko ty, fa anako, zafiko*); similarly, he did not like to be referred to as their *rafoza* (father-in-law), for in fact he regarded himself as their father. He explained that marriage is an exchange of a woman for a man (*ampela takalo johary*) in which the two sides say to each other: 'here is my child, it is not mine but it is yours' (*anako ty tsy anako, fa anakinao*).[13] Hence, a son-in-law becomes like a son, a daughter-in-law becomes like a daughter, while a father-in-law becomes a father, a mother-in-law a mother.[14]

For Dadilahy, therefore, marriage was a way of acquiring other people's children – of increasing the catch in his net. Understandably, he was far less anxious to surrender his own; despite the alleged equality of the exchange, he took without ever giving any away. Dadilahy, of course, was not alone in carrying out this act of plunder. Those from whom he took were simultaneously taking his children away from him: they insisted, just the way he did, that marriage had transformed their children-in-law into their children.

The point is that such multiple and overlapping claims over the same people are a characteristic feature of Dadilahy's vision of relatedness, as well as of the vision of many other old men and women who, like him, imagine themselves as the generative source of their numerous descendants. Inevitably, when casting their net over their own children, over their (own or classificatory) sisters' and their (own or classificatory) brothers' children, over all of these children's children, and over all of their respective spouses ... each of these old men and women 'catch' people who are also simultaneously 'caught' by other nets whose origins lie elsewhere. This is because each of these old men and women is only one of the multiple sources which have contributed to the generation of their descendants, so that when Dadilahy's children, grandchildren, and great-grandchildren look upwards at their ascendants, they find that the path that leads them to and past Dadilahy is only *one* of the many that they can follow. Their view branches out and expands in all directions: it moves upwards on both their father's and their mother's side, and moves back through their four grandparents, their eight great-grandparents, and so on. Thus, although it pleases Dadilahy to look down at his grandchildren as if they all 'belonged' to him – 'look, these are all *my* children (*anako*), *my* grandchildren (*zafiko*), *my* great-grandchildren (*kitroko*)' – his grandchildren do not in fact 'belong' to him any more than they 'belong' to any other of their many grandparents.

This is of course what happens in those non-unilineal systems of descent which occupied the minds and the writings of so many British kinship theorists in the 1950s and 60s. The problem they faced was to explain how *unrestricted* descent groups of the sort envisaged by Dadilahy could be transformed into discrete groups of the sort created, simply but ingeniously, by unilineal descent – how, in other words, membership of non-unilineal descent groups could be effectively *restricted* through non-kinship criteria (such as choice of residence or actual landholding) so as to sort people out into *de facto* discrete and non-overlapping groups.[15]

What is striking when one rereads this literature with Dadilahy in mind is that this particular preoccupation with restricted group membership is wholly foreign to him and to all the other elderly men and women who, like him, are pleased by the sight of their many descendants. This is because what they are all seeing through their gaze is not a corporate group, membership of which must be, in principle or in practice, asserted univocally against competing claims; what they are all seeing and admiring through their gaze is the making of their mature, fully developed, and wholly realised person: a person who has been successful in multiplying itself into such a vast multitude of descendants. There are moments, of course, when the inclusive vision of these old men and women is realised in practice: when all their descendants gather around them for one of the ritual undertakings which require the mobilisation of all of one's relations. In those moments, the casting-net described by Unggat unfolds before their eyes as they sit and admire its formidable extension.

Unilineal descent

Now that he is dead, Dadilahy no longer enjoys the sight of his many descendants. Next to other bodies, he now rests within the walls of a tomb. He has become a member of a *raza*. To understand, or rather imagine, Dadilahy's new existence, I first of all need to introduce this new term – *raza* – and explain its different meanings. These depend on whether *raza* is employed in the plural (*valo raza*, eight *raza*) or in the singular sense (*raza raiky*, one *raza*).

The Vezo, like other people in Madagascar, say that 'living human beings have eight *raza*' (*olom-belo valo raza*). When I asked what the word *raza* meant, I was given a superficially simple definition: 'people of the past who are dead' (*olo taloha fa nimaty*). To state therefore that living people have eight *raza* means that they have eight (dead) great-grandparents, four on their mother's and four on their father's side; *olom-belo valo raza* is thus a statement about people's multiple sources of generation.

In another context, however, the term *raza* is used to define a *single* entity. This occurs when the Vezo refer, once again, to dead people, but only to those who are buried in the same tomb; in this instance, a plurality of individuals ('people of the past who are dead') who in life possessed *many raza* are grouped as *one raza*, as '*one* kind of people' (*raza raiky*).

One way of imagining Dadilahy's present existence is to consider the effects of the transformation of 'plural' into 'single' *raza*, and the drastic loss of relatedness that this entails. As we have seen, towards the end of his life he had come to acquire an ever increasing number of descendants, gathered indistinctly from all sides (including his descendants' spouses). Acting like the ancestor he was soon going to become, Dadilahy looked down at his descendants and liked to think that they were all 'his' grandchildren. With death, however, Dadilahy's vision was suddenly curtailed. As he was lowered into his tomb, he became part of an exclusive and bounded group, a group made up of only '*one* kind of people' (*raza raiky*). From now on, his sight will only reach those descendants who are or will be buried with him: the children on his father's but not those on his mother's side; his brothers' but not his sisters' children; his sons' but not his daughters' children. Death, in other words, disposes of Dadilahy's cognatic descent group, and forces him into a different kind of kinship order: unilineal descent.

This order is created through a restrictive choice – the choice of *one raza* among the many that living people have – which is the effect of the transition from life to death; for whereas a *living* human being can be *related* to many different *raza*, the dead cannot belong to eight 'single' *raza* all at once. That *raza* membership is and can only be exclusive is self-evident for the Vezo: the reason is that *raza* membership is membership of a tomb, and since corpses cannot be cut up into pieces, one party taking the head and the other the feet (*tapa roe, raiky mahazo lohany, raiky mahazo tombokiny*), one can only be buried inside *one* tomb and only belong to *one* 'single' *raza*: either 'here' or 'there'. Non-exclusive relatedness (on which Dadilahy's inclusive vision of his many descendants depends), and exclusive belonging to 'one kind of people', thus pertain to two different and incommensurable domains of existence, to two different and incommensurable types of person.

I suggested earlier that the view over human relatedness which Dadilahy shared with me before his death revealed his mature and fully realised person, multiplied and refracted in his many descendants. What Dadilahy lost at death are these almost infinite refractions of his own self onto other people; for now he can look at himself only through those descendants who *belong* to him by being the same as him. As he enters the tomb that contains 'one kind of people', he becomes the same as all the other members of that kind – the same unitary person. In the process of operating this closure – from plural to singular, from infinite refractions to single reflection – membership of the single *raza* is established, and with it the existence of a corporate discrete bounded group which did not exist in life,[16] and which must be kept separate from it.[17]

The transition experienced by Dadilahy is of some theoretical importance in kinship studies. Marilyn Strathern (1992c) has suggested that the reason why cognatic kinship proved so problematic for British anthropologists in the 1950s and 60s was that it failed to create 'society': instead of creating groups and establishing boundaries, it produced overlapping webs of relatedness. Given the assumption that 'groups were the vehicles through which societies presented themselves to their members, then without group membership what was a person part of?' (p. 80). However, in so far as cognatic kinship was also considered to be a universal natural feature of human relations, linked to the universal recognition of both maternal and paternal parentage, it became the background against which unilineal descent groups could emerge as one line of filiation was chosen to the exclusion of the other. As Strathern suggests, in kinship theory of the 1950s and 60s the transition from the undifferentiated field of cognatic kinship to the social difference brought about by unilineal descent amounted to the creation of society out of nature (p. 88; see also Edwards and Strathern, this volume).

Dadilahy offers an interesting perspective on these questions, for his long life and his final death both resolve and reinstate the classic problems associated with cognatic kinship and cognatic descent. In life, Dadilahy resolved these problems by being a different kind of person from the one envisaged by unilineal descent theory: not determined by membership of *one* group, of *one* kind of people, but constituted through the multiple, infinite refractions of himself onto the many descendants captured in his cognatic net. In death, however, Dadilahy somewhat vindicates the preoccupations of so many kinship theorists of the 1950s and 60s by proving that cognatic kinship and cognatic descent are ineffective when it comes to establishing exclusive membership of a bounded group; in joining his tomb and the *raza* therein, Dadilahy is forced to opt for unilineal descent. In this case, however, unilineal descent does not so much create society out of nature; its realisation marks instead the painful intrusion of death into life.

Conclusion

In this chapter, I have presented three points of view from which Vezo people at different moments of their lives (and deaths) look at human relatedness. Following Dadilahy's gaze through time, we have seen how cognatic kindreds transform themselves into cognatic descent groups, and how these in turn are transformed into unilineal descent groups through an act of closure. This transformative process is marked by continuities as well as discontinuities. Most notably, while we have seen that death engenders the most radical break and painful loss in Dadilahy's view of the relatedness he had created throughout his life, one cannot fail to notice how, as an old man, Dadilahy began to act as if he already were an ancestor. For in his old age, he no longer looked at the vast but flat expanse of relatedness *centred* on him, but began to look downwards at all the descendants grouped *below* him. In this sense, Dadilahy's cognatic descent group represents the critical conversion point between cognatic kindreds and unilineal descent groups, sharing bilaterality and inclusiveness with the former and a vertical orientation with the latter.

The general point underscored by this type of analysis is the intimate connection between the changing nature of the person through time – through life and death – and the particular perspective people take over human relatedness, which in turn determines and shapes the changing nature of their selves. This means that if we are to understand how people come to be related to one another, we cannot restrict our analysis to any one moment in time. For even if relatedness is created through shared links of procreation, as it is among the Vezo, the best part of the story is what comes after that initial moment of instantiation. And for this, we will need to describe, analyse, and understand how human relatedness grows, ages, and dies along with the growth, aging, and death of the people who have created it.

Notes

The two periods of fieldwork among the Vezo of western Madagascar on which this chapter is based (1987–9; July–August 1994) were supported by Wenner-Gren Grant-in-Aid, and by grants from the Central Research Fund, University of London; the Centro Nazionale delle Ricerche (CNR), Rome; the Istituto Italo-Africano, Rome; the University of Siena; the British Academy. I thank all these institutions for their support. I would also like to thank Maurice Bloch, Karen Middleton, Janet Carsten, and the other participants in the session on Cultures of Relatedness for their comments on an earlier version of the chapter. Above all, I thank Dadilahy, whose blessing I still seek.

1 My description of Dadilahy's vision inside the walls of his tomb should not be taken literally. Dadilahy never described to me what his experience was going to be like as a dead person, nor did others discuss their own or other people's future existence in the tomb. What I say about Dadilahy's curtailed vision of *filongoa* as he is lowered in his tomb is based on my interpretation of the ritual activities Vezo people endure in order to keep the dead happy and separate from life; what these occasions reveal is the acute longing felt by the dead: longing for life and for the very many descendants they could claim as theirs in life (cf. Astuti 1994, 1995).

2 Crucially, the image of the net captures something different from the standard genealogical diagram which, as argued by Bouquet (1996a and this volume), reproduces an 'arboreal' vision of kinship as pedigree. I was reminded of the difference between the expansive image of the net and the vertical image of the tree when I first approached Dadilahy with an A4 notebook in my hands and asked him to tell me about all the people he was related to. Dadilahy looked at me with disbelief: how could I ever imagine that my little pieces of paper could ever be enough to contain all of his relatives?

3 I should add that my reading of Freeman's interpretation of Unggat's casting-net differs from that of Errington 1989: 244ff.

4 Grandparents for second cousins, great-grandparents for third cousins, great-great-grandparents for fourth cousins, and so on. Cf. Freeman 1961: 206–7 on eighteenth-century English lawyers' fascination with the geometrical progression through which the kindred achieves its 'amazing extension'. On the notion that bilateral kinship extends forever outwards to include all humankind, see also Edwards and Strathern (this volume).

5 A descent group whose non-exclusive members are the descendants of an apical ancestor/ancestress through any combination of male or female links of generation.

6 Freeman thereby distinguishes 'the kindred, as an undifferentiated category as in bilateral society', from 'cognatic kin as an internally differentiated category, existing in societies with unilineal descent systems', and argues that 'whenever, in a society, special functions attach to either agnatic or uterine kin in contra-distinction to other cognates, this renders impossible the existence in this society of undifferentiated bilateral kindreds' (1970: 204).

7 The distinction between ancestor-focused descent groups (whether unilineal or cognatic) and ego-focused kindreds is most clearly drawn by R. Fox 1967: 163–9.

8 For a similar appreciation of the almost infinite extension of bilateral kinship, see Bodenhorn (this volume).

9 In this context, I have heard more than once the suggestion that perhaps other people in Madagascar have better 'ways of doing things' (*fomba*) than the Vezo since they allow children of brothers to marry (a practice which was otherwise considered to be 'pointless').

10 Dadilahy's statement could be interpreted as meaning that marriage is divisive, because some people, normally one's daughters, are 'lost' as they move out to follow their spouses. Given the context of the conversation, and

the fact that daughters or sons who move out at marriage remain within Dadilahy's inclusive vision of *filongoa*, I find this interpretation unconvincing.

11 Sary and Lefo are *ampilongo* because Dadilahy is both Sary's father and Lefo's grandfather; Dadilahy's mother was the sister of Sary's father, and Dadilahy's father was the brother of Lefo's grandfather. According to this reckoning, Sary is Lefo's mother; however, Sary and Lefo can also be considered siblings (the father of the mother of the father of Sary's father was a brother of the father of the mother of the father of Lefo's mother).

12 Cf. Carsten 1997: ch. 8 for an extensive discussion of how the paradoxical nature of affinity among the Malays of Langkawi (i.e. that affines should be indistinguishable from consanguineal kin, while at the same time remaining distinctly affines) is largely resolved through the sharing of grandchildren by the two sets of parents-in-law (*bisan*): 'it is through shared grandchildren that the relation between *bisan* – a relation of affinity – is actually transformed into one of consanguinity' (p. 241).

13 For a fuller discussion of equality and hierarchy in marriage, cf. Astuti 1995: ch. 4.

14 See Bloch 1995 on how Merina marriage should be seen as an act that creates double filiation rather than affinity.

15 Some perceptive comments were made in the course of these often heated discussions. Most notably, one finds the suggestion that the contrast between the rigidity of unilineal descent – in which membership is established at birth once and for all, with no need to 'realise' it through one's behaviour – and the flexibility of cognatic descent – in which restricted membership to one's descent group is achieved through the exercise of individual choice – may have been overdrawn, given that even in strictly unilineal descent systems a degree of ambiguity with regard to group membership is likely to remain (Firth 1963), and that even in these systems birth ascribes only a potential status to the child which needs to be realised by assuming appropriate obligations and exercising corresponding rights (Forde 1963, in polemic with Leach's distinction (1962) between individual choice of filiation and the automatism of descent).

16 However, one's membership of the *raza* one will join in death is prepared during one's lifetime. As discussed extensively in Astuti 1995, a person's place of burial (whether in mother's or father's tomb) is established through the performance of the ritual of *soron'anake*, performed by a father for his children. Through this ritual, 'one doesn't buy the child's mouth or the child's flesh; what one buys are the child's bones' (*tsy mivily vavany, tsy mivily nofotsiny, fa taola iñy ro nivilin'olo*). If the father fails to perform *soro*, the children may thus live with him – as mouth and flesh – but their bones will not be buried in his tomb (they will be buried in their mother's tomb).

17 Cf. Astuti 1994 and 1995 on the emphasis the Vezo place on the separation between life and death.

6   How Karembola men become mothers

Karen Middleton

'I am his mother. He is my child. Born of my own belly. Made living by me. Longing for me. Crying for the breast.'[1]
                                    A Karembola man speaking of his sister's son

In her book *Gender Trouble*, Butler makes this observation: 'That the gendered body is performative suggests that it has no ontological status apart from the various acts which constitute its reality' (1990: 136). In this paper, I propose to explore Butler's observation in the context of Karembola cultural practice around mothering. I shall take a fragment of Karembola ethnography which appears to lend strong support to the notion of the gendered body as performative: namely, the sense Karembola men have of themselves as mothers with breasts. Tracing this sense of self back across the contrastive connections that make up Karembola kinship, I shall suggest that this seeming epitome of the gendered body as performative, in fact, depends inextricably on a *sexed* body.

In reading the claims of Karembola men to be 'mothers' against the radical social constructivism represented by Butler, my broader aim is to throw some issues in the study of relatedness into sharp relief. The mutual constitution of 'gender' and 'kinship' is now widely acknowledged in anthropological analysis. However, the relationship of 'gender' and 'kinship' to bodily experience remains contentious. Most notably, Yanagisako and Collier have argued that the same folk theory of biological reproduction that has informed our theory of kinship (Schneider 1984) has informed our analyses of gender, and that to understand 'kinship' and 'gender' as 'cultural systems', gender needs to be prised apart from 'sex' and biological reproduction, and treated as the study of 'pure' difference (1987: 31–2, 15). Doubts as to the viability of this project are voiced by Howell and Melhuus, who, while agreeing 'with the gist of their argument', feel unable to 'go along with the complete open-endedness with regard to biological sex' (1993: 46). Other critics reiterate a reservation Collier and Yanagisako themselves express as to the possibility of knowing 'what gender *or* kinship would mean if they are to be entirely disconnected from sex and biological reproduction' (1987: 34; Peletz 1995: 348; Moore 1993: 196). Errington perhaps makes the most telling criticism when she observes that the project would 'leave unresolved the issue of the relation between men and women as socially constructed beings and their physiological functions and anatomical attributes' (1990: 10, 27–30). I shall argue that the project is particularly problematic in the case of motherhood, almost certainly obscuring more than it will illuminate. At the same time, in writing about the maternal body I hope to draw attention to an issue which, despite thirty years of 'gendered' anthropology, and its own centrality to human experience, remains among the most untheorised issues in the study of 'gender' and 'kinship'.

To be sure, writers working in the 'feminist' tradition generally criticise 'traditional' anthropological models for taking the mother–child relation largely for granted, treating it as somehow more natural and therefore invariant, 'the kin relationship most expressive of biological fact' (Moore 1988: 24; Collier and Rosaldo 1981: 315). Three writers are commonly chastised in this connection: R. Fox (1967: 31) for describing the mother–child tie as 'inevitable and given', one of the two 'rock-bottom facts of physiology' which all 'kinship systems have to take into account' (p. 36); Goodenough (1970: 392) for suggesting that 'motherhood and fatherhood cannot be defined in the same way for comparative anthropological purposes' because 'procreation associates children directly with women but only indirectly with men'; and J. A. Barnes (1973: 71) for asserting that, while virtually all cultures attach symbolic value to both fatherhood and motherhood, 'fatherhood is the freer symbol, able to take on a wider range of culturally assigned meanings, because it has a more exiguous link with the natural world'.

It has been suggested that similar assumptions carried over into the work of alliance theorists. However, Lévi-Strauss himself places greater emphasis on the value of women as a 'natural stimulant' (1969: 62; cf. 32–41) than on their fertility when explaining why in his view the 'elementary structures of kinship', are characterised by the exchange of women by men. The exchange value of women as reproducers of life is more deeply inscribed in the ethnography for asymmetric alliance in eastern Indonesia (e.g. J. Fox 1980; R. Barnes 1974). I return to this ethnography below.

What *is* certain is that the two best-known essays in early feminist anthropology (Ortner 1974; Rosaldo 1974) sought to account for the supposed universal subordination of women in terms of a symbolism that was not so very different from descent theorists' models of maternity. Their assumptions were soon challenged, however, by a number of

studies documenting considerable cross-cultural diversity in practices
and beliefs around 'motherhood' (e.g. Stack 1974; Boon 1974; Drummond 1978; MacCormack and Strathern 1980; cf. Moore 1988:
23–30). This diversity led Collier and Rosaldo (1981: 315) to conclude
that 'there are *no* facts about human sexual biology that, in and of
themselves, have immediate social meanings or institutional consequences. Mothering is a social relation, much like fathering, judging, or
ruling, whose meaning and organisation must be understood with
reference to a particular configuration of relationships within a complex
social whole.'

Writers began to move beyond the documentation of cultural difference to asking sociological questions about why such differences exist.
For instance, Collier and Rosaldo (p. 275) pointed out how in 'very
simple societies' themes of motherhood and sexual reproduction are far
less central to peoples' conceptions of 'woman' than they had expected
and set about explaining this apparent puzzle in terms of a contrast
between 'brideservice' and 'bridewealth societies'. A similar concern
with sociological explanation is evident in Ortner's essay in the same
volume: from her review of the Polynesian material, motherhood
emerges as 'weak and, if not easily "broken", then certainly easily
attenuated', a characteristic which Ortner links to the local 'prestige
system' (1981: 392; cf. Ortner and Whitehead 1981). Likewise, Sacks
(1979: 66) seeks to refute the axiom that motherhood, political power,
and economic and personal autonomy are incompatible by tracing the
axiom to the development of industrial capitalism.

In her book *The Gender of the Gift*, Strathern seeks to extend the
critique of anthropological models of maternity by problematising 'the
indisputable fact that women give birth'. In the context of an innovative
exploration of gender, person, and gift exchange in Melanesia, she
writes of 'the *illusion* that "Women make babies"' (1988: 311; emphasis
added), and suggests a number of reasons why such a proposition might
be considered 'ethnocentric'. To begin with, as part of a more 'general
set of theoretical assumptions (on the part of anthropologists) about the
intrinsic and visible value of women, particularly in terms of their
fertility' (p. 100), it implies a view of the intrinsic attributes of things
that is typical of a 'commodity logic' (p. 314). Inextricably linked to the
root metaphors of Western culture – property, ownership, and control –
such a view of persons as individuals naturally owning themselves and
the products of their own labour is incompatible with the form of social
relations known as gift exchange, where the individual person 'is the site
at which its own interactions with others is registered' (p. 132). 'What is
drawn out of the person [in the gift economy] are the social relationships

of which it is composed' (p. 131). This premise, viz. that the 'singular person can be imagined as a social microcosm', is 'particularly significant for the attention given to the images of relations contained within the maternal body' (p. 13). For if 'a series of events is being revealed in the body, which becomes thereby composed of the specific historical actions of social others' (p. 132), and if the 'act of birth is taken as the point at which the multiple constitution of the child is made known' (p. 316), it becomes inappropriate to say either that 'women make babies' or, *pace* J. A. Barnes (1973: 72), that 'the mother–child *relation* in nature is plain to see'.

Embedded in a model of the 'partible' person, Strathern's placing of the maternal body in the particular cultural configuration of a 'gift economy' is also a view of the person as composed of both male and female relations. Since 'each constitutive relation is gendered', we here find images not 'of a totalistic sexed identity of a Western type. On the contrary, maleness and femaleness seem defined to the extent in which persons appear as detachable parts of others or as encompassing them' (p. 107). This view of gender as constituted relationally has led several authors (e.g. Battaglia 1992: 15 n. 5; Moore 1993; Morris 1995) to draw parallels between Strathern's work and Butler's (1990).[2] Comparable arguments are made by Gewertz (1984) and Battaglia (1992) for other Melanesian peoples, and by Atkinson (1990) for the Wana of Indonesia. Gewertz (1984: 618–19), for example, suggests that among Tchambuli a person may be thought to acquire the appropriate genitalia because of what she or he does.

At first sight, the ethnography of the Karembola of southern Madagascar presents yet another 'of a large number of cases where it is the performance of particular kinds of activities or tasks which guarantees gender identity rather than simply the possession of the appropriate genitalia' (Moore 1994: 39). After all, if Karembola men describe themselves or are described by others as 'mothers' or 'mother people', then, one might reason, this must mean that for Karembola being a 'mother' can have little to do with biology. Indeed, Karembola men present strong echoes of Gewertz's Tchambuli data when they speak of suckling the children they nurse. And yet the issues around gender, sexed bodies, and relatedness are not so simply resolved. To begin with, there is the tricky question of why I gloss the local statement *rene zahay* in English as meaning 'we are mothers', given that it is spoken as often by men as it is by women (cf. Milton 1979). The same conundrum also arises with the meaning of Karembola dialect words I translate as 'breast' and 'milk'. The difficulties of severing 'gendered' words from sexed bodies become more apparent when we examine the ways in which Karembola men become or imagine themselves to become mothers or mother people.

If, as Butler argues, the gendered body has no ontological status apart from the various acts which constitute its reality, then in principle we should be able to specify the performative acts that constitute the reality of these mother men. In practice, however, we find that this key idiom of Karembola relatedness is not particularly accessible to performative models. This is because if Karembola men are mothers, it is less that they 'perform' as mothers than that they are held to be the 'root' or 'source' (*foto*), the hidden but effective cause of growth, the power that makes others give birth. Their mothering is read in and through the manifest embodied acts of others, acts which it either claims to encompass or which stand in antithesis to it, but it is not particularly performative in and of itself. Exploring the relationships Karembola pose between what is hidden and what is manifest, I shall suggest that the ethnography in the first instance points up some difficulties in applying performative models of gender in the analysis of cultures whose ontologies pose real or effective causes that lie beyond the visible and material world.[3]

This does not exhaust the difficulties that arise in applying performative models of gender to the Karembola ethnography, however. For if, on the one hand, the mothering undertaken by Karembola men depends upon an ontology in which the real source or root of things lies in what may be hidden and unseen, then, on the other hand, it also requires to be 'proven', made visible in a material form. And when we look at how their mothering is made manifest in a form people can apprehend, we see that Karembola men can only become 'mothers' through acts that place them as 'source' or 'origin' in relation to sexed bodies, those of women, cows, and nanny-goats. They cannot 'mother' any 'child' without this third presence, this middle term. Paradoxically, their disembodied mothering must be embodied in the manifest acts of female people and female livestock in order to be known.

Much of the ethnography will appear to echo Strathern (1988: 131) on 'source' and 'display'; viz. 'Information, sexual organs, and a capacity to grow are all made known or valued by reference to their source. Yet the source lies beyond the person who displays it, by the same token that its efficacy must be registered in another.' However, the *irreversible* relationship Karembola pose between men as 'source' or 'efficacy' and women as embodied display in the case of making babies requires a rather different emphasis in the conclusions we draw about the role of *sexed* bodies in the Karembola ritual economy.

The power of mothering

As a pastoralist people who live in the arid south of Madagascar, Karembola take great pleasure in the sight of a cow with calf at heel (*rene mianake*). They love it for its promise, for its ability to replicate and reproduce. For not only will the calf suckle at its mother's udder and bear its mother's earmark, but if it is a heifer, then, with good fortune, it too in time will become a cow with calf at heel. This asymmetrical pair forms a contrast with the 'ox of ten cattle years' (*vosy folo'ay*). Great in body, bearing splendid horns, this also is a sight that pleases Karembola. However, the ox's destiny is invariably to be slaughtered in one sacrifice or another, because, Karembola explain, it will not give birth.[4]

Contrastive imagery of the cow with calf and the single ox is woven into Karembola understanding of the relationship between affines. For Karembola there are two kinds of marriage. On the one hand, there is 'marriage within the hamlet', 'between close agnates' (*fanambaliañe añate tana, anak'mpirahalahe*, lit. 'the marriage of brothers' children, patrilateral parallel cousins'). On the other hand, there are marriages beyond the hamlet, with 'people of a different kind' (*ondate karazañe hafa*). Marriage within the hamlet is associated with the transmission of an unchanging ancestral essence across the generations, and with the creation of identity and equivalence among agnates. It is the epitome of 'a world in which one might *keep to oneself*' (Lévi-Strauss 1969: 497). The idioms that inform 'marriages with people beyond the hamlet', on the other hand, are very similar to those which govern the asymmetric alliance cultures of eastern Indonesia. That is to say, affinal relations are pictured as oriented, asymmetrical, and repetitive; the wife-giver ranks higher than the wife-taker; and Karembola generally avoid giving and taking wives in one place. Placing Karembola ethnography within the framework of Errington's (1990) regional model of South-east Asia,[5] we could say that Karembola marriage practice encompasses both the endogamous marriage of the 'centrist archipelago' and the asymmetric alliances of 'eastern Indonesia', and that the particular shape of Karembola society derives largely from the articulation of these two very different ways of marrying.

As in the asymmetric alliance cultures of eastern Indonesia (e.g. R. Barnes 1974; J. Fox 1980; Needham 1962), the principles of dualism, asymmetry, and orientation that organise marriages between Karembola hamlets are embodied in the gifts that affines exchange. Thus, certain gifts go in one direction, and other gifts return, and the directions in which gifts move between wife-givers and wife-takers cannot be reversed. For Karembola, gifts of cattle are constitutive of this asymmetry, because cows and nanny-goats are sent by wife-givers while grooms offer bullocks and castrated billy-goats in return. These gifts embody acts of life-giving and the debt that life-receiving incurs, because with their female livestock wife-givers are said to 'make grooms living' while grooms 'honour' their life-givers, as they do the ancestors, with typical 'sacrificial' victims. At the same time, the contrasting reproductive potential of the livestock also embodies and substantiates the unequal capacity of wife-givers and wife-takers to leave enduring marks (debts) upon each other's social domain (Middleton n.d. a).

For Karembola, however, the key present in these exchanges is without doubt the bride. Not only is she known as *the* present (*enga*), but Karembola constantly emphasise the immensity of this gift. Nothing, they say, is commensurate with the gift of a woman; thus, nothing can free the debt that the groom incurs. It is this gift which makes the wife-giver superior to the wife-taker. 'We are their mothers, they are our children. They have rooted upon us. We have given them life.' Indeed, Karembola emphasise the groom's indebtedness to such an extent that they appear to deny the 'reciprocity' between affines that the ethnographies for asymmetric alliance in eastern Indonesia tend to stress (but see McKinnon 1995).

This irredeemable debt not only hierarchises particular wife-giving and wife-taking affines, but becomes, in the extended series of ceremonial exchanges that accompany Karembola funerals, the basis for an imagined transitive order of descent lines. In this respect, Karembola draw on idioms of asymmetric alliance, not to construct imagery of groups 'marrying in a circle', as in much of the ethnography for eastern Indonesia, but rather to make a picture of a social order that is explicitly ranked. Yet Karembola society is not actually a ranked society, and to this extent participation in the ritual economy is associated with a high degree of alternicity as Karembola act out an imagined hierarchy organised in no small part around mother–child ties.

This, then, is 'no narrowly conceived image of maternity' (Strathern 1988: 85). Analysis is no longer simply a case of exploring whether or not motherhood is compatible with political power and autonomy; but rather of acknowledging that mothering *is* the key idiom in which Karembola imagine power and rank. Its centrality to the Karembola political imagination has implications for anthropological discussions of maternity. For instance, in his much-maligned essay, J. A. Barnes argued that agnatic idioms are more widely used in 'pre-scientific' cultures to make the connection between taxa in adjacent levels – so that *A* is father, and not mother, of *B*, *C*, and *D* – 'because the symbol of fatherhood is largely a cultural construct, unfettered by evidence from nature' (1973: 72). This is not true of the Karembola, for whom motherhood provides taxa for an (imagined) polity. The power Karembola ascribe to mothering is also difficult to reconcile with some more recent theories of gender such as the argument Ortner and Whitehead (1981: 16) make about 'the universal male face of prestige'. To be powerful, that is, to project themselves beyond their own domain as persons who 'command' those of other hamlets, Karembola must imagine they are the mother and nurturer of other men. 'Is it not mothers who rule in the Karembola?', people ask. 'Is it not they who have authority here?'

It is on this very point of mothering as constitutive of power over *other* people (i.e. non-agnates) that it is worth *contrasting* Karembola culture with the asymmetric alliance cultures of eastern Indonesia. A basic theme of the published ethnography is that 'alliance in eastern Indonesia is concerned with the transmission of life' (J. Fox 1980: 12). Clama-girand describes this for the Ema as 'the flow of life which circulates by means of women', and Fox explains how 'the very notion of alliance implies a direction to the flow of life since it is women who are perceived as the providers of this life' (ibid.). Reading this literature from the Karembola perspective, I am struck by the paradox that, although the affinal relationship is said to be based on life-giving through the gift of a woman, the relationship between superior wife-giver and inferior wife-taker is seldom if ever conceptualised as a mother–child bond. This curious fact, together with other characteristic features of the regional ethnography such as the proliferation of botanical idioms,[6] raises many more comparative questions about bodily metaphor and gender hier-archisation in hypogamous forms of asymmetric alliance than I have space to consider here. The point I wish to make at present is simply that Karembola men, by contrast, have a keen and unashamed sense of themselves as 'mothers', and draw constantly on imagery of the mater-nal body to claim pre-eminence.

The strong link Karembola make between political power and motherhood reinforces the sense that being a 'mother' in this culture is a sociopolitical status that has little, if anything, to do with biology or domestic kinship. And yet this is not the case, as we shall see.

How men become mothers

It is, I think, significant that I learned about 'male mothers' in the Karembola through what I heard people say rather than what I saw them do. That is to say, while I saw, and indeed spent much time with, women nursing their newborns and administering herbal balms to the tears they had sustained in childbirth, I did not see men perform any work that *I* readily glossed as 'mothering'. I learned that Karembola men are or imagine themselves to be mothers only because Karembola repeatedly employ the same term *rene* as they use of *mother* and child, or *cow* and calf, to explain what they or other people were doing or what they expected of or felt about another person, or how particular individuals were related amongst themselves.[7]

The question naturally arises as to whether such statements are of metaphoric power rather than literally meant.[8] When Karembola men talk of being mothers, they do not present this in any obvious sense as metaphor. For example, I never heard them say that the mother's brother is 'like a mother', 'a kind of mother' *(sahale rene)*. Likewise they could describe him as a 'picture of a mother', rather as they describe a male transvestite as a 'picture of a woman' *(sarin-ampela)*, or perhaps as 'mothers with penises' or even 'mothers without breasts' (De Boeck 1994: 460), but in fact they do not qualify the statement in any such way. Only when Karembola add the qualifier *lahe* (male) to the term *rene* (mother) (e.g. *renekolahe*, 'my male mother') can their speech be said to carry something of the sense of metaphor – that the mother's brother is like a mother, but not exactly the same. I return to the significance of this below. For the most part, men not only describe themselves as *rene* without qualification but draw freely on an 'embodied' maternal sub-jectivity in describing their sister's son 'as born from their own belly' *(an-troke teña)*, 'as crying for their breast' *(mitomany ty nono)*.

Of course the lack of a qualifier does not necessarily mean that the idiom is not figurative. Metaphors are known to figure in the way people in many cultures think and talk about relatedness (J. Fox 1971; De Boeck 1994). At the same time, it is often very difficult to establish for certain how people in other cultures view and use different kinds of trope. As I understand it, the statement that men are 'mothers' is more than a 'turn of phrase' in so far as Karembola men believe, and social debts depend on the fact, that it is they who 'make the child live' *(mameloñe anake)*. At the same time, though, I do not think they mean to say that men are mothers in the way that women are. Thus, rather than categorise the statement as literally meant or of metaphoric power, I find it useful to explore how this idiom of relatedness is given existential reality by being conjoined with incorporated practice.

In reaction to earlier overformal 'descent' models, and in keeping with the greater emphasis upon body and practice in anthropology generally, many scholars today emphasise the importance of embodied acts of feeding, exchanges of bodily substance, sharing house and hearth, in creating relatedness (Schneider 1984; J. Fox 1987; Carsten 1995a;

Carsten and Hugh-Jones 1995). In principle, we can imagine that a culture of relatedness based on idioms of nurturing might provide the space, so to speak, for Karembola men to make themselves mothers. (On the other hand, it is worth noting that Cucchiari (1981), speculating on what a genderless society might look like, specifically wonders whether a society based *entirely* on nurturing would not *eliminate* kinship.)

Certainly it is said that for many, if not most, peoples of Madagascar, as in Austronesia generally (J. Fox 1987), relatedness is processual, fluid, and contextual, with descent identity being at most a possibility, created from *valo raza* ('eight sides'), i.e. cognatic kinship (Southall 1971; Bloch 1993; Astuti 1995). Karembola, however, take a different view of the person, presenting what Astuti (1998: 32) dubs more 'African' idioms of identity. 'Ancestry', they declare, 'comes through fathers' (*karazañe avy ama ty rae*). 'We Karembola light father's fire.' This is a 'thing God has ordained' (*raha namboarañe Ndriañanahare*). Moreover, unlike those Malagasy peoples among whom a person is 'kinded' – that is, grouped in exclusive, bounded ancestries – only or finally in the tomb (Bloch 1971a; Astuti 1995), Karembola believe that *living* people are kinded, and that ancestry shapes the *living* person in important ways.

There are of course problems with the primordialist model Karembola have of themselves. To begin with, as anthropologists *we* know that people are not born kinded, i.e. arranged in patrilineal ancestries, because this does not happen everywhere! Thus we find that, paradoxically but perhaps inevitably, Karembola are completely taken up with proving their 'intrinsic' kind. From a particular perspective, 'kindedness' looks very much as though it were 'performatively' constituted, that is, made contextually and processually through the practice of social relations in the course of a person's life, as indeed it is. If, however, we listen to Karembola, we shall have to acknowledge that *they* construe this activity as a matter of showing forth what already lies within. Agnates don't *become* agnates. They *are* agnates, 'in perpetuity', 'way back from the beginning, from the very root' (*hatra hatra, boak'añe, boak'am-poto añe*). 'Doing' here is held to be the outward manifestation of the essential 'being' that exists prior to the act.

Siblingship is conceptualised in terms of this essential kindedness. 'Brothers' and 'sisters', Karembola explain, are 'one people', 'people of one kind'. 'They own one another.' 'They are rooted in one another.' 'They are consubstantial because they are agnates' (*miharo raha, ondate vata raike, fa sambe mpirae*). Their consubstantiality is given substantive expression in a set of embodied practices which includes the literal exchange of bodily substances through sexual partnering and spouse-sharing (Middleton in press). Above all, agnates act out their primordial connection in a silent, giftless type of union. 'There's no exchanging, no ritual, nothing to see, when agnates marry.' 'They simply enter the house.' This is because, by marrying together, agnates are simply *being* what they *are*.[9]

The consubstantiality of brothers and sisters has a direct bearing on what happens when agnates marry out. First, the suitor is made to kneel at the cornerpost 'to beg' for what is not his, and then if the woman's agnates agree to the marriage, they impose a heavy fine for giving up what is rightly theirs. 'Keeping-while-giving' (Weiner 1985), they continue to 'command [the groom] fiercely' (*mandily mafy*) throughout the term of the marriage, because, they say, a Karembola woman 'always keeps her root or kind' (*manam-poto, manan-karazañe, tsy afake*). This is why the groom is obliged to take his wife home to her 'father people' when she is seven or eight months pregnant with their first child. 'The first belly must be conveyed to its hearth-of-origin', Karembola explain, because the mother's people are the baby's *foto*, its 'origin' and 'cause'. If a man fails to acknowledge his wife's rootedness by failing to pay homage to her kin, the latter grow so angry that their malice is likely to kill the child.

During her confinement and postpartum seclusion (lasting six months if the baby is a boy; slightly fewer if a girl), a woman is housed by her father-people and nurtured with vast quantities of the finest body-building foods they can afford, for instance, millet cooked in milk rather than plain boiled manioc. These foods, together with the heat of the hearth, fatten and strengthen her body, causing a thick milk to flow to feed her child. Again, Karembola do not see such acts as making kinship, for they are simply the way agnates behave. A woman returns to her father to give birth and to be heated, Maraze noted, because she is of his 'house' and 'hearth'. A father who neglects a daughter, she explained further, brings sadness to the ancestors, and their regret soon makes him ill.

It is worth asking why Karembola should put so much visible effort into housing, heating, and nurturing their kinswomen during and after childbirth, given that they are held to be the source and root of the child, the invisible potency (*asy*) that lies behind the manifest birth. This points to a basic tension in Karembola ontology, namely that, even as Karembola insist upon the pre-eminence of the *fo*, the hidden but effective cause of being, growth, and life, they also insist that a thing or force can be known only by being seen, touched, heard, and felt (Middleton n.d. a). 'Has it been seen?' (*tsy trea vao?*), they ask. 'How can we know a thing if it has not shown forth?' (*fanta'ay vao ty raha tsy nitrean'teña ndraike*). 'If we have not seen it, how can we be sure that it even exists?' Thus, it is not enough for Karembola men to claim to be mothers, i.e. to be the invisible, mystical agency that makes children be born, live, and grow. They must substantiate their efficacy in the real world by visible acts. Otherwise how are people to know?

From the perspective of gender performativity, what is significant about the set of acts by which Karembola men document their birth-making powers is that they are all concerned with demonstrating a primordial connection between their sisters and themselves. Men make themselves visible as 'mothers' by nurturing a sister's body, and by reabsorbing her in their house. More precisely, they become 'mothers' in practices focused on a *sexed* body, a body that is about to give or has given birth.

The Karembola ethnography presents many parallels to Strathern's (1988) model of 'personhood' in a 'gift economy'. For example, it would be true to say that a Karembola woman's pregnancy is read as 'the site at which [her and her baby's] own interactions with others is registered' (p. 132), and that for Karembola the source of a capacity to grow often lies beyond the person who displays it; by the same token, its efficacy must be registered in another. However, to sustain a view of the gendered body as truly performative would require that all the terms (the gendered body parts) might be as easily reversed: that is to say, the 'effect' (the pregnancy) of the specific historical actions of social others might be read in *any* body, and this would not apply to Karembola, who know that the 'effect' (maternity, the birth of a child) can only be produced ('read') in and through *sexed* bodies, the bodies of women. Even as they insist upon being mothers, Karembola men know that they depend upon a kinswoman's body to make their life-making efficacy known. Theirs is a mediated motherhood, because they are never mothers in and of themselves.

It is precisely for this reason that the *enga* – the great present – is always *sexed*. Karembola are very clear that men cannot perform the 'gendered' role of the *enga*. Indeed, as we shall see, Karembola mortuary ritual involves an extended parody upon what happens to uxorilocal men who try to do just this. Even if they pass between hamlets, men 'cannot substitute' *(tsy misoloho)* for women as 'presents', because the essence of *the* present is that 'it will give birth'. It is this that creates the irredeemable debt. Significantly, the party of women that escorts the bride to her groom's village always includes a woman with a babe in arms. This is a child strong enough to venture beyond its own hamlet strapped to its mother's back but still suckling, and therefore close enough to the moment of birth to impress upon the groom's imagination what he may be tempted to forget: that only women give birth.

The most obvious way in which men *nurture* their sisters and their sisters' children is with gifts of cattle. Every bride ought to be accompanied by a cow with calf at heel when she 'walks across the land', or at least a heifer and some nanny-goats, for, as Maraze put it, even if the heifer has not yet given birth, she almost certainly will. Flows of 'gendered' wealth subsequently play a critical role in constituting the sister's son's experience of the mother's brother as mother, life-giver, and nurturer. And yet it is important to note that this wealth is not only 'gendered' (compare Battaglia 1992). It must be *sexed*. Making a bullock *perform* the 'gendered' ('female') work of dowry cattle will prove unsuccessful (*tsy manjary*), Soatse explained, because the whole point of the dowry is that it 'should give birth' (*ho terake*). 'Cows and bullocks are not equivalent', he reminded me gently, a grin beginning to tug at the corners of his mouth; 'both may be cattle, but the bullock can never accomplish what the cow can.' According to Ilina, *her* kin had put the matter to the test when, in desperate straits, they had sent an ox, their only livestock, as a wedding gift. It was a very bad present, Ilina complained, which made her feel ashamed. In any case, the substitution was 'pointless' (*tsy misy dika*). The ox will only grow old pulling carts, and then die, and when it's dead, everything is lost. There'll be no calf to carry its earmark, because the ox will not give birth. My agnates might just as well have been the 'supplicants' (i.e. grooms), she concluded, because they will see no *fiasiañe* (honour) from their gift.

With cattle as with people, Karembola depend upon *sexed* bodies to make their life-giving power known, and to this extent there is some sense in which the Karembola ethnography, while contradicting the greater part of J. A. Barnes's argument, meets up with his sense of the mother–child relation in nature being plain to see (1973: 72).[10] Thus, even as Karembola talk as though men had the body parts of women, making the gendered body appear fluid, contextual, and performative, they draw unhesitatingly upon bodily difference between the sexes in the practices that shape their ritual economy. For the most part, knowledge of the bodily difference between brothers and sisters, and the part this plays in local cultural practice, remains implicit. It is knowledge that not only 'goes without saying', but is obscured by language Karembola employ to describe relatedness. It is, however, made explicit on those occasions when Karembola state that 'what makes a man a mother is the fact that his sister has given birth' (*ty maharene aze, fa niteraha ty rahavave'e*), or, more indirectly, that 'he has given a kinswoman to be another man's wife'. It is also disclosed whenever Karembola refer to their mother's brother as *renekolahe*, 'my male mother'.

The couvade

I now turn to another type of birth practice that involves Karembola husbands in the nurture of a mother and her newborn child. This is the ritual which is observed in unions between hamlets when a man's wife gives birth to their second or later child.

Not long after arriving in the village I was to study, I met Saotse returning from the forest bearing a great bundle of herbs. He looked remarkably scruffy: his hair unkempt, his beard unplucked, and his clothes tattered and torn. He had been collecting medicines for his wife, who had just given birth to a daughter and was heating in the house. Back at the village, I watched Saotse pounding millet with the pestle in the mortar in readiness to cook porridge for his wife. The other women were laughing because Saotse was clumsily performing 'women's work'. Saotse, I learned, was 'nurturing his partner' (*mamahañe valy*), 'making her live' (*mameloñe aze*). Besides fetching firewood, food, and water, and cooking during her postpartum seclusion, Saotse had to protect his wife and baby by observing a number of prohibitions: for example, he could not groom himself or eat certain foods or have sex with other women.

Interpretations of the couvade – of which this clearly is an instance – have moved from the typically functionalist, which saw the practice as establishing social paternity for the child (e.g. Malinowski 1960: 214–15; Douglas 1968), to the typically structuralist, which interpreted the couvade as 'but one way of dealing with what is an almost universal problem concerning the nature of man, the conceptualised dualism of body and soul' (Rivière 1974: 430). More recently, the practice has figured in debates on gender and reproduction, where it is cited to support the point that women have no monopoly on birth (e.g. Paige and Paige 1981: 189; Moore 1988: 29–30). In the Karembola case, the couvade is undertaken by a groom partly to *counter* the excessive pre-eminence claimed by his wife's agnates in the act of creating the child. In response to men who insist upon re-encompassing their kinswoman's swelling belly within *their* house (i.e. descent group), the groom envelops his wife and baby in *his* care. In the context of an ideology of exchange that diminishes his reproductive contribution in favour of the mother's brother's agency, the groom puts *visible* effort into documenting his own consubstantiality with his wife and child. In the context of an ideology that insists that 'ancestry lies on father's side', a father shows how he 'gives life' to his child.[11]

We could say that in performing the couvade a Karembola man seeks to demonstrate *paternity* over and against the maternity claimed by his affines, if it were not for the fact that the couvade also involves him in a kind of maternity. During the couvade, Soatse's daily routine had undergone an explicit gender reversal. The women had laughed to see him do 'women's work'. Yet again Karembola men are 'regendered' in relation to birth as a father now proves his substantial link to and effect upon the child by mothering the mother and baby in the house. What *is* common to the maternity of both groom and mother's brother, however, is that each seeks to encompass birth and life-making in his own person by expressing a close identity between his body and the body of his sister or wife. Neither the disembodied mothering of the mother's brother, so crucial to the debt he claims upon the groom, nor the performance of the husband in the couvade would make sense without a *sexed* body newly delivered of a baby within the house. Thus, while the couvade is cited as cross-cultural evidence to show that women have no necessary monopoly on birth, it is worth reflecting upon the fact that it is invariably practised in relation to a *sexed* body giving birth.

Nursing the corpse

The third type of 'mothering' I shall consider is one that few Karembola men willingly undertake. This is the work performed by the *tsimahaive-loñe* (lit. 'who does not know the living') during funerals when he is called to tend the corpses of his 'mother people' (see n. 7). When a man or woman dies among the Karembola, his or her dead body is kept in the dwelling while preparations are made for the first mortuary feast. Within a few days, the corpse has swollen, just like a pregnant belly, and before long 'its waters break'. All the while the corpse is 'housebound', the *tsimahaiveloñe* stays with it, watching over it and wrapping it in shrouds. As I show elsewhere, Karembola draw explicit analogies between the work of the *tsimahaiveloñe* and the seclusion of a mother and her newly delivered child (Middleton n.d. b). The *tsimahaiveloñe* 'cares' (*miambeñe*) for the dead body of his 'mother' as a mother cares for her newborn. Nothing the corpse does will cause the *tsimahaiveloñe* to reject it and to abandon it in the house. 'Whatever foul fluids or vapours the corpse expels, the *tsimahaiveloñe* is not repulsed.' Using words they use of maternal love and forbearance, Karembola describe the *tsimahaiveloñe* as one who 'withstands all trials' (*mahatante ty hasarotse*).

This evocation of mothering is not coincidental, because the service the *tsimahaivelone* performs for his mothers' corpses is said to follow from the irredeemable debt he owes to them for the life he has received. *Tsimahaivelone* are very poor men, usually (though not always) uxorilocal grooms. They are men who have left their hamlets to 'root' exclusively in their mothers, men who have 'accepted women' and been unable to maintain a separate identity with counterprestations of any kind.[12] Encompassed by their mothers, they are obliged to care for their dead bodies because they while alive mothered them.

And yet the 'mothering' that each undertakes for the other – the one in life and the other in death – is less than 'balanced'. To begin with, there is an asymmetry in the fact that, while Karembola men 'mother' their sisters' sons in a rather disembodied, tangential way, the 'mothering', which constitutes its return or complement, has an undeniably visceral and embodied form. The *tsimahaivelone* 'sits day in, day out with the decomposing body', 'never leaving', 'always caring', 'no matter what it does'. At the same time, Karembola draw important contrasts between the work of nursing babies and the work of caring for corpses. The one is the work of 'making live', 'bringing into being', and 'making flourish', while the other is concerned with 'what is dead' and 'has no more use'. And if one looks carefully at birth and death ritual, one sees that, behind the extended analogies, Karembola mark out this difference in many ways (Middleton n.d. b). For example, the *tsimahaivelone*, while showing great forbearance towards the dead body placed in his care, also does weird unmotherly things like (symbolically) feeding on it. Instead of his nurturing his charge, it nurtures him (*mamahane aze*). Accordingly, the 'mothering' the *tsimahaivelone* performs is best understood as a parody of what 'mothering' means to Karembola. It is but one of a series of ways in which Karembola mortuary ritual transacts the life-giving value of mothers: for instance, the *castrated* steers that are slaughtered in honour of the deceased are left all day in the burning sun until their bellies become so swollen that their legs stick up in the air (Middleton n.d. b).

I am reminded here of the argument Bloch and Parry (1982) make about the importance of antithetical symbolism in creating imagery of an ideal order which would otherwise be difficult to apprehend. To be sure, Karembola ethnography does not tally with the specific argument they make about the devaluation of women's birth in mortuary ritual in so far as the maternal body is the metaphor for political power in the Karembola social imaginary (Middleton n.d. b). Nonetheless, the way the work of the *tsimahaivelone* relates to the social construction of power is a good example of their general principle. For if Karembola men can never realise their all-important claims to be 'mothers' in the tangible shape of bodily acts, the reverse or the corollary – the 'mothering' of the corpse by the sister's son – *is* experienced during funerals in a very real and concrete way.

I am suggesting, then, that the work of the *tsimahaiveloñe* not only stands in antithesis to the real embodied birth of women, but also helps to substantiate the disembodied mothering of men. It is the sight of the *tsimahaiveloñe*, sitting with the corpse by night and day, being made to live his irredeemable debt for the mothering he has received, that in no small part makes visible the invisible life-giving efficacy of mother-men. And it is precisely because the mothering undertaken by the mother's brother is unseen and unseeable save through the 'performance' of a kinswoman's body that the embodied performance of the *tsimahaiveloñe* is a parody, *not* of what the mother's brother does to make his sister's son live, but of what a mother can be *seen* to do as she sits caring for her baby in the seclusion of the house.

Experience and embodiment

'The relationship between mother's brother and sister's son', Lewis writes in his work on Gnau ritual, 'is complex, desired and enduring and I believe they think of it as a kind of whole or entity or thing. *It is not the kind of thing which can be seen, grasped, touched or smelt, or heard as a whole.* The relationship is given or axiomatic, qualities formulated in ideal terms by people who see them as good and right. As ideals, they go beyond what can simply be pointed to and seen. The nature of the relationship is not shown in a single concrete experience but it may be more accessible in symbolic form' (1980: 197–8; emphasis added).[13]

The same might be said of the efficacy of the Karembola male mother, which is made manifest through work performed by a sister's body, and then sustained in antithesis through the *tsimahaiveloñe* expressing his gratitude for the mothering he has received by caring for the corpse. What links together all the ways Karembola men 'mother', whether in the disembodied form of mother's brother/wife-giver, the embodied debt of the *tsimahaiveloñe*, or the counterpoint of the couvade, is a reference to a *sexed* body delivered of a baby sitting in the house.

I suggested earlier that the contrasting ways Karembola have of knowing the world easily give rise to discord. For even as Karembola insist upon invisible but all-powerful roots or causes (*fo*), they are driven to authenticate them by their manifest outcomes. Documenting an invisible *fo* by its visible effect inevitably carries the possibility that the 'effect' (what is known because it is seen, heard, or smelt) may turn out to be the root or cause. This paradox, which pervades local musings on experience (Middleton n.d. a), is very clearly the focus of an extended discourse around the roles of men and women in mothering. To begin with, I lost count of the number of times Karembola women asked rhetorically, 'Where is the man made tired and thin by childbearing? Show me the man with hollowed-out cheeks and sunken eyes on account of the children he has borne.' What Karembola women seem to be saying at these moments, when they sought to make me *see*, is that, if it is not exactly an illusion that men make babies, then there is at least some problem in understanding the agency or power men, the root of growth and birth relative to women, actually expend in birth. The sense women have that it is their own bodies that bear the cost of bearing the child, of losing teeth, of growing thin, even of haemorrhaging to death, is matched conversely by their evident pride when they can count on all ten fingers the babies they have carried, or touch their breasts to remember the children they have fed. Nor indeed is this sense of children being rooted in women's bodies confined to women, for Karembola men also tell a story of how once upon a time women were 'owners' (*tompo*) of the child. Karembola men strive to grasp and to incorporate mothering, yet both sexes know that men cannot perform as mothers even if they try, and to this extent they know that the invisible *asy* (agency, power) that men claim as 'mothers' must always partner 'the indisputable fact that it is women who give birth'.

Long before they learn to read a woman's pregnancy as 'the site at which [her and her baby's] own interactions with others is registered' (Strathern 1988: 132), Karembola children have made a more substantive, bodily connection between the actual mother and child. This is because, when they are very small, they spend their days playing in and around the houses where mothers sit nursing their newborns. Long before they learn that the mother's brother is the 'mother' or the 'breast', they have smelled the breastmilk upon swaddling, they have seen infants sucking at nipples, they have heard crying babies quietened upon being put to the breast, and to this extent we could agree with J. A. Barnes that 'some aspects of nature impinge more obviously and insistently on the human imagination than others' (1973: 73).

Indeed, my sense is that it is often not until much later, perhaps well into their teens, that Karembola women learn to read their own bodies as the site 'in which the specific historical actions of social others is revealed' (Strathern 1988: 132). Let Maraze, a woman of around twenty-three years, explain:

When I was young, I never took *hakeo* [moral blame] seriously. I heard people talk about it but didn't believe that my agnates had such power over me. I just thought it was something grown-ups said, so I laughed and did as I pleased. But then when I married, I had a baby which lived only a few days. Then I miscarried another pregnancy. During the months that followed I was very sick. I learned then that I should respect my father, my brothers. Now I know to fear their power for Nirisoa's sake, for they are her root, her mother. If they grow angry, then she will fall sick, perhaps even die. Everyone likes to play around and be headstrong, but sooner or later one realises as one grows older that it's vital to respect one's origin, one's source. Then the self is wise.

If Maraze's learning experience is typical of Karembola women, the agency of the mother's brother in making babies is (again) in no small part constructed through antithesis. It is 'proven' or 'made known' as often in the interpretation of cases where women remain infertile, miscarry, or suffer stillbirths or neo-natal infant deaths as in instances where babies are born safely and live. The high incidence of such bodily events among the Karembola provides constant opportunity for diviners to read women's bodies in terms of *hakeo*, 'moral blame', stemming from her agnates.

Two kinds of roots

I have highlighted the continual tension between the invisible and invisible in Karembola understandings of procreation. At the same time, I have indicated that a Karembola man's ability to 'mother' rests upon both the consubstantiality of opposite-sex siblings *and* their difference. I want now to suggest that the uncertainty that always surrounds 'mothering' needs to be viewed against a deep uncertainty about the meaning of bodily difference that comes between brothers and sisters as 'people of one kind'.

Despite their gender-bending, Karembola in fact show no hesitation in drawing on the visible genitalia to class newborn babies as 'boy' *(ajaja lahe)* or 'girl' *(ajaja ampela)*. A woman, Seva declared, 'has what makes her a woman, and a man has what makes him a man'. Or as Temere'e put it, 'the root of us women is in the vagina while the root of men is in the penis'.[14] It should be noted that Karembola use the same term *foto* (root) of the genitalia, so visibly manifest in physical form, as they use of the fertile but *invisible* ancestral root from which living people grow.[15] This striking synonymy not only indicates the great importance Karembola attach to the genitalia as a marker of difference between people, but also indexes a profound ambivalence around how this visible bodily difference relates to kind. In effect, Karembola constantly wonder whether this other root of being means that male and female agnates are not actually different 'kinds' of people, after all, divided and bounded against each other by bodily difference (Middleton in press).

Errington has suggested that the two major variations in the marriage-cum-political systems of island South-east Asia are linked to different models of siblingship (1990: 53–6). In 'centrist archipelago' societies, opposite-sex siblings epitomise the unity and similarity associated with cognatic kinship and endogamy, while in the 'exchange archipelago' the practice of asymmetric alliance depends upon *difference* between brother and sister and their enforced separation at marriage. It will be apparent that Karembola must play upon both tables, however, since patrilateral parallel-cousin marriage keeps together brothers and sisters as 'people of one kind', while asymmetric alliance divides them by their sex, because only women can move between hamlets as 'gifts'. The articulation of these two contrastive forms of marriage in the endless constructions of everyday life inevitably imparts an essential instability to siblingship.

This indeterminacy more broadly lays the basis for mother's brother/sister's son relationships to undergo politically significant value trans-formations: from bonds of consubstantiality, 'nobility', and purity between a man and his sister's child when agnates marry, through the almost playful alternicity of hierarchy in equality that characterises most marriages between hamlets, to the profound otherness of the *tsimahaive-loñe*, who becomes 'akin to a slave' (*sahala ondevo*) by living his 'uterine kinship' with a corpse.

Concluding remarks

In this paper, I set out to read the claims of Karembola men to be 'mothers' against the radical social constructivism represented by Butler. Variously foregrounded, transfigured, and mimicked, being a 'mother' in the Karembola in fact shows much of the indeterminacy that one associates with theories of gender performativity, and yet, I have argued, it resists the 'fantasy of utterly unfettered, purely elastic gender' (Morris 1995: 585) in so far as the unfolding chain of meanings that Karembola weave around gifts, debts, and persons of value is anchored in 'the indisputable fact that women give birth'.

At the same time, being a 'mother' in the Karembola has emerged as more complex, more various, more surprising, more imaginative, a 'freer' symbol, than Barnes ever supposed. Lending support to a view of 'kinship as a primarily *creative* (rather than a merely necessary) aspect of human life' (Wagner 1977: x), many of its linked or contrasting associ-ations differ radically from European cultural conceptions of kinship (Schneider 1984). And yet it is fastened in bodily sexual difference, with all that this implies about the embodied, material nature of one's relation with the world (Errington 1990: 30). It is this common fastening in a sexed body that gives meaning to the interplay between the power of the mother's brother and the couvade, between the two types of marriage, and to the work of nursing the corpse.

In tracing out this key motif in Karembola understandings of relatedness, I have also sketched in a ritual economy based in no small part on the gift of sexed bodies. This is a ritual economy in which Karembola women have a value, a value that is not arbitrary but is inextricably linked to *intrinsic* properties of the female body, properties that men can emulate, encompass, and parody but never replace. This is not to say that Karembola women have only this value; nothing could be further from the truth.[16] Nor is it to suggest that 'women' are valued for their fertility in all cultures, for this is very clearly *not* the case (Collier and Rosaldo 1981; Bodenhorn, this volume). What we can say, however, is that in the specific context of the Karembola ritual economy, and perhaps other ritual economies such as those of eastern Indonesia, women have acquired a social value that is inextricably linked to natural capacities of the female body, to 'work' this body *alone* can perform. Indeed, we can almost speak of Karembola 'harnessing and organising the natural resources embodied in women' (Strathern 1988: 100) in the construction of their imagined polity.

In Strathern's typology, this would appear to make the Karembola ritual economy a 'commodity' rather than a 'gift' economy. And yet it is evident that 'relatedness' as lived by Karembola has many aspects that would 'fit' a 'gift' economy as defined by Strathern. Perhaps, then, the material points up the difficulty in applying ideal types to the analysis of real societies. For even supposing that scholars could agree in formal terms as to what is meant by 'gifts', as over and against 'commodities', the distinction between two kinds of economy must remain a kind of 'fiction' (Strathern 1988: 18–19) in so far as societies are almost always more complex than ideal types (see Thomas 1991; Valeri 1994). To the extent that it *is* a fiction, however, it is difficult to know what sense one is to attach to the stricture that notions of the intrinsic value of women can have no place in the analysis of a 'gift' economy.

Notes

Fieldwork was carried out in southern Madagascar from November 1981 to October 1983 and from March to August 1991, under the auspices of the Regional University Centre at Toliara, with grants from the Economic and Social Research Council and the Leverhulme Trust. An earlier version of this chapter was presented to the panel on Cultures of Relatedness at the conference on Boundaries and Identities, University of Edinburgh, 24–6 October 1996. I should like to thank Janet Carsten, the organiser, and fellow-participants, especially Rita Astuti and Marilyn Strathern, for their comments. I am also very grateful to Cecilia Busby, Jennifer Cole, Philip Thomas, and the two anonymous readers for Cambridge University Press for their careful readings of an earlier draft.

1 *Rene'e raho, anako re. Niteraham-troke teña, nivelomako. Maniñ'ahe, mito-many ty nono.*

2 Strathern, however, refutes such a reading of her work. She states that, for Hageners at least, sexual ascription on the basis of anatomy is unproblematic. Her point rather is that it is relatively insignificant, being merely a starting point for the process of 'making visible' what is already there (personal communication, 25 October 1996). In the words of *The Gender of the Gift*, the problem Melanesians set for themselves is 'how to draw out of the body what it is capable of' (1988: 103). What perhaps requires further clarification for the Melanesian data therefore is how unambiguous cognition of anatomical difference based on sexual dimorphism *articulates* with gender that is seemingly lived or experienced as performative, shifting, and contextually defined.

3 Errington (1990: 5–8) remarks the prevalence in South-east Asia of similar ontologies which stress the pre-eminence of invisible power over visible form. She argues that this may require anthropologists to reconsider earlier conclusions about the high (visible) status of South-east Asian women (see also Atkinson 1990). Neither she nor the other contributors to Atkinson and Errington (1990) address the potential of this kind of ontology to generate uncertainty around and conflicting local interpretations of power, cause, and agency (see Middleton n.d. a). Nor do they explore how this might bear on the analysis of gender difference and power in the asymmetric alliance cultures of eastern Indonesia, where a man is held to be the (invisible) source of life for his sister's child.

4 Karembola also sacrifice female cattle, but only when they have proved infertile or are well past calving age. The expression *folo'ay* (ox of ten years) is often used in exasperation of big-bodied but clumsy, 'useless' young men.

5 Errington has been criticised for misrepresenting the two variations as though they corresponded to a *geographic* distinction between centralist maritime south-east Asia and eastern Indonesia. Recast as 'conceptual spaces rather than geographical ones' (Errington 1990: 54), the contrast has proved very useful for exploring the articulation of contrastive types of marriage among the Karembola. For a comparable but not identical combination of marriage practice, see Boon (1990) on the endogamy (FBD marriage) and exogamy (hypergamy) of Balinese ancestral houses.

6 As J. Fox observes, 'throughout the area [the relationship] is linguistically marked by cognates of a single Austronesian term meaning "trunk", "base", "root", or "origin". Thus the Rotinese suffix the cognate *hu* to the terms for the mother's brother and the mother's mother's brother to signify these men as the "origin" of their sister's children, who are described as their "plants". Similarly, the Sumbanese refer to their mother's brother as their "tree trunk" (*pola pu*), the "trunk from which they grow"' (1980: 23). As Fox notes, '[s]uch cognate terms ("*epu*", "*pu*", "*hu*", "*fu*", "*uf*") give a definite botanic cast to affiliation and alliance relationships' (cf. J. Fox 1971).

Karembola also use plant imagery to describe the alliance relationship. For instance, they talk of the wife-taker 'rooting' upon the wife-giver, employing a cognate (*mifototse*) of those Fox lists. Plant imagery does not eclipse the maternal body, however, in conceptualisation of these sociopolitical bonds.

7 Since nouns in the Malagasy language do not change according to whether they are singular or plural, the term *rene* in the Karembola dialect may mean 'mother' or 'mothers', and *rene ondate* 'mother person' or 'mother people'. As 'mothers' or 'mother people' it can designate all kin on the 'mother's side' (MB, MMB, MBS, MMBS, and, depending on context, MZ, MBW, MMZ, etc). *Ondate* is also employed to distinguish human mothers from animal mothers (*rene osy*, 'nanny-goats', *rene añombe*, 'cows').

8 I am uncertain of the place afforded to metaphor in theories of gender performativity. In her discussion of Gewertz's data, for instance, Moore seems to rule out the possibility or usefulness of asking whether a statement is literally or metaphorically meant: 'the issue here is not whether the Tchambuli do or do not think that Gewertz really acquired male genitals' (1994: 39). One reason why the status of metaphor in theories of gender performativity is uncertain would seem be that, as heir to two traditions – Austin's speech-act theory and practice theory (see Morris 1995) – the relationship between gender as the effect of discourse and gender as the effect of habitual forms of embodied practice in this theory is itself unclear. Failure to explore resonance *and* dissonance between discourse and embodied practice is a common source of confusion in the analysis of gender, however. For instance, Howell asserts that among the Northern Lio of Indonesia 'both male and female characteristics are *incorporated* in [the mother's brother's] body' (1995: 294; emphasis added), without in fact tracing this out in 'incorporating' practice.

9 Actually, these marriages take place between patrilateral parallel cousins rather than actual opposite-sex siblings. However, in casting endogamy as 'a world in which one might *keep to oneself*', Karembola tend to obscure the taboos that exist on marriage and sexual relations between actual siblings.

10 Critics have noted some confusion in Barnes's argument as to whether by the 'mother–child relation' he is simply talking of acts of gestation, parturition, and lactation or also the subsequent work of caring for a human child which extends over many years. In cultures like that of the Karembola, where reproductive technologies are limited and there are no substitutes for human breastmilk, birth and lactation are functions tied inextricably to *sexed* bodies, although it is not necessarily the birth mother who breastfeeds the child, and other childcare can be undertaken by people regardless of sex.

11 I should point out that Karembola do not conceptualise the difference between matrilateral (affinal) relations and agnatic relations in terms of an opposition between blood (flesh) and bone (Lévi-Strauss 1969). On the contrary, relations between fathers and children and between mothers and children are both conceptualised in idioms of vital life substances (milk as well as blood). Significantly, both sides are merged in marriages within the hamlet, since 'all are of one kind'.

12 This, of course, contradicts Karembola representations of marriage alliance, which insist that grooms can never redeem their debts because it shows that

there is, in fact, a very great difference between those wife-takers who can be forced to perform the *tsimahaiveloñe* and the majority who defend their honour by responding to the gift of a woman with countergifts (sacrifices) of wealth. For an impressive analysis of another culture based on asymmetric alliance in which the status of wife-takers hangs in comparable balance between autonomy and encompassment, see McKinnon (1995).

13 It is curious to remark how many anthropologists, sensing something 'insubstantial' and 'abstract' in the mother's brother/sister's son relationship, have turned to an examination of how it is created and sustained in 'ritual'. J. Fox (1980), for example, speaks of the 'mother's brother, acting in his *ritual* role, [being] the source of life for his sister's children' (emphasis added). This inevitably raises the question of whether people in other cultures make a distinction between what is 'said' about gender and kinship in ritual and what 'goes without saying' in everyday life, and whether such a distinction might be usefully introduced into discussions of gender performativity in Melanesia.

14 *Foto tika ampela ty raha boribori, fa ty fotorahañe ty lahelahe avy ama ty voto'e.* Temere'e used the inclusive first person plural (*tika*), as opposed to the exclusive form (*zahay*), thus counting me among those whose essential root of being lies in the vagina.

15 Feeley-Harnik (1991: 136) reports similar usage for the Sakalava (northwest Madagascar), while Astuti (1998) argues that the genitalia ('sex') are important in defining the limits of the negotiablity of the person among the Vezo of the west coast. Unlike Karembola, however, who constantly turn over the problem of identity and difference between brothers and sisters, Vezo generally downplay the significance of bodily difference. This ethnographic difference makes sense in terms of the contrasting models Karembola and Vezo have of kinship and marriage (see Astuti, this volume).

16 For instance, I show elsewhere how Karembola women are key actors in the ceremonial exchanges that configure the imagined polity, and, indeed, that Karembola are unable to explain important aspects of their ritual economy save in terms of women's rivalry (Middleton, n.d. c).

7   'He used to be my relative': exploring the bases of relatedness among Iñupiat of northern Alaska

Barbara Bodenhorn

Over the past fifteen years, many conversations I have had with Iñupiat – whalers of northern Alaska – seemed to assign relatively little significance to what bodies 'are' and to give rather a lot of weight to what they 'do'.[1] Iñupiaq kinship relations are central to social life; according to many people, they allow you to survive in difficult situations. However, as I have argued recently (Bodenhorn 1997), the relations are so potentially transformative that there is virtually no immutable basis for putting forward a claim on kin-related resources. If the state of being related is infinitely negotiable, then ways in which the conditions of birth may act as a fixed basis for property claims in many cultures ('you must do this for me because I bore/sired you'; 'I have a right to resources because we share "blood", "DNA", "ancestors"', and so forth) are not salient in this one. One consequence of this negotiability, I argued in 1997 and will explore further here, is the protection of individual autonomy to a very great degree. In the present chapter I want to push this exploration of the bases of individual autonomy further, examining not only the negotiable but also the non-negotiable grounds on which claims to resources may be made. These latter, I shall argue, lie largely in the non-negotiable rights earned through labour undertaken by autonomous individuals. How 'the negotiable' and 'the non-negotiable' enter into the enactment of kinship relations is a central focus of the chapter. I shall suggest that whereas both 'biology' and 'acting' are categories Iñupiat use when talking about kin, it is the latter category that renders kinship 'real'. In curious ways, then, 'labour' does for Iñupiaq kinship what 'biology' does for many other systems.

It is of course clear that individual autonomy in itself is a way of organising social relations; the degree to which that includes intense social interaction varies widely. Valued as the idea of individual autonomy may be on the North Slope, Iñupiat are not social isolates. In Barrow, Alaska, categories of collective belonging – community, whaling crews, and households, for instance – are recognised and valued as fundamental to social life. Their boundaries are both clearly marked to a degree unusual in many hunting and gathering societies and highly permeable. Utqiagvik (Barrow) itself has been permanently settled for close to a thousand years. The idea of 'community' is celebrated throughout an annual cycle in a series of feasts, dances, and games; its most explicit expression as *an* entity is seen perhaps in the definition of the whale as a communal resource ('the whale gives itself to all of the community' and thus must be shared throughout the community).[2] Whaling crews are highly organised and likewise endure through time. Houses are the locus of marriage and 'should' be peopled by adults and children. Ways in which individuals may decide to move across the boundaries of these collectivities form one of the focuses of this chapter.

In some societies virtually all social relationships are in some way articulated through an idiom of universal kinship: 'we are all kin' is heard on the tundra (see Guemple 1965) as well as on the savannah (see Woodburn 1982). Such is clearly not the case everywhere and certainly not in Barrow today. To be *Utqiagvingmiu* (person of Barrow) or *Ahmaogatkunni* (person of Ahmaogak's crew) is to imply participation in a set of social relationships that may well include but are not exclusively collections of relatives. Nor are they presented as definitions of collectivities of relatives. Indeed, when I asked people how they would translate the English word 'family' into Iñupiaq, there was much metaphorical scratching of heads. The post-base *-tkut* was most frequently offered, but then instantly qualified: *Ahmaogatkut* could refer to the representatives of the Ahmaogak family attending a wedding, for instance. But it could equally signify the employees of a business owned by Ahmaogak, or, as in the example above, refer to a crew headed by Ahmaogak. Thus, *Ahmaogatkut* are people whose relationship to each other is defined as a collectivity through their relationship to Ahmaogak. The state of being kin is one of the bases on which such relationships might rest, but it is by no means the only basis.

Iñupiaq 'kinship' cannot be defined as a collectivity in the same sense as the categories outlined above. Despite the apparent lack of any Iñupiaq collective term that seems translatable as 'family' into English, the term *ilya* was consistently and without qualification translated as 'relative'. The term literally means 'addition' and is most correctly complemented by the post-base *-giich*, indicating a two-way relationship (see Burch 1975). In a way that resonates strongly with Edwards and Strathern's material in this volume, *ilyagiich*, as we shall see, are not only linguistically but also practically persons connected through networks of relatedness that may be defined in multiple ways. When I speak of

Iñupiaq kinship, then, I refer to the institutionalised processes by which Iñupiat recognise specific relations as those they define as *ilya* – their additions – as well as the institutionalised practices through which these relationships are enacted.

The category of *inuk* (individual) as a moral person is an important one in understanding at least some of the ways in which Iñupiat social lives are carried out.[3] This is revealed perhaps most clearly in terms of the claims one can put forward on the basis of one's labour – claims which accrue unambiguously to individuals regardless of gender, generation, or kinship ties. At the same time, however, with regard to kinship relations, Iñupiaq selves are significantly multiple – 'dividual' to use Strathern's (1988) phrase. The possibility that Iñupiaq as well as other human beings may be simultaneously individual and multiple (and perhaps more importantly that cultural categories recognise that possibility) may present logical dilemmas, but not, I think, experiential ones. Within this context, both possibilities support each other. Indeed, I suggest, a fixed basis for individual claims to resources and a transformative basis for relationships that are continuously made rather than affirmed through birth, jointly underpin a system which protects individual autonomy and institutionalises a high degree of sociability to a degree rarely found elsewhere.

Relatedness, kinship, biology, and rights: locating some cultural categories

Recent discussions about the nature and importance of Inuit kinship have been heavily informed by the wider debate of the 1960s concerning the 'biological' or 'cultural' basis of kinship discussed in the introduction. Whereas Burch (1975) argues that Inuit kinship is biologically determined and structurally central, Guemple (1988) asserts that 'kinship' is simply a general metaphor for alliance among Inuit and not terribly important at that. While challenging biological determinism, I agree with Burch, nonetheless, that kinship for Iñupiat is of profound rather than superficial importance. In fact, I suggest that only by getting away from the assumptions about kinship-as-biology prevalent in Euro-American systems can one fully appreciate the central importance of kinship, not only in Iñupiaq social life but as a structuring principle of Iñupiaq social organisation.

Schneider (1968), of course, argues strongly that the argument above itself depends on the culturally framed category of 'biology'. American kinship, he insists, is a metaphor (of relatedness) based on another metaphor (blood). Taking this further, Carsten (1995a) points out how narrowly many anthropologists have defined 'biology' when restricting their focus to reproductive processes *per se*. She suggests that on Langkawi the crucial physical process in the generation of kinship is feeding. Carsten's challenge to the narrow definition is apt. In Barrow, however, the term 'biological' *is* used in English conversations about kin. 'George often hunts with his biological brothers', for instance, would not be surprising to hear. It refers to people who are related through birth and often identifies activities and relationships that might not otherwise be recognised as ones occurring between relatives, that is, between kin who have been separated through adoption. As I shall show in this chapter, this use of 'biology' as a marker of relatedness corresponds at one level with the usage heard throughout the United States. It is a reflection of the narrow definition of 'biology' critiqued by Carsten above. At another, crucial, level however, the significance of 'biology' for kinship differs radically in these contexts. It is not that 'biology' is the single 'real' basis for being *ilya*, but rather that it is one of a number of possible bases for reckoning this particular kind of relatedness.[4] Feeding is also crucial to creating important social connections, but, unlike in Langkawi, these are not necessarily defined as the connections of relatives. Feeding is fundamental to the proper conduct of human/non-human relations rather than of kinship relations, and the consumption of 'real', or Iñupiaq, food is in itself often a marker of Iñupiaq identity.

In order to consider 'cultures of relatedness' on the North Slope and their roles in the exercise of autonomy, then, we must include Iñupiaq persons as individuals, persons as dividual-relatives, and persons as members of collectivities. In order to do so, we must examine some of the assumptions behind a number of concepts so prevalent in social analysis: 'individuals', 'rights', and biology, as well as the bases for what is considered 'real'. I want to examine these assumptions somewhat obliquely in connection with the ways Iñupiat talked about links between parents and children. In many societies, parents' claims to rights over children stem from the fact that they have produced them through the labour of childbirth (see, for example Astuti 1995). To deny that claim is to deprive parents of their rights 'to' their offspring. To grant that claim is to obviate the offspring's own autonomy (see for instance Collier 1988). On the North Slope, virtually no aspect of kinship – not even the bond between parent and child – is so linked to bodily processes that it provides a fixed basis for putting forward a claim to the very strong obligations relatives feel towards each other.

Linguistically and on the ground, Iñupiat identify categories of belonging that are spoken of as highly valued, enduring, and morally obligating networks and collectivities of relationships. At the same time, however, Iñupiat value individual autonomy highly and protect it assiduously. Using information gathered in Barrow and Wainwright, Alaska, since 1986, I shall argue that since the immutable is not linked to the enduring obligations of reciprocity, Iñupiat are not faced with the contradiction posed by the possibility of 'possessing' others – whether as spouses or parents – while simultaneously valuing individual autonomy. What *is* immutable, however, is the right to put forward a claim generated through one's labour. And it is that immutability – which underlies the definition of marital, of kinship, and of hunting relations – that forms not only the basis of Iñupiaq autonomy but of Iñupiaq sociability.

The setting

Iñupiat are one of the circumpolar peoples now collectively known as Inuit. They have lived on the edge of the Arctic Ocean for two millennia, establishing settled communities strategically located in the migratory path of *arviq*, the bowhead whale. One of these may provide as much as sixty tons of edible food which, thanks to freezing Arctic conditions, can be stored for up to a year in ice cellars. It is not surprising, then, that much of Iñupiaq spiritual and economic life is organised around the whale hunt. Whales are not the only food, however; the 'subsistence diet' includes a wide variety of land and marine resources.[5] For centuries, their abundance not only permitted the growth of permanent villages, but also provided the goods (hides, ivory, baleen) with which to enter trading networks extending from Siberia to eastern Canada. European and American commercial whalers appeared in the mid nineteenth century, introducing several decades of virtually uncontrolled predation on the region's marine resources; they left gradually in the decade before the First World War, leaving behind them a small institutional Euro-American presence in the form of teachers, a missionary, and a small hospital, all located in Barrow, the most centrally located of the original Iñupiaq villages. Iñupiat were then essentially left to themselves until the middle of the twentieth century. Unlike the experience of so many other hunting peoples, Iñupiat did not have to fight farmers, loggers, and others for control of their territory, simply because the Arctic environment has prevented such economic enterprises from taking root.

With the discovery of oil in 1968, the rules of the game changed; control of the land (rather than of removable, renewable resources) and its non-renewable resources became a major issue. For reasons much too complex to go into here, the Iñupiat were not simply squeezed out of the process, although the fight they are continuing to fight is by no means balanced. Against the active opposition of the oil companies as well as the State of Alaska, the Iñupiat managed to have 88,000 square miles (227,900 sq. km) of their territory declared a Home Rule Borough, now governed by an Iñupiat-controlled Assembly and funded primarily by property taxes on oil development. Today Barrow is a regional capital, with a population of around five thousand people, just over 50 per cent of whom are Iñupiat. Wainwright, the other community upon which this paper is based, is a much smaller village; its five hundred inhabitants are virtually all local. The Iñupiat define themselves primarily as whalers; although not everyone hunts, all of the households I have worked with thus far have access to hunted food through sharing networks. They must also have access to money; income ranges from about $6,000 annually (for a single mother with one child receiving public assistance) to $80,000 or more. People use their money to buy rifles, boats, snow machines, and other means of hunting/production. They also purchase colour televisions, microwave ovens, videos and, vacations in Hawaii. The argument I put forward here is based on what these people do. It is not a reconstruction of past practice, unless such reconstruction was explicitly used by people to explain their understanding of present circumstances.

Labour, individuals, and shares

Let us begin by asking what may constitute a non-negotiable basis for interpersonal claims. The search for the animals of the land, sea, and air may be conducted alone, with spouses, with partners (who may or may not be kin), or in crews. Access to these resources is generalised: 'If you can get out there, you can go hunting' (Ernest Kignak, in Bodenhorn 1989: 85). The organisation of labour with relation to hunting is primarily gendered, in that men and women have specific tasks, defined predominantly as work that husbands and wives do for each other. One of the most desirable characteristics of an eligible spouse is that she or he be 'hard-working', and indeed Guemple (1986) suggests that the marital bond is primarily defined as work done explicitly for one's spouse. For the most part, men kill animals, fish, and make tools; women fish, gather berries and greens, sew, butcher, preserve and prepare food, and share it generously. This division is explicit, but not determinist. As long as one's gendered tasks are fulfilled, expertise in the other's activities simply makes one skilled rather than anomalous.[6] The activities of both men and women are thought to be perceived by the animals, who have intent and give themselves up to be killed. In that they give themselves up to men whose wives are generous, the actions of both men and women – gendered as husbands and wives – are defined as those of hunting.[7]

Distribution rules fall into two major categories: *ningik*, or 'shares', and 'sharing'. Sharing encompasses many ways of building and maintaining social relations;[8] it is the social glue holding humans and animals together and is often identified as the most pleasurable aspect of village life. Human generosity in sharing *niqipiaq* ('real' or hunted food) attracts the animals. With large animals (bowhead whale, beluga, polar bear), this should be done in a generalised way throughout the community. Smaller animals may be shared according to individual or marital decision. Who gets what and when, however, is not predetermined. Sharing thus is very much connected to decisions made by the giver, who may well be 'generous' to some and 'stingy' to others. As we shall see, relatives are expected to share with each other, but this process too is highly negotiable. Shares, on the other hand, are an entitlement and not a function of the generosity or goodwill of one person in relation to another. They are earned by contributing labour, material, or intellectual technology to the hunting effort; if you contribute to the hunt, you collect 'your share'. Access to shares is governed neither by kinship nor gender: a woman may own a 'male' tool, such as a harpoon, which she loans to the harpooner of a crew, or she may engage in 'female' activity, such as butchering. Both actions earn her a share if the hunt is successful regardless of kinship or marital connections.

Women as individuals (not as wives; not even necessarily as women) customarily had access to both hunted and traded resources and today have access to and take part in the market. They can instigate divorce as easily as their husbands; by earning shares or earning money, a divorced woman can avoid dependent status *vis-à-vis* male kin. Women as well as men thus have considerable scope for movement through the entitlements accruing to them through their labour.[9]

Even generation, which in many ways seems to dominate gender as an ordering principle for Iñupiaq social relations, may lose relative importance in the earning of shares. An increasing emphasis on fall whaling's importance for collecting winter supplies has been accompanied recently by a number of shifts in the ways labour is divided and shares earned. Twice during my stay in 1996, four or more whales were brought on the beach simultaneously, each weighing several tons. As unbutchered, unstored meat can spoil in a very short time (and in the autumn might well attract polar bears), the pressure on labour under such conditions is enormous. Everyone was helping; men worked not only with 'their' crews but with whoever needed their particular skills.

Unusually, teenagers participated in full force. More striking was the number of girls among them – something I never saw during the spring. Recognition of their contribution came in two ways. Both girls and boys got full adult shares of whale meat and *maktak* (prized edible skin and the fat immediately beneath the skin) delivered to their doorsteps. And at the subsequent communal feast hosted by the successful whaling captain, all teenagers were given adult portions of food. For this moment, teenagers 'were' adults. The individual share, earned through individual labour, went to individual young men and women. For the communal distribution, the category teenager was redefined as adult, and all teenagers benefited – regardless of whether or not they personally had helped in the butchering.

Individuals, then, in many ways seem to be independent agents. Autonomous control over their labour and the non-negotiable claims generated thereby which adhere to the person, regardless of age, gender, or kinship connection, suggest the primacy of individual rights – of entitlement – embodied through labour. I have never met any Iñupiat, however, who saw themselves as free-floating autonomous agents earning individualised shares throughout the day. As I said at the outset, daily social life in Barrow is awash with kinship connections, and it is to the question of what it means to be a relative that I now turn.

Kinship and negotiability

On the North Slope, kin are reckoned bilaterally: birth, names, adoption, and marriage may all add on separate kin networks. As I have already mentioned, *ilya*, the Iñupiaq word for relative, means addition. Anyone considered a relative to anyone you consider a relative may be your relative. And if a clear line is impossible to establish, *kinguvaaqatigiich* (through the generations somehow) will do.[10]

How one becomes a relative and what that means in terms of expected behaviour need some elaboration. Heinrich and Anderson (1971: 542–5) posit two analytically separable domains of kinship terminology among the Bering Strait Inuit: one defining the 'mode of recruitment' and the other describing the 'moral content' of a given relationship. *Nukaaluk* identifies the category of younger brother, a category which includes a number of moral commitments. There are a number of ways one may be eligible to belong. *Aniqati* are siblings by virtue of having been born of the same womb (*ani*, to go out; *qati*, companion); *tiguaqti* (lit. taken) are siblings through adoption; *qatangutit* are siblings by virtue of an acknowledged sexual union outside marriage. They might be, but are by no means necessarily, the offspring of such a union.

Rather such siblingships would customarily be established between any and all offspring of two people who had ever slept together and admitted it in public. As such, the existence of such offspring created no enduring relationship between the adults, but was a way of creating sibling alliances (governed by an incest taboo) over time and space. Indeed, such siblingships continue to be referred to in Wainwright as 'keeping the peace'. Male *aniqatit, tiguaqtit,* and *qatangutit* younger than ego would thus all be referred to and addressed as *nukaaluk,* younger brother; the moral content of the relationship would remain the same regardless of how one came to 'be' there. Of the three modes of recruitment, only one is biological in the sense used by both Iñupiat and Euro-Americans. The three are descriptive terms, not modelled after the biological one.

The expansive potential of adding on relatives of course does not mean that all kinship links are permanently active. The universe of potential kin is much larger than one could maintain if one were to satisfy the obligations that kinship entails: shared food, labour, company, child care, political support, and so forth. Heinrich (1963) identifies what he calls 'optative' and 'non-optative' kinship spheres. Parents, grandparents, and siblings fall into the latter category, for their relatedness cannot be denied without incurring social disapproval. The optative category describes virtually everyone else – kin who are kin because they – and you – act like kin. If the action ceases, the relationship does as well. It was not uncommon to hear the comment 'He used to be my cousin.' This, as I explore later, is not a case of fragile fictive kin versus the more durable 'real' kin described by Bloch (1973) for the Merina. Cousins are equally 'real' whether established by virtue of a natal link or not; and equally optative. The fact that one may choose to recognise or not the players who may fill these roles creates enormous tactical potential, a point made by Bloch as well (1971b: 81–2).

Becoming a person: names, souls, and personal identity

I was struck by the very early age at which children were expected to make autonomous decisions.[11] Indeed, just as animals are thought to choose to be killed by a hunter, infants are thought to choose when to be born (and, according to Saladin D'Anglure (1986), may even choose their sex).[12] One might say that the mother did not so much 'give birth' as the child 'was born' or (as English does not have an active form of the verb 'to be born') 'took life'. However, small humans who are autonomous and capable of decisions are not yet social Iñupiaq beings; animals are likewise considered to have intent and control their actions. Names play an important role in this transformation. Names contain personal essence which attaches to the human being and creates individually unique social connection through time. Names travel through the generations, embodying a kind of reincarnation that accrues to individuals rather than classes of people. 'A kid is only a vehicle for the name is the way they put it in the Iñupiaq language', according to Raymond Neakok, Sr, but 'the vehicle' is never absolutely the same. I give you an extended quotation from an interview with Neakok, since it brings this out so well.

I was already named even before I was born by which are now my parents – that's Arthur and Hesther Neakok. If I was a girl, I was going to be called Lolly. If I was a boy, I was going to be called Raymond. But my Iñupiaq names – the ones that were given to me – that's another thing. When an Iñupiaq wants to recognise the fact that a person has lived, they'll use his name over – they'll give his name to another kid. They don't consider it a kid – it's a continuation of that person – a kid is only a vehicle for that name is the way they put it in the Iñupiaq language ... I want to be remembered as I am – my *ilitqusiq* – the way I live. I want somebody to remember it, so I name you me.
   When a close relative is going to have a baby, the relatives themselves will go ahead and say, 'Here, let this one be so-and-so.' All the families together – not just the close family – would say, 'Here, we have named you this because of this.' They'll tell you why they have named you. Your ancestral tree was intact that way because other than the father and the mother, the brothers and sisters, aunts and uncles, your grandmothers would select at times which name will be used. My mother named me Uiññiq, after her father, but there were also the other names I've been given ... These were not given by my mother, but by people who were alive at the time ... They gave the names – the Iñupiaq names. They will identify me as that person in that family. I cannot be four or five different people at the same time, but whatever family wishes to identify me as that one person, then I will be that one – for them. And that's how the whole village would look at you. If you are named that, you cannot be somebody else – you cannot be identified by another name if they choose to remember you by that name – the name of the person that was given to you. So, the name is not just from one generation, but generation upon generation – that's the social structure of the Iñupiaq. (Bodenhorn n.d.: 16–17)

People who give you names may be, but do not have to be, relatives; they are never uniquely parents, who may be left out of the process entirely. The names you receive may be, but often are not, those of your deceased relatives. Generally the name-giver decides the proper name because he or she has recognised something about you that indicates a specific connection with someone who is deceased: you may seem to be familiar with a certain place, or to recognise a particular person the first time you come in contact with her or him. Rather than noting that a child 'has her father's eyes', then, a doting visitor will find parallels in much more distant identities (see also Guemple 1988). This is not gendered. Although names convey personal essence, people can and do inherit names – and personae – of men and women.

Names may not only reflect personality, they can confer personality, particularly in the way they combine. 'Someone named my son every place we stopped coming back from the hospital (in Anchorage)', a friend told me when talking about her somewhat hyperactive child. 'He's got too many names; they fight all the time!' was her final diagnosis. Unhappiness may also be a sign of the improper fit of a single name. My Wainwright grandmother, Mattie Bodfish, was being visited by a great-granddaughter with her youngest child. 'Ah – that baby is crying too much', Mattie worried; 'maybe it's got wrong name!' She took the infant in her arms, gently rocking it while crooning names. When the baby stopped crying, Mattie handed it back to her mother. 'There, that's her name', she said.

In addition to personal essence, names confer personhood in so far as one enters into the kinship roles of the person whose name has been given. Thus, a young girl may be addressed as '*aapa*', grandfather, by those who are grandchildren to the original name-provider. Persons, then, are multiples of personal essences. As Raymond explained, you cannot be more than one at a time, but, depending on the context, you become the name at the forefront, are treated as that person, thus learning how to react as that person. An individual may choose the name he or she goes by in public. Alternative names may be preferred by others. There is no 'proper' number of Iñupiaq names: some people have one or two; others have several. Nor is there a point in the life cycle when names should be 'complete'; people often continue to gain names well into adulthood. Thus, no two people are likely to carry identical name sets. The multiple essences which make up their personhood may be at one and the same time 'dividual' in that one is different people depending on context and individual in that each configuration of names is unique.

As in many societies, then, names and naming carry a significant moral load over time: past made future. Unlike in many systems – in Amazonia, among the Nuer and the royal families of Europe – Iñupiaq names tell you nothing about parentage, descent group, or sex. They mark personal essences transferred between individuals over the generations which are used to foster kinship relations in the present and guarantee continuity into the future. In quite important ways, social and psychological personhood reflects attributes of names, not characteristics inherited from biological parents. What the child does in acting out his or her personae is not evidence of 'good breeding'. Parents take neither glory from nor blame for the actions of offspring.

Adoption

Whereas naming practices highlight important ways in which individual personhood is not thought to be inherited through shared substance, adoption brings out the ways in which parenting – as action – is privileged over the acts of begetting and bearing. Throughout circumpolar North America, adoption levels are very high.[13] On Belcher Island in eastern Canada, Guemple (1986) claims that 40 per cent of all children are either adopted in or adopted out. In Wainwright, Luton (1986) discovered that 34 per cent of all households contained an adopted child. In fact, he felt adoption was the statistical norm. Most adults have either been adopted in or lived in a household where a child has been adopted in or adopted out. One-fifth of the households I worked with (combining Wainwright and Barrow) had done both.

People who adopt usually know each other, but do not need to be close kin; adoption often results in a mild intensification of relations between the adults involved (see also Guemple 1972; Rousseau 1970). The reasons given to me for adoption were numerous. Childlessness, the most common reason in many societies, accounted for only two of twenty-five cases. A much more common reason was that someone (a sister, grandmother) 'wanted to'; that 'we had too many boys, we wanted a girl' (or vice versa); 'all my other sibs have'; 'we kind of exchanged'; 'we had too many kids'; and so forth. Often it was because the children themselves wanted to. Only two kinds of adoptions did not at least slightly strengthen existing ties within the parental generation. Historically, orphans of community members would be taken in by close kin or turned into *savakti*, literally workers, and never truly incorporated into another family.[14] The final category, one forcefully pointed out that I had missed when charting reasons for adoption, is that of 'miracle baby'. These were infants left beside the trail and found before they froze to death. These have often been treated in the literature as victims of infanticide, although Burch (1975) argues that putting a child by a well-travelled route may more accurately be thought of as an attempt to save rather than take a child's life. I knew of three (adult) miracle babies – two women, one man – all involving families who had been travelling through the region during difficult times. They would have been relative strangers, who certainly could not afford to intensify ties but instead were being forced to break them. That the infants themselves are identified as miracle babies testifies to their special status as adopted children.

Important to the present argument is that several of these reasons suggest that birth parents do not necessarily have 'first rights' to their offspring. Young mothers occasionally joked that their older sisters or their mothers might try to take a child away from them. Children often decide themselves that they should be adopted and by whom. It is considered a legitimate choice for them to make, even if a parent may not wish it.[15] In many cases, the shift may be to everyone's satisfaction, but even when it is not, the question as to where a child 'should' go was never in my experience grounded in biological argument. The natal home is not assumed somehow 'naturally' to be the 'right' one. In general, adopted children feel special and talk of it positively, occasionally in terms of dual family membership. Mattie Bodfish was one of these. When I asked if she knew her biological family, she chuckled and said, 'I knew them – because my father and his brother always work together – hunting together. They love each other – and I loved them both ... I like it myself. When I want to stay in the other family, I go move to other family. That's the way I was ... we always stay together' (Bodenhorn 1989: 154).

More often, however, the primary relationship is transferred to the adoptive family, and natal ties are residual. Sometimes what was thought to be temporary fosterage becomes adoption when the child appears to bond closely to the new family. Birth parents may occasionally bring over presents; adult children may hunt with biological siblings, or bring food over to parents. The degree to which these ties are maintained is left up to the individual child, and may range from virtually no contact to regular shared activity. The biological relationship then becomes optative. Someone who did not 'act like' a son or daughter to adoptive parents would incur social disapproval; the recognition of that link is not left to individual whim. Ignoring one's biological parents as an adopted child, on the other hand, did not, in my experience, excite comment. Adoptive parents are, in Raymond's words, 'real – they're real to me'.[16]

The issue of who Iñupiaq parents 'are' exactly may seem somewhat perplexing. E. N. Goody (1982: 8) suggests that parenthood may be subdivided into five tasks: bearing and begetting, endowing with status, nurturing, training, and sponsorship. In Iñupiaq families, most of these tasks are spread out, and none is restricted to the natal parental domain. Bearers and begetters are no more 'real' candidates for parenting than adoptors, nor do they provide any more enduring status. Personal essence and character is largely influenced by names rather than inherited through shared substance. It is often up to grandparents to provide moral upbringing, and left to aunts and uncles to furnish discipline. Everyone nurtures. What, in short, do parents do? We turn to Raymond Neakok once again: 'My people believed at the time when they were growing up, that parents only had one thing to do with the children – just love – *nakuaq* – their whole heart. They brought me up that way. Though it has changed, it hasn't changed much – the only thing they could give me was love.'[17]

Human beings bear children, just as children take life. Neither physical act creates personhood, either in the form of 'parent' or of 'child'. Giving birth thus does not necessarily create 'rights' in these children that have primacy over other potential rights. Parents are the ones who do the parenting, who love them. This role is not necessarily restricted to one set of people. Biological kinship is rarely denied, but the *primary* relationships, both in affect and in moral weight, are formed with those who brought you up. If there is a hierarchical principle, it emphasises generation over anything else. For parents, however, even this source of privilege becomes relatively unimportant.

Discussion: 'real' kinship, authenticity, and permanence

To return to one of our original theoretical dilemmas – the place of biology with relation to kinship and its connection to personal identity and personal claims on others – this material presents a social world in which natal bonds are recognised but given virtually no *determining* character whatsoever. It is not somehow what makes kinship 'real'.

The child chooses when to be born; it may choose which sex to be; the begetters and bearers have relatively little to do with the process. Non-parents give the names which bring personhood; the child may choose which name to use in public; it may choose, in fact, whether or not to remain with its natal home, and whether or not to maintain those bonds if it leaves. The hierarchy of generation is de-emphasised so that parental bonds are thought to carry much affect but little moral authority. Children are reflections not of parental but of named selves.

If giving birth does not entail the status of parent, we are forced to look at the question of what is 'real' about kinship from new angles. Bloch (1973), following Fortes, suggests that the morality of kinship is based on its irrevocability, thus leading to tolerance of unbalanced reciprocity over the short term. He discusses how the Merina were not – as one might expect – likely to call on 'real' but on 'artificial' kinsmen in times of need. The distinction, he asserts, is theirs; 'real' relations, being permanent, needed no renewal, they said. Artificial kinship needed constant strengthening through bonds of favours that would be reciprocated in the short term (pp. 78–9). This makes absolute sense, not only in Merina logic, but in that of many other societies as well. It does not work at all in Iñupiaq logic, for although Iñupiat are explicit about the long term – both past and future – their language of kinship seems neither anchored nor legitimated in a language of permanence or authenticity.

This assertion calls for further examination, as it bears directly on a number of current Euro-American conversations concerning the 'real' bases of kinship. The assumption that 'real' kinship is somehow fixed in the physical processes of reproduction is, I think, related to another assumption: that giving birth makes a child 'really ours' and that this generates for the bearer not only obligations towards, but rights over, the child. In the Fortesian view of kinship, this is regarded positively. It is what gives kinship its character of long-term, irrevocable morality which is obligated through nurturing. The Marxist view is more negative, for within this framework, 'kinship' functions as ideology, naturalising asymmetrical power relations via gender and generation. The fact that someone is 'your' spouse, 'your' child, gives you rights over their person. If property can be defined as rights claimed over resources, then the potential immutability of kinship in this sense, like the categories of race, gender, and ethnicity, can clearly be used as a basis on which property claims may be put forward beyond the control of individual actors.

That the category 'real' might be as unstable as that of 'biology' should come as no surprise. Its instability causes difficulties for actors as well as anthropologists. Many current court cases concerned with the implications of new reproductive technologies revolve precisely around arguments over the 'real' basis of legitimate claims, particularly to the status of parenthood. In these cases, conceptions of biology are called on not only to identify the 'real' basis, but also to define what is 'natural' (and therefore acceptable) in these relations. Both categories – the 'real' and the 'natural' – are called into the service of legitimising the claims at stake. The ways in which these recent technological developments have highlighted and complicated the assumptions behind these categories in Euro-America have been thoroughly explored in recent anthropological discussions (to name but a few: Cannell 1990; Stanworth 1987; Strathern, 1992a, 1998a).

Whether we consider the question of surrogacy in Great Britain, or of artificial kinship among the Merina, the categories of 'authenticity' ('real' *v.* 'fictive') and of 'permanence' must be examined. These of course are not always separable, for, as Weston (1995) suggests for the United States, authenticity and permanence are in some senses held to be synonymous; blood ties are assumed to be permanent and are therefore more real than non-biological friendships, which are classified as non-permanent. Gay challenges to this ideology invert the notion 'what's real is not subject to change' in order to argue that 'whatever endures is real' (p. 100). 'Permanence in a relationship', she goes on to argue, 'is no longer ascribed ('blood is blood'), but produced' (p. 101). Weston's material clearly resonates with the ethnography presented here but does not replicate it. The category 'real' is important in Iñupiaq conversation: *niqipiaq* is 'real (because hunted) food', Iñupiat are 'real people', and, as Raymond Neakok said of his adoptive parents, 'they're real, they're real to me'. The use of *piaq* in Iñupiaq or 'real' in English does indeed mark a category of value; to be 'real' is in many ways to be 'good', but it is not defined as real-because-essential and therefore unchangeable. Nor is it necessarily opposed by a category that is somehow 'not real' – or false. In Weston's challenge to the notion that real family ties must somehow be located in biological relations, the validation continues to be located in permanence. Iñupiaq material challenges the assumption that 'real' must be either biological or permanent. Permanence lies in the ever present potential for revivifying dormant relations, but these must be enacted by individuals with intent. What is real is acted on and mutually recognised.

Among Iñupiat, labour that earns individual shares regardless of social category serves to guarantee individuals access to resources without dependence. It is labour that may be undertaken alone or in groups. It is impossible, however, to be 'kin' on your own, and the basic idiom with which to talk about daily life revolves around interactions among relatives. And daily life is intensely social, involving many people in a wide variety of activities. But because it is disconnected from anything permanent, it must be constantly reconstructed: kinship bonds renewed and kept viable through a myriad of reciprocities: shared tools, food, labour, political alliance, ceremonial participation, and simply company. These links are made through individual negotiation: *ilyagiich:* my additions; in a two-way relationship; living. Sharing may be both uncalculated and balanced, but among kin it is not dormant. It is *this* labour – the work of being related – rather than the labour of giving birth or the 'fact' of shared substance that marks out the kinship sphere from the potentially infinite universe of relatives who may or may not belong. And it is hard work. Having to construct and reconstruct one's social world virtually on a daily basis can be stressful stuff. People develop ulcers wondering whether they are 'getting it right'. But they have no doubt that it is real.

Labour, then, plays a tremendous role in defining social relations and their identities; it allows individuals to earn shares; it defines spousal responsibilities; and it enacts kinship. Bodies are indeed sites of both identity and boundaries, but more in terms of embodied action than of bodily substances. The obligation to labour is a constant – if you are to earn shares, if you are to have relatives – but how you do this in many ways is highly negotiable at the individual level.

Conclusions

Several of the chapters in this volume present material in which the boundaries defining 'kinship' seem to revolve around processes and perspectives at least as much as around anything as concrete as substances, genetic or otherwise. 'Real' Alltowners, according to Edwards and Strathern, define themselves through an intertwined history of shared place and shared 'blood' – forming the basis for what the authors describe as a series of links along which claims of kinship can travel. Occasionally people reported that kin were 'cut off' or 'took [themselves] out of the family sphere'. The explanation for inclusion or exclusion was sometimes given in biological terms ('well, she was adopted ...') or in purely social terms ('he moved away and we lost contact'). The potential for opening up or closing down these links means that an individual kinship universe may shift repeatedly during a person's life.

Astuti's account in this volume describes how the perspective of Dadilahy, a Vezo elder, shifts in terms of *filongoa* (relatedness), depending on his position in the life cycle. As he moves from the universe of the living to the universe of the dead, his view of his universe of relatives changes from cognatic to unilineal reckoning. Perspective and process thus profoundly influence both Vezo and English kinship boundaries, but in very different ways.

As with Alltowners, Iñupiat describe their state of being related as potentially expansive ('our additions; in a two-way relationship') and contractive ('he used to be my cousin'). Whereas the net result in Alltown ultimately is that people are more likely to drop off than to be added on, the opposite is true on the North Slope. Individual relatives may be sloughed off (at least temporarily), but it is always 'good to have relatives', and proper behaviour generally results in incorporation into broadened kinship relations of some sort.

The ways in which these systems resonate *vis-à-vis* each other deserve further attention. Rhetorics of kinship in 1990s Britain use 'biology' to frame multiple discussions of what it means to 'be related'. Alltowners may slough off kin with or without reference to 'biology'. Arguments over new reproductive technologies, by contrast, always assume that there must be an unsloughable-off biological something on which claims to be the 'real' parent may be based. The essential category may have been rendered uncertain through technological developments, but the assumption that it entails something about the parent/child link remains. For Alltowners as well as Iñupiat, kinship may be optative as well as non-optative; for Iñupiat as well as Alltowners, the parent/child bond is assumed to fall in the latter category. The grounds on which the status of 'parent' is made 'real' (that is, non-negotiable) differ radically, as we have seen.

In a recent paper, Strathern (1998b: 226) invites her readers to consider the possibility that Mount Hageners may have *anticipated* some Euro-American ways of thinking about ownership. It is a provocative challenge to the continuing impulse to think evolutionarily – to assume that if people change, they will move towards European modernity. And it invites us to consider the same challenge with reference to the particular relationships parents and children are thought to have. The idea that adoption does not entail a break with the natal parent/child link is increasingly common across Euro-America. The idea that a child's 'legitimate' status does not rest on the marital status of its parents has also recently been changed in British law. Both notions are of course long established in Iñupiaq ways of thinking about parents and children. Iñupiaq ideas about being a relative depend on a category of subject whose personhood is multiple and constantly transformative through performance – a thoroughly post-modern-sounding notion. Whether its increasing currency in Euro-America allows the possibility of recognising two maters as a way of resolving the dilemmas of identifying 'real' parents in the wake of technological developments remains an intriguing question.

For many Euro-Americans, strategies for coming to terms with the implications of biotechnological shifts echo those discussed by Edwards and Strathern: in a universe that has the potential to expand as well as to contract the parameters within which humans are recognised as related, the net result so far seems to be a drawing in. Ever smaller 'biological bits' are assigned ever more determining effects. Iñupiat, not being charged with the task of reproducing 'their own' children, are not faced with the same dilemmas. Iñupiat social organisation contains an intriguing mixture of characteristics, protecting individual access to resources, for instance, but allowing individual accumulation of goods. Iñupiaq kinship relations are perhaps the most perplexing of all, for whereas much of the labour involved in hunting, butchering, and distribution emphasises the claims on resources rather than on relationships, the obligations of relatedness may be enacted through labour, but they are clearly social and explicitly moral. It is precisely the non-biologised character of Iñupiaq kinship, however, which allows for moral obligation *and* autonomous control together. One consequence of this – and, I would suggest, perhaps the key difference between the systems described by Edwards and Strathern and by myself – is that 'kinship' does not act as a controlling element in the property system. Individuals are free to move within families as well as across space, preventing interdependent actors from becoming dependent relatives. That these relations do not fit easily in property systems defined through capitalism is something that people on the North Slope are aware of. Parents in Alltown and Barrow are of course contemporaries. In both places the conditions of late-twentieth-century life challenge foundational ideas of what it means to be social, moral human beings. How they are worked out is, of course, another story.

Notes

The fieldwork upon which this paper was based was conducted with the joint support of the North Slope Borough Iñupiat History, Language and Culture Commission and the Alaska Humanities Forum during 1983–4 and by the Alaska Eskimo Whaling Commission and the National Science Foundation between 1994 and 1996. In addition, I learned much from my co-workers while I worked for the Iñupiat Community of the Arctic Slope (1980–3). As always, I must thank Marie and Raymond Neakok, Sr, Mattie and Waldo Bodfish (now deceased), Leona Okakok, and James Nageak for what I have learned from them both formally and informally. Nancy Ahsogeak, Wendy Arundale, Sue Benson, Nurit Bird-David, Ernest S. Burch, Jr, Janet Carsten, Melba Collette, Kathy Itta Ahgeak, Benjamin Macias, Edna Ahgeak MacLean, Frances Mongoyak, Frances Pine, Marilyn Strathern, and James Woodburn among many others have provided stimulating insight and criticism. From Cambridge, I received support from the Audrey Richards Fund, a Chadwick studentship, Pembroke College, the Smuts Fund, the Department of Social Anthropology, and Wolfson College. Earlier versions of this material, focusing on some of the implications of these ideas with regard to 'property', were presented at the Oxford seminar on ecology and identity (Bodenhorn 1997) and at the faculty seminar at the University of Sussex. Although this chapter deals with quite different issues, discussions following those presentations as well as the very lively discussions at the conference out of which this volume emerged have all contributed to its final form.

1 Iñupiat, literally 'real people', occupy the northern and north-western coast of Alaska. The singular as well as the adjectival form of the word is Iñupiaq. The practices of people who call themselves Iñupiat vary; most of the material in this chapter reflects things said to me between 1980 and 1997 by people living in the Barrow region.

2 See Patrick Attungana (1986), in Bodenhorn (1993).

3 I employ this term in the Maussian sense: individuals *qua* individuals have
   recognised standing, rights, and so forth, and are assumed to be agentive,
   exercising intent and accountability (see Carrithers, Collins, and Lukes
   1985; Lukes 1973; Strathern 1988). I am not thereby suggesting that
   Iñupiaq ideas of sociality are defined through an ideology of individualism.
   Far from it. The practices of maintaining individual autonomy found on the
   North Slope are in marked contrast to those of mainstream United States,
   whose political foundation rests on the language of what Lukes (1973: 596)
   defines as U.S. political individualism. That distinction is not the object of
   the present chapter. The importance of acknowledging Iñupiaq categories
   that consider individuals as moral, social persons is, however, central to the
   argument.
4 From here on I shall use biology without inverted commas, since in terms of
   kinship both the Iñupiaq and the Euro-American on the street refer roughly
   to the same thing even if they do not accord it the same significance.
5 'Subsistence' in this sense refers to a lifestyle centred on the pursuit of
   hunted food.
6 I certainly know women who are skilled hunters, and men who are good
   cooks and handy with the sewing needle. Both Burch (1975) and Jenness
   (1985; cited in Cassell 1988) point out that within the privacy of the marital
   unit, men and women might switch off on their duties simply to make things
   more interesting.
7 See Bodenhorn 1990.
8 This is reflected in the numbers of words depicting different kinds of
   actions, all of which are translated by Iñupiat as 'sharing' when they speak
   English; see Bodenhorn 1989: 100–5; Burch 1988: 104–5.
9 There is, in fact, considerable sentiment that a wife without a husband is
   better off than the reverse: 'This is what we have always known. When a
   mother loses a husband, she can sew, or she can get food by begging or
   working for it. But when a husband loses a wife, he can't do anything'
   (Bodenhorn 1989: 135). See Bodenhorn 1990, 1993.
10 Literally, a companion (*qati*) moving back (*kingu*) in a two-way relationship
   (*-giich*).
11 One friend related how her seven-year-old son had decided to move to his
   grandparents', some seventy miles away. She laughed as she described how
   he had even gone to school to get his papers so that he could change schools.
   I chuckled as well and asked her how she had responded. 'He went,' was her
   reply, somewhat surprised that I should have had to ask.
12 According to Iqallijuq, a woman shaman from Iglulik, human bodies are
   formed through the provision of semen, which is transformed into bone;
   menstrual blood, which becomes the child's blood; flesh from the animals;
   and spirit from the names (see Saladin D'Anglure 1986: 40). A child is thus
   very much a product of its parental substances, but those substances are by
   no means sufficient to create another human being. Its gender, however,
   may be a function of whether or not the foetus picks up male or female tools
   on its way out of the birth canal (ibid.).
13 Adoption practices differ among Siberian Inuit for reasons too complex to
   explore here. In short, however, access to wealth through whaling and

trading was historically controlled through kinship. Sons whaled with fathers and inherited from them. Adoption was considered a last resort for childless couples (Schweitzer, nd).

14 Burch (1975) suggests, and I agree, that this is not adoption. Kin terms of address would not be used, and appropriate cross-generational kin behaviour would not be observed. Such children now become wards of the state.

15 One woman told me that her daughter had essentially moved into the house next door; when the woman complained to her husband, his response was, 'But if she is happy . . .' Another related that she had been taking care of an infant who was beginning to bond with her own children. She called the natal mother and said, 'You'd better come get your baby; it's getting attached to my kids.' 'Keep it!' came the reply. In neither case was there any suggestion that the 'birth mother' was in any way lacking in motherly feelings or proper behaviour.

16 See also Pitt-Rivers 1973: 90, who noted with some bemusement that Inuit seemed to make no qualitative distinction between natal and adoptive parents.

17 In Bodenhorn 1989: 158 or, for a fuller context, Bodenhorn n.d.: 18ff. Neakok was discussing this in relation to conflicting expectations of 'proper' parental behaviour as defined by Euro-American teachers or social workers and Iñupiaq parents. The former might well expect that parents should 'set limits', make sure their children were at home at a certain time, had done their homework, eaten a proper supper, and so forth. Neakok's point was that moral discipline was the area of aunts and uncles rather than of parents, who 'had only one thing to do with the children – just love . . .'

8   Including our own

Jeanette Edwards and Marilyn Strathern

In March 1995, a child was born from an embryo that had been frozen for more than four years, implanted by clinicians at the Bourn Hall clinic in Cambridge and carried to term by a friend. The gratitude of the child's mum and dad[1] towards the surrogate mother was voiced by the eventual mother in a double idiom of ownership: 'No words can express how I felt – my own perfect baby girl, given to me by my best friend in the world.'[2] The child was her own, by the combined virtues of a tie of substance (genetic connection) and the gift that having been given cannot be given back.

One would not ordinarily think twice about the idioms of ownership here. English-speakers know that what is claimed as one's own may encompass as much a claim to identity, adduced in ways of 'belonging' to a place or a family, as it does to rights of possession. Consistent and subtle pressure in idiomatic usage keeps the connotations apart. One may claim a person as one's own but not that one owns him or her.[3] At the same time, equally subtle and consistent idiomatic pressure keeps these connotations in tandem. There is a moral propriety to the indigenous English concept of 'ownership' which suggests that it is as natural to (want to) possess things, as part of one's own self-definition, as it is to be part of a community or to belong to a family. This gives rise to proprietorial identity being claimed over a large range of animate, inanimate, and quasi-animate entities, such as one's own past, the place where one lives, inheritance, family names, and so forth. These associations hold some interest for 'cultures of relatedness'.

Narrating such associations makes a chain out of them, and claims can travel along chains. The child belongs to the parents not just by virtue of the genetic connection or the gift by which the surrogate mother gives it up, but also through the effort they had to make in going to Bourn Hall, through the skill of the clinicians who implanted the embryo, through the cryopreservation techniques to which they agreed, through the support of family and friends, and so forth. These activities may be claimed as part of the history of the life in which the parents shared, though any one of these could also be claimed as parts of other people's lives and histories too. What is true in the way the parents consider their connections to the child is also true when families consider themselves as people who belong to one another.

We seek to sidestep one of the impasses into which contemporary discussion has fallen. We refer here to discussion outside as well as within anthropology, notably that stimulated by the new reproductive technologies, and to the impasse set up by imagining kinship as divided between social and biological manifestations of itself.[4] Our lead is given by Janet Carsten's (1995a) illuminating critique of that divide. However, rather than going beyond the 'Western thought' which produced it, as Carsten and many of the contributors to this volume have done so effectively, we offer a critique from the inside. We draw on material from the north of England for the insights it gives us into indigenous English concepts of relatedness. In so doing, we follow Bouquet (this volume) in foregrounding certain aspects of Euro-American kinship thinking which have been foundational in the development of anthropological analysis.[5]

To address the divide between social and biological kinship face-on would simply reproduce the terms of the debate. We propose to sidestep the issue by drawing on theoretical resources which have not to our knowledge been applied to kinship thinking in quite this way. These we make explicit in the final section of the chapter. The preceding sections provide a context from which it will become apparent that the divide (between biological and social kinship) is also a combination or association (of disparate elements), and belongs to a whole range of possibilities for the inclusion and exclusion of persons. Our interest in this chapter is less in what is counted as 'biological' or as 'social' than in the power of imagining their intersection. The terms operate within a field of operations repeated over and again on a daily and ordinary basis.

Belonging

The concept of 'belonging' has such an embracing (inclusive) effect in English that it can encompass any form of association, including narrational or logical association, as in stories or classificatory systems, and appropriations which draw any manner of human or non-human elements towards one: 'my colleague', 'my illness', 'my house', 'my cat', 'my way'. In turn, entities traced, assembled, classed together, or juxtaposed, in English idiom 'belong' to one another thereby, although the links through which they are brought into association may be diverse.

The English residents of Alltown, in Lancashire (Edwards 1993, 1998), construct chains of association that enlarge their own sense of belonging to families by belonging to a place (and see A. P. Cohen 1982). They also enlarge their sense of belonging to a place by belonging to particular families. Persons claim Alltown is theirs as members of families rather than as individuals, and residents who define themselves as 'Alltown born and bred' talk of how their 'family' migrated to the town in search of employment or housing and of how 'whole families' used to work in the cotton mills or shoe factory. Certain patronyms are readily identified as 'real' Alltown names, and are associated with 'original' Alltown families. It is just such a name, or parental occupations or housing histories, that constitute a person as 'proper Alltown',[6] and it is these diverse connections which enhance the connotations of belonging.

A common observation in and about Alltown is that in the past 'cousins married cousins', and that 'original Alltown families' were all related to each other. Similar ideas of interrelatedness are deployed in descriptions of present-day Alltown and are used to portray either its 'parochial' or its 'friendly' nature. The notion that Alltown people are interrelated is put to work, on the one hand as evidence for the mutually supportive community and on the other for its cliquishness.[7] There is in this sense a constant interweaving of 'family' and 'community' in Alltown talk. Community is described in terms of stability and communication, and its 'breakdown' is linked to the loss of these things. Like communities, families are said to be 'tight knit' and, like communities, they are also said to be 'breaking down'. For members of an Alltown youth club, the elements that compose community are 'people living together', 'being nice', 'respecting each other', 'being able to borrow off each other', 'communication'. Community, like family, connotes these qualities and more, and not only in Alltown. Indeed, the analogy between community and family is common in English social commentary in general, including here anthropological and other academic studies of English society. However, while it is well known in Alltown that families are marked as much by antipathy as by mutual support, and that community is as much a forum of gossip and the generation of stigma as it is about communication and respect, this divisive side is often missing in academic commentary, a point to which we return.

A claim on the place entails a claim on those things that belong to the place. Hence belonging to Alltown entails a prior claim on, amongst other things, its housing, its moorland, its clubs, pubs, factories, informal organisations, education, health and social services, and its past.[8] It also embraces claims on ways of doing things: 'our ways' as opposed to 'their ways'. While recent 'incomers' are unable to mobilise the same set of connections to the town as those who claim 'born and bred' status, they note that their commitment to Alltown – their intentional activities of dwelling, of neighbouring, of preserving history, of conserving amenities, and of joining in – attaches them. They too create chains along which claims can travel. Claims, moreover, travel in more than one direction, and places exercise claims as much as persons. A claim on Alltown requires reciprocation, so that one must 'put back' something; an often heard criticism is that incomers do not 'put anything back' – they do not, it is suggested, reciprocate in appropriate manner. If certain Alltown families are potentially all linked up, as much with themselves as with town history, or with the ups and downs of employment in the shoe factory for that matter, and others are linked in the activities of dwelling, joining, and conserving, then anything can become a link in a chain of attachments or relationships by virtue of 'belonging' there.

These are not value-free ideas. 'Belonging', like 'association', 'relationship', and a host of similar connective terms, carries positive overtones.[9] It is almost as though there were something productive and generative in making connections as such.[10] At least for English-speakers, it seems natural that persons should want to belong (to whatever it is), as it is natural to want to have things in one's possession which belong to one, or as it is obvious that there is analytical virtue in making connections and tracing sequences of events. What is true of the citizen or author is also true of the text: everything in a narrative 'belongs' to the account, even where the account may be about things which supposedly do not belong to one another.

The analogy between social and intellectual engagement (making connections) that strikes Strathern (1995) is of a piece with the sentimentalised view of sociality as sociability and of kinship ('family') as community that pervades much Euro-American commentary of an *academic* kind. Perhaps one counterpart to the romantic view of connections as benign and community as harmonious, or logic as satisfying for that matter, lies in a salient cultural fact of English and Euro-American kin connections: the significance of an emotionally binding core in the positive affect ('love') that links persons together (Macfarlane 1986, 1987). Connections appear intrinsically desirable. People take pleasure in making links of logic or narrative, as people take pleasure in claiming personal links. Linkages may also appear exciting, especially when they cross apparent boundaries. Moving along a chain of associations may confirm the (homogeneous) replicability of shared values; but it may equally well bring into view (heterogeneous) elements regarded as inherently diverse, as disparate from one another as a shoe factory and local history records appear to be.

We have with these few words created a very simple type of chain, based on contiguous associations of meaning in English, from ownership to belonging to association to link. But every such conceptualisation of inclusion also excludes. The most explicit double pointer to inclusion and exclusion alike is the concept 'ownership', with its Euro-American connotations of alienable possessions and inalienable possessiveness.[11]

Exclusion is not value-free either. It frequently carries negative overtones, connotations of marginality or loss or deprivation. It may point to an antithesis between those who belong and those who do not, those who have title of possession and those who do not: the excluded are excluded by virtue of their failure to be part of something.[12] Of course, the excluded may also be identified by virtue of their own power or other characteristics (class, accent, lifestyle) which set them 'off' from others, as ethnic minorities appear to be set off (Stolcke 1995). Yet perhaps some of the awkwardness with which English-speakers deal with exclusion, having to justify it on grounds of difference, dislike, people cutting themselves off, not keeping up, finds resonance with the kinship interplay between the characteristics one owns and the people claimed as one's own. We refer not just to the boundary that 'our own' is supposed to throw up against outsiders, strangers, offcomers (Rapport 1993), and foreign families, but to the way the relatives can be disowned. For whatever reasons, they cease to belong.[13]

Mediating

Key kinsfolk may act as links, and links act as mediators (Edwards 1993: 51–3); we might say they afford a passage from one entity to another. Any entity may serve as a link for another. Thus the mediating gift of the surrogate mother enables the intending mother to relate to the child by claiming the child as her own. The same gift also links the 'two mums'; for the donating woman, it is the child who is the mediating node in her link with the other woman. If persons belong to one another through what belongs to them, then these mediators may be other persons, possessions, individual characteristics – in short, things material or immaterial, human or non-human. So persons can belong to one another through living in this or that part of Alltown, or going to work in the same factory, or indeed imagining giving their 'own' embryos to another.[14] But the belonging produced by kinship has, for these people, a whole further dimension to it. It lies, idiomatically, in the difference between relating and being related.[15] While relatedness is not restricted to biological connection, biological connection signals the reference to a mutual history which gives it a dimension in time.

English images of kin relatedness include limitless chains of relatives stretching back to remote ancestries, so that links between kin could ultimately link all humanity. An emphasis on biological connections allows for links to be extended to all humans, and even between human and non-human animals. Listen to the way in which Martin Johnson, an embryologist, traces the development of his own identity, and by implication that of all human beings, to unknowable ancestors of a dim and distant past.

My emergence as a unique individual with my own identity began back in the ovaries and testes of my parents when they themselves were embryos in the grandparental womb. The events occurring then were in themselves linked via a continuous thread back through successive ancestral germ lines to the emergence of humanity itself. Just as an anthropologist cannot define an exact and absolute point during evolutionary time when our ancient ancestors became human, so I cannot define any single developmental transition at which I became an individual with a clear identity. The evolution of humans and the development of my identity are both continuous processes. (Johnson 1989: 41)

The links which are thought to connect us to, say, primate ancestors are traced, in this mode, through idioms of biology. Within the compass of a rather narrower horizon, such links can be co-opted to serve claims about the antiquity of connections with localities, as when Alltown residents trace local connections through the origins of families and their neighbours. Such links are made effective through the mediation of persons.

Now the manner in which persons are linked by other kinds of mediating entities can qualify such relations. Biological ties may themselves be more or less diluted. Step-siblings, for example, share one biological parent, rather than two; they are said to have in common half the substance transmitted from their parents. In terms of biology, they might not seem so tightly or so all-embracingly linked to each other as they might be if they were to share two parents. Yet in terms of other kinds of links, they may be tightly connected to each other; and more tightly connected than if they were to share two parents instead of one.

Jane Griffiths, in her early forties and a relatively recent incomer to Alltown, explained to Edwards that as far as family were concerned 'we should do our best to [help] our own'. She says she would not expect to have to go to the assistance of her cousins, as they have 'their own family', but she would *know* if they needed help. She and her husband, Malcolm, explain how far 'our own' stretches.

JANE: It's always my belief that we should do our best

MALCOLM: Yeah

JANE: to make sure that our own

MALCOLM: I would say financially and physically, I was going to say when they're ill, you go and look after them, don't you? you know? As far as my mother-in-law's concerned, if she's got any little job she wants doing, she can't do it herself, she usually asks. But it's a reciprocal thing, because if I want my trousers shortening, she shortens them for me.

JEANETTE: How far though does 'our own' extend; how far is the, like, the bounds of family?

MALCOLM: That's difficult to say.

JANE: If for instance, one of my nieces were to really get into debt and were to be faced with losing her home, whether we could [. . .] help her get on her feet, we would do.

MALCOLM: In the sense of nieces, yeah.

JANE: Certainly. I mean there was four of us [siblings] and there's three of him [nodding towards Malcolm]. Those and the children.

JEANETTE: And do your parents have brothers and sisters ? So do you have aunts and uncles?

MALCOLM: Well, my mother was an only child. Her father had one

JANE: So we've got one on his side

MALCOLM: and I don't see him.[16] Because he was, he never, in fact, made himself part of the family.

JEANETTE: This is your uncle?

MALCOLM: He's a half-brother, 'cause me father's mother married again and he never, sort of, made himself part of the family, you know, he didn't – he was invited, for instance, to weddings, to my parents' golden wedding celebrations and he just never came.

JEANETTE: So how's he related to you?

MALCOLM: He's my father's half-brother. 'Cause he was – my father's mother married again and had another child. In fact he's called Butterworth, not Griffiths, you see?

JEANETTE: Right . . . do you class him as family?

MALCOLM: Well he was when we were younger. When he was Uncle Frank, yeah, and we used to go and visit and everything else. But, I think he just – for all I know he may well be dead, you know? – so I think he sort of took himself out of the family sphere by not, you know, communicating sort of thing.

Mr Butterworth is related, but he 'took himself out of the family'; an intentional act on his part which suggests that were he not to have done so he would still belong. But for Malcolm the link between himself and his uncle was already attenuated: Mr Butterworth, he notes, is his father's half-brother. The single rather than double ply of Mr Butterworth's link with Malcolm's family is implicated in his disappearance, in his having left the 'family sphere'.

Jane Griffiths has a similar figure in her family: an adopted cousin, Phoebe Taylor, with whom she is no longer in contact.

JANE: Well, one of my cousins was adopted.

JEANETTE: Is this one of your mother's or father's brothers or sisters . . .

JANE: This is one of my father's sister's children – was an adopted child . . . I mean, it's never occurred to me in all these years, until tonight, but we've virtually lost contact with her

JEANETTE: And that's unusual?

JANE: Well it is in the rest of the family. Yeah. Yeah. It's only because we've been talking about it tonight that I actually realised that. Because, as I was saying about other cousins, I wouldn't see myself as being primarily responsible for caring for them if they were ill, because they had other members of their family. But I would know if they were ill. Whereas I've no idea where she is or what she's done or – we've just more or less cut off contact with her.

The realisation that kin are no longer in touch and that attachments have been broken, either intentionally or by accident, and a juxtaposition of their absence with already attenuated links through, in Malcolm's case half-siblingship and in Jane's adoption, leads Jane to wonder, unhappily, whether this is what might be in store for children born through assisted conception.

I mean, I wonder if this is the kind of treatment that, in fact, these children are going to have . . . because they're not genetically . . . I mean, you think about it, I've never set eyes on Phoebe Taylor for thirty-odd years.

The 'disappearance' of Phoebe Taylor, conflated with the fact that she was an adopted child, preoccupies Jane, and she returns to it later in the conversation.

JANE: All I can say is that not until tonight, when we started talking about it, that I considered the fact that this adopted baby had virtually disappeared.

MALCOLM: Perhaps it's – it doesn't show itself initially when they're growing up [and] part of the family, but when eventually they've reached . . .

JANE: Then their parents die.

MALCOLM: Then the connection's lost.

JANE: And there's no longer any connection with the family. Is there, then? I wonder if that's the case.

MALCOLM: Yeah. Yeah.

JANE: Yeah. 'Cause, I mean, it's not something I've even considered, you know, until tonight . . . Well, we're talking about only our family . . . it is a big family, 'cause my father was one of eleven. And all *that* family is in touch with each other. I don't mean in a direct way, but anything that happens, we know about.

MALCOLM: [It] goes down the telephone tree.

JANE: It does, yeah. You get, you know, anything that happens to them . . . We are interconnected, and we've always kept connected.[17]

JEANETTE: But this person was just dropped

JANE: Has – has just dropped out.

Adoptees or step-relatives, connected by less concentrated ties than 'full' relatives, might 'drop out'. The suggestion is, in these examples, that they take themselves out, perhaps because they do not perceive themselves to be so securely connected. The dilution of substance attenuates the link. From this perspective, the greater the number of persons that mediate the link the more tenuous it becomes. But ideas of shared substance are only ever one side of the story; connections are also broken through lack of attention.

In English homeopathy, trace amounts of remedies are potent, but they are potent only when the remedy and the person interact. The remedy has to be carefully matched to the make-up or to selected characteristics of the recipient. In ideas about relatedness, as in homeopathy, the trace element – in this case the biological vestige – is only potent when it reacts with a particular person. The 'microscopic blip', as one Alltown man called it when thinking of the relationship between a sperm donor and the ensuing child, requires the context of an active and intentional parent.

> Without the mental and physical connection, the microscopic blip will become lost on the floor of the laboratory ... There is no mental and physical connection between the donor and the baby ... there's a huge gap. However microscopic, there's got to be a connection.

Self-limiting

Given these ways of counting and discounting connections, an indigenous English person might query the ideological weight given to the open-endedness so often said to be characteristic of bilateral or cognatic kin reckoning. An image of people imagining ties going on for ever is one which has passed into general anthropological analysis. The ties were – rather unidimensionally – imagined as non-divisive: division lay beyond them. Thus the received wisdom behind many mid-century accounts of cognatic kin systems and bilateral reckoning outside Europe was that truncation had to be brought about by other than kinship means. Such limiting devices would be external to kinship itself. Who were and who were not included in particular groups would depend on a diversity of factors, of which kinship *per se* could never be the only component (others might be residence, access to land, opting for certain associations). It seemed particularly important to demonstrate this in societies where kinship appeared a significant organisational base even though kinship alone did not define discrete groupings.[18]

In many Euro-American societies, however, the truncation of chains of connections, like kinship itself, seemed to mid-century academic anthropologists a much less important matter. Theoretically speaking, the tracing of ties created by links of biological substance could extend for ever outwards. There seemed no limit posed by the way people thought of the distribution of such material itself – any more than a narrative, or knowledge, need ever end. Here biological ties (a sign of relatedness) merge with other mediating (relating) entities. Indeed, one could make a similar claim for social relations opened up these days through telecommunications and information highways. Human relations are theoretically inclusive up to any imaginable scale, as in Johnson's imaginative connection with the emergence of humanity itself. So the potential extensiveness of genealogical connection is one among the several global extensions (such as information, desire, consumerism, technology) that Euro-American academics imagined operating against external rather than internal limits.[19] The checks and stops come from outside, as one may think of human emotions as natural expressions checked by social rules. However, these (constructivist) formulae that led social anthropologists to see social actions as extraneous to natural ones also suggest an alternative state of affairs for twentieth-century Euro-American kinship.

Kinship reckoning appears endless only when a chain is created through a series of similar (homogeneous) elements. Thus one could count for ever the reach of genetic ancestry, or the contacts of contacts. But in practice few such chains ever get very far. They quickly encounter other elements (thereby heterogeneous to themselves). A purist might point to these as non-kinship factors; we think that it is the interdigitation of diverse kinds of linkages that gives English kin reckoning not just an expansive but also a *self-limiting* character, and that this self-limiting character is fruitfully regarded as part of kinship thinking. This is where our view parts company with Schneider's views on relatedness.

In the Alltown conversations in which Edwards participated there is an occasional metaphysical hint at the unity of humankind, but generally connections were made not in the abstract but through mediating human beings. Links might be traceable for ever outwards; in practice they require mediators. For example, Alltown thinking about the donation of gametes includes the notion that gametes not only link the donor, recipient, and ensuing child – 'you are connected, and always would be' – but also predecessors. These predecessors are identified and identifiable as kinsfolk: 'The egg is part of me, but I am part of me mum.' It is also key kinsfolk who act as a link to the past, or as caretakers of family relationships (see e.g. Macdonald 1997; Edwards 1993; Finch 1989). And while the 'dropping out' of relatives appears trivial theoretically, when the person who 'dropped out' is identified, the way Phoebe

Taylor was, then it matters, because now the severance might have been deliberate.

It is arguable that what makes twentieth-century English kinship, and its Euro-American cognates, distinctive is precisely the division and combination of social and biological facts.[20] The distinctiveness becomes evident through comparison with some of the other material in this volume. Bodenhorn's chapter is particular apt. She describes the endless Iñupiaq 'work' of relating in the sustaining – and abandoning – of specific relations drawn from an infinite universe of relatives; yet there is no tension here between birth and nurture, and 'biology' neither extends nor cuts off relations.[21] By contrast, social and biological claims of the English kind, each endlessly ramifying in themselves, serve equally to link and to truncate *one another*. Both afford perspectives from which kinship can be claimed, and the one may either lead to or be played off against the other. Limits are set by how far one wishes to claim – or own, or own up to – such connections.

As in the case of the surrogate mother who nurtured the frozen embryo, reproductive medicine may create ties of substance (carrying the child entailed the surrogate's 'nurture' of it) that do not get translated into social kinship. The surrogate mother, so called, transferred her claims to the commissioning mother through the sacrificial Euro-American gesture of alienation, the gift. Indeed, the gift appears to dominate popular parlance as a solution about how to think of the transfer of human capacities in procreation: predictably, the *Sun* quotes the receiving mother saying of the surrogate, '[She] has given me the greatest gift of all – something I'll treasure for the rest of my life.'[22] We would suggest that the gift is a suitable medium in this context precisely because it is, in its English-culture sense, an alienation which mobilises bonds of attachment (Abrahams 1990; cf. Cheal 1988).[23] The gesture is of course a nice dovetailing of – keeping consonant but separate – the twin ideas of what one owns (as property) and what is one's own (as persons may be). The gift that links the two mothers also divides them. A potential future chain of relationships and claims that could have been traced through the child's tie to the gestational mother is truncated, deactivated in advance, by pitting one set of truths ('biological') against another ('social').[24] It is not surprising that donation remains ambiguous in this respect, at least as some Alltown people see it (Edwards 1993: 52).

But there is another cause – powerful, and also more routine and ordinary – of severance: lack of interest. Blood ties might theoretically allow connections through genealogy and procreation to be traced in ever widening circles, but if it comes to recognising persons as relatives, then in the English experience social exhaustion intervenes. Only in rather restricted circumstances might one wish to claim the world as one's family. Ordinarily one is protected from endless ramification by the people who get lost – they fail to make the claims on their relatives that will activate the relations. Forgetfulness plays an important role here.[25] Since English-speakers generally take forgetfulness as natural failure rather than as social action,[26] the droppings-out come to seem as natural as the claiming of one's own. Hence they may appear trivial. So a person who could be claimed in terms of blood ties may be disowned through lack of social interest, which might or might not be a matter of consequence. Conversely, someone who was forgotten may be claimed back through resurrected biological links.

Kin may act as (social) mediators regardless of how weak or strong the (biological) link is in someone's narrative. To return to the simple connections between a woman and her mother or a woman and her mother's mother: in terms of blood, the second seems to Alltown people more attenuated than the first, since the more mediators on a chain linking persons, the smaller the amount of shared substance. Yet 'amount' may *or may not* be relevant to the strength of the connection. The dilution of shared substance in the course of its flow does not lessen its ability to connect, and biology is never the full story. So while many mediators might dilute the blood tie, it is precisely many mediators that suggest 'large' and, to use the Alltown idiom, 'tight knit' families.

To describe oneself as belonging to a 'close' family in Alltown is not necessarily to talk about biology. The social relationship between a woman and her mother's mother may be 'closer' than her relationship with her mother. Spatial proximity may map onto emotional proximity so that families are regarded as 'close' because they live near to each other and members interact frequently. Or 'closeness' may evoke the quality of affective ties: mutual support and the ability to confide in, depend upon, and trust. This is the way Alan Gray, an Alltown man in his late twenties, and the youngest of eight children, described his relationship with his siblings.

> We've always been a close family, even though we don't see each other much. I could tell them anything and they could tell me anything ... If I could help anybody out, I would, but more so family, no matter what it meant.

'Closeness' summons affective ties, the obligations and duties such ties entail, and the warmth and mutual care with which relationships are sustained. 'Closeness' also points to distance, and 'distant relatives' are those with whom interaction is infrequent, with whom obligations are at a minimum, and with whom confidences are unlikely to be shared. From this perspective, close relatives can become distant ones.

Biological and social ties do not provide the only intersections with which people deal. But they have their counterparts in other domains. In so far as relatives are social persons, the bonds that grow over time to unite friends or are dissolved in disagreements between club supporters are similar to those which join kin together or set them at one another's throats. In so far as they are biologically connected, the moulding effects of a person's birthplace or mother tongue, immutables not open to choice, echo the definitive transmission of substance at conception.

The combination/division of biological/social elements is paradigmatic for what we might wish to call kinship over other Euro-American forms of association. But if it creates the conditions for relatedness, that is only in conjunction with/in separation from other forms of relating. Part of the persuasiveness of kinship derives, we would suggest, from certain routinisations, from the fact that it 'belongs' to a wider field of combinations and divisions. This field is constituted in the acts by which persons make things belong to them. Kin connections (and disconnections) thus belong to the myriad and quotidian ways in which people divide their social universe. As a consequence, if kin ties may be created through links, then in various circumstances they may also work as links or mediators or nodes themselves.

Networking

We have talked of links and chains but not used the term that frequently springs to mind in discussions of the ramifications of kin links: network. And that is because of its contemporary saliency.

'Network' is not a new term; but, as Price remarked (1981: 283), all metaphors (mediators) require vigilance. It is impossible to deploy these days without carrying some of its recent baggage. There is the explosion of net terms that have accompanied the computer user's Net, constituted through 'the myth of the synapse, the "I join together"' (Pound 1995: 529), with its illusory ramification, where 'each new connection appears as a new origin for a new branch of the network' before being overrun by other networks (p. 530). Networking has become a buzzword in NGO circles for empowering persons who become the central nodes of their worlds (Riles 1996). Network is Hannerz's (1992) reduplicated metaphor for the global ecumene (network of networks), for the distribution of meanings across numerous channels of variable distance, for chains of relationships that are transnational at one node, local at another. We have referred to the benign aura in such usages, to the touch of sentimentality which renders ties somehow productive and generative in themselves, as though long-range contact with people or information flow were good things in themselves. It is even arguable that some of the emotions anthropologists once saw flowing towards groups as objects of sentiment are now equally in evidence along pulsating networks of persons and instruments – rather like extensions of people's alleged liking for connection and relationship.[27]

What distinguishes some of the contemporary interest in networks from earlier usages is the explicit attention paid to the interdigitation of the material and immaterial, the human and non-human. Networks are not just relations between persons: they are, like the Net, both the effect of vehicles mobilised to carry messages and the resultant passages and translations which co-mobilise different orders of phenomena.[28] What is interesting about some current theorising on networks is that hetero-geneity is written into them.[29] Like the quasi-objects that Bouquet (this volume) describes, networks have become, definitively, links between the disparate. In this view, they are found in those contexts where one makes a passage from one domain of materiality to another (the nature–society combination/divide is archetypal in Latour's (1993) theorising). Actor-network theorists have developed these suppositions to a fine point. What is benign about their networks is their narrative power, the way they empower the making of stories to which whole sets of otherwise disparate entities belong. Influence consists in enrolling 'others' to come to one's aid (Singleton and Michael 1993: 229).[30]

We have indicated that there is, as it were, an inherent network capacity in the way English-speakers do not just trace ties between kin but narrate them. They enroll all manner of others – gametes, aunts, a sense of place, giving a gift, and forgetting a half-brother – and they do so in the context of a specific cultural preconception about relatedness based on kinship. For that relatedness was never one thing, and definitively never either a matter of social or biological connection alone. We have also suggested that networks truncate themselves through the very constructs that carry them[31] – on the one hand the combinations and divisions that create kin persons as a hybrid of different materials, and on the other hand claims of ownership and belonging that include or exclude them.

The old network theorists traced ties between persons (friends, associates, kin, as so many points on a graph) (see Price's review of 1981; Scott 1988). Law goes out of his way to observe that the actor-network theorists' deployment of the concept of network has little to do with (does not belong to) 'standard sociological usages – for instance as found in the tradition of kinship studies' (1994: 18). But that depends on the tradition. If we take seriously the interdigitation of social and biological accounts of relatedness, we can see that the instruments by which people reckon connections with one another create mediators of diverse kinds. At the core of English kinship thinking for much of the twentieth century has been the combination and division of phenomena for which at the end of the century we are just beginning to find metaphors. It might even be that indigenous kinship thinking has something to do with the attraction of 'networks' to theorists who still wish to tap into the power of making and unmaking connections.

Notes

1 The terms used by the *Sun* (28 March 1995), from which this account is taken. Frances Price sent MS the cutting, but we both wish to thank her, and for much more than that, in relation to the ideas developed here.

2 The newspaper article laid great stress on the bond that grew up between the eventual mother and the surrogate mother. Its header read: 'Miracle "frozen baby" unites two mums in joy'.

3 The idiomatic usages we are thinking of here include, for example, 'our Billy' and 'my mum', phrases which distinguish a particular Billy and one mother from amongst many. Such idioms also make manifest a commonality between those who are able to claim the same person as 'their own'. We note the cultural specificity of this observation; under other authority regimes, the father's proprietorship over his children has provided a powerful analogy for property claims, notably in relation to the history of copyright (reviewed by Coombe 1994; see the discussion in Franklin 1996). A full review would need to ask whether a child regarded parents as belonging to him or her in the same way that parents may claim the child belongs to them, a point prompted by questions from Barbara Bodenhorn and Sari Wastell, to whom we are grateful.

4 Originally in part learnt from anthropology, it has become an obsessive issue in many NRT contexts (see the several contributions in Eekelaar and Šarčević 1993).

5 A general discourse, at once analytical and folk, that we dub 'Euro-American' is the source of the divide between social and biological kinship which is our focus here (cf. Strathern 1992a). We draw on particular ethnographic examples from England, conscious of differences elsewhere, especially in southern Europe (e.g. Bouquet 1993a).

6 'Proper' in the sense of strictly so called rather than decorous.

7 The inextricable links within and between Alltown 'families' are imaged in evocative expressions such as 'Kick one and they all limp'; from a different perspective these same expressions are used to refer to Alltown as a whole.

8 Just as 'real Elmdon' folk of East Anglia in the 1960s belonged to families who had a claim on local occupations (Strathern 1981).

9 Which is why a relational exposition can appear sentimental or romantic (for instance, as in Macintyre's 1995 critique of relational analysis).

10 Including the academic creation of relationships between parts of data (e.g. Riles 1994).

11 For a consideration of cultures of relatedness, there is much more to 'ownership' than possessive individualism, property and rights and claims. We go on to comment here on how it serves to cut networks and truncate chains of relations. Mary Bouquet (pers. comm.) observes the mixed arboreal and metalwork metaphor in this last phrase of ours ['link' is an Alltown word; 'chain' is ours]. For a metaphorically sensitive account, see e.g. Bouquet 1996a; and on 'dropping off', Bouquet 1986.

12 In contrast, say, by virtue of being part of the opposite moiety or of another clan or caste. (There are of course many English contexts in which, contrary to this sentiment, virtue is attached to not belonging, e.g. people may claim not to belong in order to accord themselves superior status over those who do.)

13 Abrahams (1990: 141) observes apropos of claims following organ donation that it is in 'the nature of our kinship system' that 'people generally appear keen[er] to limit their kinship ties than to extend them'. The cutting off of relatives has its own history in English inheritance practices, specifically in primogeniture and shedding of the cadet line, and in the possibility of disinheriting kin who might otherwise have been heirs. In Elmdon, branches of families moving up and down the class ladder shed connections.

14 A potential for diverse claims based on people and places is encapsulated in an Alltown idea that 'all eggs and sperms' should be named (Edwards 1995).

15 Thus one can 'relate' to this or that person without 'being related', a phrase which English-speakers tend to reserve for kin.

16 This is transcribed from a tape recording of our conversation. Later, Malcolm is referring to his own father's brother, not to his mother's father's brother, as here.

17 This is an example of how the two elements identified by Edwards (1993; after Schneider 1968) as constitutive of 'English' kinship – ideas about relatedness and affective kin ties – are juxtaposed. Lambert (this volume) writes also of how in quite a different context consanguinity and affection are mutually constitutive.

18 This became a search for the principles of inclusion and exclusion that could come to rest in (be specified by) 'boundaries'. (Strathern 1992c revisits some of the issues.) Carsten's account is an interesting departure (1997): she shows in the Malay case that boundaries, such as those defined by house membership, solve nothing if they are elusive in themselves.

19 Hence perhaps the 'need for limits' perceived by indigenous Euro-Americans with reference to medical intervention in conception. The need for limits may be expressed as an effort to enunciate rules for behaviour (Hirsch 1993).

20 This is a combination which is also a 'part' of a field of combinations, notably in kinship thinking the combination of law and nature (Schneider 1968; for a recent commentary see Simpson 1994). Strathern calls these merographic connections ('The popular supposition that kinship is only a "part" of society rests on the fact that it is also a "part" of biological process.

Such parts are not equal to one another. The perspective that gives each of them its distinctive nature appears always as a different order of phenomena. Each order that encompasses the parts may be thought of as a whole, as the individual parts may also be thought of as whole. But parts in this view do not make wholes' (1992a: 76).) See Hayden 1995 on the *simultaneous* placement of biological connection as fundamental and contingent.

21 Without the 'biological' dimension, in this context, it becomes redundant to refer to Iñupiaq arrangements as 'social'.

22 Ragoné (1994) comments on similar sentiments proffered by women acting as surrogates in the United States. These connotations of the term are not to be confused with those of its dominant analytical usage in social anthropology, where 'the gift' often points up the inalienability of bond-creating substances. Note that in this case the commissioning mother was also the 'genetic' mother: the surrogate's gift was to give life to the previously frozen embryo.

23 The bond may be to other persons or be manifest as a flow of sentiment towards 'society', as in anonymous donations to charity.

24 By way of exploring the possibility of predicting, for specific cases, what will and will not count as a basis for connection, Cussins (1997) takes diverse accommodations to such facts made by couples seeking fertility treatment in the United States. Of the various intermediaries through which a pregnancy is established, some are opaque (become the basis for relatedness and kinship), while some are transparent (admitted to have a consequence for relatedness without, as she says, getting configured in the web of kinship relations).

25 Among other factors. See Simpson (1994) for the divisions and combinations of relatedness that follow divorce. He refers to Finch's (1989) term 'working out' for the process by which some relations are preserved and developed and other relations become attenuated and atrophied.

26 Implicit (Carsten 1995b) or explicit (Battaglia 1992).

27 Price (1981) offers a critique of an older network theory whose problematic revolved around questions of density and intensity: intensity implied an order of trust and reliance ('positive values'), but these were pitted against the 'negatively valued' narrowness of networks too folded in on themselves. After all, the 'openness' of potentially unbounded fields is what attracts commentators to the metaphor of networks in the first place (e.g. Hannerz's [1992: 40] observations on the double openness of networks and network analysis).

28 The Net 'is always a plural object with neither inside nor outside, as much an artefact of discourse and imagination as a thing of glass, metal, and plastic' (Pound 1995: 527). In his usage it corresponds to no one computer network but evokes the rationality that hinges on the invisible world of information networks, 'not a thing but a work of translation' (p. 532).

29 Singleton and Michael (1993: 258), quoting Callon: 'an association of heterogeneous elements each of which associates its own elements'. We must thank John Law for this and other materials, and for the introduction to actor networks.

30 But Law (1996), considering diverse examples of what might constitute

actor-network analysis, shows that every passage or rerendering of the theory (translation) is also a betrayal. From a kinship perspective, one might remark that persons never reproduce themselves in identical form, a tenet of biological understandings of the recombination of characteristics that get transmitted over the generations.

31 Here we follow Singleton and Michael's (1993) argument about ambivalences and uncertainties. The gift of the child would cease to be a mediating link in the relationship between the two mothers if the status of the child became indeterminate, the focus of dispute perhaps – the one could not 'give' it to the other if there were a question mark over to whom it 'belonged'. However, they suggest that such indeterminacies, far from confounding or defeating networks, lead to the fresh building of them, with different sets of elements in focus.

9   Figures of relations: reconnecting kinship studies and museum collections

Mary Bouquet

'I am inclined to think that you would not wish to see *your* sister make such an exhibition.'

Jane Austen, *Pride and Prejudice*

Kinship and collections

Two lines of thought inspire this chapter. The first concerns the division, questioned by Carsten (1995a: 235), between the biological and the social in studying kinship. Edwards and Strathern (this volume) argue that 'to address the divide between social and biological kinship' (among ourselves, i.e. Euro-Americans) 'would simply reproduce the terms of the debate' and devise a way of sidestepping the issue. But who counts as ourselves in this debate? I propose that the biological/social divide within the classic domain of kinship reiterates another division, between the material and the social, within certain national traditions of anthropology. More specifically, I take historical ethnographic collections that were jettisoned by modern social anthropology as 'the material', and the study of kinship – especially in the Anglo-Saxon tradition – to represent 'the social'. I suggest that an understanding of this divide may, in turn, illuminate the biological/social division in kinship.

Here the second line of thought stemming from recent work on the history of anthropology comes into the picture. There are those who seem to consign museum collections to anthropology's prehistory. Van Keuren (1989: 26) contends that modern anthropology is grounded in university departments with an emphasis on first-hand field experience. Stocking (1990: 722) too refers to the pre-academic museum period as being largely oriented to the collection of material objects. Both write in an American tradition. On this side of the Atlantic, however, Vermeulen and Roldán (1995: 2) identify as an essential *difference* the fact that what is the territory of professional historians in the USA is written in Europe by anthropologists themselves. Kuper (1991: 139), furthermore, sees this combination as offering the possibility of a really challenging reflexivity, by making the practitioner aware of the historical forces shaping practice.

This chapter takes heart from these European ideas about practice and history in trying to make sense of what can appear simultaneously as a gulf between academic and museum anthropologies and as a convergence between the two.[1] The possible connections between kinship systems and museum collections are puzzling to anyone moving among the guardians of each across Europe. Some might ask, 'Why on earth *should* they be connected?'.[2] I propose to explore this division by drawing on some ideas from Latour's *We Have Never Been Modern*. Part of Latour's (1993: 51) thesis is that the relation between two sets of modern practices, the work of purification and the work of translation, has yet to be made explicit. These practices underscore what he calls the modern Constitution, dating from the seventeenth century, whereby politics (sometimes Society) and science (sometimes Nature) were effectively separated from one another, as instantiated by the respective work of Hobbes and Boyle. Latour argues that Boyle's experiments with the air-pump were in fact intricately connected with political matters: 'it associates, combines and redeploys countless actors, some of whom are fresh and novel – the King of England, the Vacuum, the weight of air – but not all of whom can be seen as new' (p. 72). Latour's view is that such quasi-objects should be given official representation as the point of departure – rather than Nature or Society – for the investigation of networks that 'are simultaneously real, like nature, narrated, like discourse, and collective, like society' (p. 6). The Middle Kingdom is the place where everything happens (unacknowledged) by way of mediation, translation, and networks (p. 36). Might Latour's notion of the Middle Kingdom facilitate an understanding of the relationship between anthropological matters assigned to museum and academy respectively?

What if, for the sake of argument, we took kinship studies and museum collections to exemplify the two poles (of Society and Nature, respectively) which became separated in anthropology through the working of the modern Constitution? Historical collections look like the substance or material that has been cast off by modernising social anthropology as it has moved on to new fields. Kinship looks like the opposite end of the spectrum: the study characteristic of *social* anthropology in the British tradition *par excellence*. Considered historically, indeed, the demise of anthropology in museums (by the end of the nineteenth century) coincides with the beginnings of social anthropology as an academic discipline. A similar division emerged within the study of kinship itself, in the distinction between a biological basis (conceived as the universal facts of procreation), and the social/cultural interpretation of those facts, as a speciality of the anthropologist.

These separations were partly achieved through the detachment of data from the mechanics of their collection. Another way was through the creation of new visual and plastic forms whose existence was typically unacknowledged. Separation and re-presentation imply an area of middle ground within anthropology itself, which I will try to concretise through two rather different kinds of figures, used to exhibit collections of different sorts. The figures I shall refer to, one a genealogical diagram and the other a museum prop, correspond with Latour's hybrids or quasi-objects: whilst serving to mediate and present knowledge, it is their *unacknowledged* presence that interests me here and which I think connects them, helping us to understand the divide between biological and social as a reflex of the broader material/social divide within anthropology.

The museum prop is set in a Norwegian museum, while the genealogical diagram is used in a British monograph. The historical fields of the two figures are thus European, and, although similar figures are certainly found in American anthropology, their historically specific uses in European contexts makes me wary of labelling them Euro-American. I shall consider the extent to which the museum figure relies upon the genealogical model, and the implications of connections through such quasi-objects for contemporary practitioners.

Two figures

Let us start with the museum prop, the model of a Papua New Guinean Bedamini dancer, in the Norwegian context.[3] The social/material divide within modern anthropology assumed very physical dimensions in mid-1990s Oslo. What were seen as the social parts of the discipline (and hence most of the academic anthropologists) at IMA (the combined Institute and Museum of Anthropology, University of Oslo) were housed on the 1960s university campus in suburban Blindern. The material (historical, ethnographic collections), together with a few anthropologists associated to greater and lesser degrees with the museum, was accommodated some kilometres away in an art-nouveau building, which the Ethnographic Museum shares with the Numismatic and Archaeological collections, in central Oslo.

There had been much heart-searching among staff at both the Institute and the Museum about the relevance of each to the other, ever since the Faculty of Social Sciences ordered an administrative reunion in 1990. The Institute, which was founded initially *at* the museum in

1964, moved up to Blindern in 1967/8. Norwegian anthropology, as it developed after the Second World War, was strongly influenced by the British tradition – especially through Fredrik Barth. Some took the hard line that a complete divorce would be preferable, while others were more nuanced and cautious about cutting the ties. The fact that university museums fall under the authority of the Ministry of Education, rather than the Ministry of Culture, was the political context of this hesitation. While museum and material culture have become priority areas in Oslo, as elsewhere, the decision was taken (in 1997) to group all the university museums together, separating them from their respective faculties. For the purposes of this chapter, it is instructive to look at the historical separation between the two, especially since the timing was later than was the case in Britain.

The separation of the social from the material in postwar Norwegian anthropology was, of course, more complicated in practice (Bouquet 1996b). During Barth's directorship of the Ethnographic Museum, from the mid 1970s to the mid 1980s, there were attempts at mediating the collections for the general public through modernised permanent exhibitions.[4] And during the preceding decade, when Arne Martin Klausen was *de facto* director, there were equally innovative attempts, in the spirit of the time, to mediate the collections in terms of exotic/modern art. Furthermore, collections continued to be made (at least by a few) as part of ethnographic fieldwork throughout the period. The Bedamini dancer figure, whose paraphernalia were collected (by Arve Sørum) in 1974, during ethnographic fieldwork in Papua New Guinea, was exhibited in 1984 as part of the Oceania exhibition.

Despite these qualifications, it could fairly be said that social anthropology took off from museum anthropology during the postwar period in Oslo, and that the two followed largely separate agendas. More important, such attempts as there were at interpreting the collections purged them of their messy intervening histories. The ethnographic present embodied in tableaux was designed to give an idea of the diversity of other people's lives – as happened in many museums (such as the Tropenmuseum in Amsterdam) during the 1970s. So the material legacy of the discipline came to be presented in a form purified of its historical specificity in the museum displays. Furthermore, the sum of the material and, in particular, its often less than edifying archival accompaniment, ceased to be matter for anthropological research, which shifted to what were seen as more exciting empirical field studies carried out mostly without any reference to the historical collections.[5]

Kinship would be placed, according to Latour's thesis, in the purified realm of the social at the academy,[6] together with politics, economy, and

Figure 1 The Bedamini dancer

religion; while ethnographic collections (and historical ones in particular) would become the 'dirty' material residue that has sedimented down to the depots and other dark places in museums. The collections in Oslo came to be tended predominantly by technical staff (curatorship having been abolished in 1990), apart from occasional selective resuscitation in permanent or temporary exhibitions. Kinship, whether in its formalist or in its more recent cultural incarnations, could not apparently be further removed. Nonetheless, kinship also suffered, if not the marginalisation that some have ascribed to material culture,[7] then at least a removal from centre stage to backstage (a kind of routinisation) in the postwar period, certainly by the 1960s. If kinship had once been seen as the foundation of social organisation, it was superseded by network and transaction. Even if, as Edwards and Strathern argue (this volume), cognatic kinship thinking was at the heart of network theory, this was nonetheless presented as a conceptual breakthrough.

But, of course, as with material culture, kinship did not somehow evaporate. An adequate description of the kinship system remained one of the minimum obligations of ethnographic fieldwork (cf. Barnes 1967: 121; Barnard and Good 1984: 1). The genealogical diagram became, indeed, a standard piece of graphic shorthand not only in mainstream analyses but also in fieldnote jottings and the kinds of simple diagrams drawn on blackboards.[8] My second figure is therefore a genealogical diagram taken from a recent monograph where, although kinship was certainly not the analytical focus of the study, it was nevertheless there. We can read from the diagram what is absent from the text: Sid and Doris, the main protagonists of the book, are brother-in-law and sister-in-law.

Would this kind of routinised kinship (a form of collection, after all) bear comparison with the continuing collections made during ethnographic fieldwork during roughly the same period? I contend that there is a line of continuity between nineteenth-century collections and the kinds of collections made during ethnographic fieldwork, although the latter are in the form of words (diaries, fieldnotes, surveys, and so on) rather than material objects. It is therefore heuristically useful to consider the revivals of anthropological interest in both kinship and museums/material culture since the early 1980s as being in some way related.

The lines of inquiry developed most notably by Schneider (1968, 1984) and Strathern (1981, 1982, 1992a) turned the tide in so far as they demonstrated that kinship as an analytical construct needs unpacking as a cultural one. Kinship, which had in a way been put on the shelf – rather as an ethnographic object after its accession to the

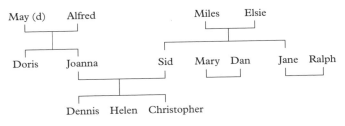

Figure 2 Sid Askrig's family

collection – was taken down again in the 1980s and given a dusting off. If some have interpreted Schneider's dusting as destructive, Strathern has demonstrated that it could actually be the starting point for a new and very challenging kind of ethnography. She has subjected a whole series of English concepts (nature, class, individual) to rigorous cultural investigation and historical specification that give new purchase on both the notion of kinship and the history of anthropology.

A renewal of interest in museums and material culture since the mid 1980s has had a similar effect. I might mention Clifford's (1988) work on the fate of tribal artefacts and cultural practices once relocated in Western museums, exchange systems, disciplinary archives, and discursive traditions; Appadurai's (1986) analysis of the social life of things once diverted from their customary paths; or Ames's (1992) ideas about the peculiar structural position of a museum in modern society, providing fertile ground for theoretical and practical work on a number of topics. Among those topics, exhibitions have received considerable attention (see, for example, Karp and Lavine 1991).

This new atmosphere in anthropology has been a source of inspiration for many of the new-style studies of kinship during the 1980s and 1990s, a number of which are represented in this volume. It certainly inspired me when I began to examine the cultural content of the genealogical method (1993a), and the visual imperative of the genealogical diagram (1996a). The new museology was equally inspiring for the work I have been doing in various museums. Here I would like to explore how genealogical thinking informed museum collections as well as kinship studies. There is evidence that biblical pedigree has been a significant classificatory principle used in collections since early modern times. Shelton (1994: 201), for example, discusses how the category *pagan*, used for New World objects filtering into Renaissance cabinets, 'admitted cultural diversity and provided it with a biblical pedigree'. The chroniclers speculated on Aztec and Inca origins: were they descended from Noah, or from some lost tribe of Israel? It was little wonder 'that racial genealogies and conjectural histories partly informed written compendiums of customs and arrangements of material culture' (p. 203).

Pedigree, later translated into scientific methodology, also proved a powerful means of collecting, sorting, and presenting material on the simultaneous diversity and interconnectedness of species as well as human cultures. It was, of course, as *ex*clusive as it was *in*clusive, as the graphic conventions for shaping the tree clearly demonstrate (Bouquet 1996a). Although Strathern has argued that cognatic kinship provided the model for cutting the network (1996), cognatic kinship was in a sense an outcome of the working of pedigree. The distinction of pedigree depends upon excluding large numbers of people, whose kinship appears relatively unbounded by contrast.

Useful comparison might be made with the coexistence between cognatic kinship for the living and unilineal descent for the dead among the Vezo, in Astuti's processual analysis (this volume). It is thanks to the work that the living perform for the dead that cognatic kinship and unilineal descent are kept separate. The coexistence of cognatic kinship and pedigree in turn-of-the-century English culture was defined by birth rather than death. Pedigree thinking was *so* important to English middle-class intellectuals that it was absorbed into the processes of making knowledge about other peoples (Bouquet 1993a: 219).

Let me try to show how pedigree thinking informed museum collections as well as kinship studies by considering the intellectual lives of our two figures, going back from the Bedamini dancer figure to the kinds of figures that graced the ethnographic museum displays from the mid nineteenth century and earlier.

The ethnographic collection in Christiania/Kristiania/Oslo

The activities of collection, analysis, storage/display, and comparison are the common denominators of both kinship studies and ethnographic collections. But it is not just the systematic collection of information and/or objects and their transportation from one place to another by a variety of persons. The further treatments they receive/d, ranging from componential analysis to purificatory baths, and translating into triangles, circles, lines, and labels, storage boxes, and display props, are the key to the Middle Kingdom. Considering the scale on which this collection has occurred since the mid nineteenth century, anthropologising the world could almost be considered as a social movement. Latour would see the lack of explicit relationship in this double movement of cleansing or purification and rehabilitation or presentation as evidence of never having been modern. Keeping the two moments apart has certainly produced the legion of amorphous lines and props, involving countless actors. What was the underlying assumption for all this activity in Oslo?

Systematic ethnographic collection began in Christiania around the mid nineteenth century, although scientific collections had been central to the Royal Frederiks University since its foundation in 1811. C. A. Holmboe, professor of Oriental languages and founder of the numismatic collection, took the initiative towards establishing an ethnographic collection. During the first four decades of their existence, the university's museums were used primarily for teaching purposes. In other words, the collections were seen as an integral part of the production and reproduction of knowledge. This point is quite evident from the architectural disposition of the university by the mid nineteenth century.

Public interest in ethnographic collections really developed only in the second half of the nineteenth century. L. C. Daa, who was appointed director in 1862, attempted to systematise the Ethnographic Museum according to more widespread intellectual frameworks of the day. Among the most important of these was the philological view of the world, which connected families of languages and, by extrapolation, the people speaking those languages, in an immense pedigree or genealogy. A new field of knowledge, variously called 'Ethnographie', 'Völkerkunde', and 'Ethnologia', arose in the late eighteenth century in central Europe, spreading somewhat later (in the first part of the nineteenth century) to Britain. The principal object of this study was to arrive at the origins of nations and peoples, and the main method was linguistic (Vermeulen 1993).

One of Daa's British contacts, Robert Latham, pursued the tradition of linguistic ethnology well into the nineteenth century (Stocking 1971: 373). Latham was vice-president of the Ethnological Society of London, an ethnographer, physician, and German scholar. Stocking refers to the biblical (or ethnological) tradition derived from the first ten chapters of Genesis as providing the dominant framework of assumptions during the period of European expansion (1990: 714). The genealogical model exercised the minds of European intellectuals in 'trying to trace the putative links between every present human group and one of the branches of a biblical tree that linked all of humankind to a single descendent of Adam and Eve' (ibid.). Since the events of Babel had brought about the diversification of mankind by confusing languages, the 'privileged data for re-establishing connections were similarities of language', combined with those similarities of culture which survived the degenerative processes identified with migration (ibid.).

UNIVERSITAS REGIA FREDERICIANA.

CHRISTIANIÆ.

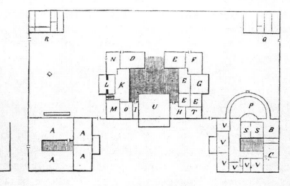

SENATUS ACADEMICUS:
Dr. Broch.   Nissen.   Ingstad.   Lochmann.   S. Bugge.

Secret. Univ. Holst.   Qvæstor Univ. Aars.

EXPLANATIO DELINEATIONUM.

A. BIBLIOTHECA ACADEMICA.
   Director: L. L. Daae.

B. NUMOPHYLACIUM.
   Director: Dr. Holmboe.

C. MUSEUM ANTIQUITATUM BOREALIUM.
   Director: Profr. Rygh.

D. MUSEUM ETHNOGRAPHICUM.
   Director: Dr. Daa

E. MUSEUM ZOOLOGICUM.
   Director: Prof. Esmark.

F. MUSEUM ZOOTOMICUM.
   Director: Dr. C. Boeck.

F. COLLECTIO IMSTRUMT. PHYSIOLOGIC.
   Director: Dr. C Boeck.

F. COLLECTIO INSTRUMENT. CHIRURGIC.
   Director: Profr. Hjorth.

F. COLLECTIO INSTRUMT. OBSTETRICIOR.
   Director: Dr. Fr. Faye.

G. MUSEUM ANATOMICUM.
   Director: Dr. J. Voss.

H. MUSEUM PHARMACOLOGICUM.
   Director: Profr. Lochmann.

I. MUSEUM BOTANICUM.
   Director: Dr. Schübeler.

K. MUSEUM MINERALOGICUM.
   Director: Dr. Kjerulf.

L. LABORATORIUM CHEMICUM.
   Directores: Profr. Waage & Hjortdahl.

M. LABORATORIUM METALLURGICUM.
   Director: Profr. Münster.

N. MUSEUM TECHNOLOGICUM.
   Director: Profr. Münster.

O. COLLECTIO INSTRUMENT. PHYSICOR.
   Director: . . . . .

P. AULA ACADEMICA.

Q. PALÆSTRA.

R. HABITATIO CHEMLÆ PROFESSORIS.

S. CONCLAVE SOCIETATIS SCIENTIARUM
      CHRISTIANIENSIS.

T. CONCLAVE SOCIETATIS MEDICORUM.

U. VESTIBULUM.

V. AUDITORIA.

HORTUS BOTANICUS EJUSQUE BIBLIOTHECA (Dir. Dr. Schübeler), OBSERVATORIUM
ASTRONOMICUM (Dir. Fearnley) ET OBSERVATORIUM METEOROLOGICUM
(Dir. Mohn) ALIIS LOCIS ÆDES SUAS HABENT.

Figure 3 Plan of the Royal Frederiks University, Christiania, around the mid nineteenth century. The Library is on the left; the museums occupy the central building, Domus Media; and the lecture theatres are on the right hand side

Daa's vision of the ethnographic museum conformed to the ethnological model: he firmly believed that *every* ethnos should have a place in it – including Norwegians and, of course, the Sami population then called Lapps (see Gjessing and Johannessen 1957). Lappish items were used in one of the earliest exchanges, initiated by Latham, who was in charge of establishing an ethnographic museum in London in the wake of the Great Exhibition of 1851. Latham offered ethnographic objects from various parts of the world, including Borneo, in exchange for a Sami collection.

Daa drew heavily on Latham's the *Varieties of Man* (1850) in his *Utsigt over Ethnologien* (1855). Latham's genealogical model envisaged three primary varieties of the human species, the Mongolidae, the Atlantidae, and the Lapetidae, who were thought to be descended from a (hypothetical) common ancestor. As Latham (1855: 13) put it: 'The questions connected with the Natural History of the Human Species are so thoroughly questions of descent, affiliation or pedigree that I have no hesitation in putting the names of the primary divisions in the form of Greek patronymics; the supposed ancestor (or *eponymus*) being, of course, no real individual, but an ethnological fiction.'

Daa also referred to more recent developments in geology, and to Darwin's theory of evolution. Darwin saw the archetype as 'an actual creature whose descendent species were united into real genealogical relations through reproduction' (Richards 1992: 131). Both Latham's 'ethnological' genealogy and Darwin's evolutionary genealogy enabled, I contend, systematic display of the peoples of the world as represented by their material culture. These genealogical relations were as basic to the 'totalising classificatory grid' which facilitated the constitution of museums as they probably were to census-taking and map-making (see Anderson 1991: 184).

Yngvar Nielsen, who succeeded Daa as director in 1877, describes the ethnographic collection as already comprising (in 1886) some 6,100 specimens. Three rooms on an upper floor of the central university building, Domus Media, contained articles illustrating the life of the Norwegian peasantry, as well as Lappish items. Australia and the South Sea Islands occupied a fourth room. Objects from the Sunda Islands, from Lao in the Back-Indies, Africa, Egypt, the Indies, China and Japan, South America, and Greenland and the subpolar regions could be seen in five further rooms (Nielsen 1886: 24–5).

Chapman argues that when the biblical chronology was undercut in the 1850s, confidence in the traditional ethnological approach was considerably eroded (1985: 21). However, genealogical *trees* (phylogenies) were used by Darwin, Haeckel, and others to represent evolutionary connections among all forms of life, including mankind (Bouquet 1996a). The great advantage of the tree image was that it could expand to cover the vastly expanded notion of time that developed through nineteenth-century geological and archaeological research, just as it could contract to represent the existence of a family through the shallows of historical time.

My argument is that the logical connections furnished by the philological/genealogical view of the world provided the underlying rationale for ethnographic collections such as this one. The objects made by people were just as separate as people themselves were thought to be. Once detached from their original environment, they had to be reconnected somehow. Considering that Darwin's tree imagery had inspired the philologist Schleicher to draw up trees connecting families of languages, and that he in turn suggested to Haeckel doing the same for all forms of life, it is not difficult to imagine the power of such a representation. It is striking but scarcely surprising that genealogical conection with even the most distant and unknown members of humanity was the underlying assumption for systematic ethnographic collections – echoing what biblical genealogy had been for Renaissance cabinets.

The systematic nature of ethnographic collecting has been distinguished by Thomas (1994), for example, from the promiscuous curiosity of common sailors in the eighteenth century. However, systematic collecting was by no means immune from certain excesses. Furthermore, curiosities from earlier times were accommodated by the Ethnographic Collection, and remain an on-going division. These were typically things that could not be assigned to one geographical locus, or were too closely identified with an event or personality to be purged of them. They represent a further internal schism within the material, between matter in and out of place, thus demonstrating one of the cut-off points in genealogical thinking and one of the ways in which quasi-objects were made (cf. Latour 1993: 55). The withered reptile in a box, for example, joined the curiosities. It was a 'mummified crocodile' presented by the director of the Zootomical Museum which could not be classified as part of nature or part of society (Bouquet 1996b: 124).

Daa's systematic catalogue appears to have been geographically based: items received a number as they entered the museum, often in batches that were sometimes of mixed provenance. Daa then superimposed a second (systematic) scheme assigning things to place (for example, Africa), and hence to places (rooms, cabinets) in the museum. The geography of the world, the territory of these genealogically connected peoples, was thus imagined into the available architectural space, where material evidence of their arts and industries was put on display. It should be noted that the collection was, at this time, the exhibition. There was no frontstage/backstage distinction between exhibitions and depots such as subsequently developed with the sheer physical accumulation of collections and later essays in selection and presentation. Collections were acquired through all kinds of intermediaries: sailors, sea captains, diplomats and consuls, missionaries, by exchange with other institutions (the Smithsonian and Trocadero as well as the British Museum). Daa travelled abroad to obtain items from dealers: he went to Holland in 1864, returning with, amongst his ethnographic purchases, a Russian 'Helvedesmaskine' (literally a devil's machine) which took its place among the curiosities.

Daa also went to northern Norway and the Kola peninsula with his cousin, the Sami philologist and scholar J. A. Friis, in 1867 (Friis 1871). Nielsen (1907: 40) comments that Daa and Friis's journey did not produce much in the way of a collection. Daa's observations on the topography of the Imandra valley during that journey, however, reflect the importance of geography for his understanding of both human variety and relatedness. The question of when and how the Scandinavian peninsula was populated beset scholars during this period (Holck 1993: 36ff). Daa refuted Munch's theory of immigration of the Germanic peoples into Scandinavia via this northern route, using the evidence of his own eyes: the valley was too narrow to accommodate such a great river of people (1870). Daa also collected from the Norwegian countryside, especially from Telemark, alarmed by the exodus of huge amounts of peasant material culture in the late nineteenth century, not least as part of A. Hazelius's collection for the Skansen open-air museum in Stockholm. This activity bears more than a passing resemblance to Malinowski's and other early ethnographers' engagement with salvage ethnography.

Modelling the varieties of man by means of man's productions was not in the first instance an evolutionary exercise. Acquisition was initially about mapping the world and charting it in terms of physically differentiated peoples whose various appearances (termed 'race' by the mid nineteenth century) somehow transpired in their material culture. As Coombes (1988: 61) has put it in her discussion of British museum taxonomies around the turn of the century, 'since culture was seen to vary according to geographical and regional factors and since environmental factors created regional affinities within the same groups, the "natural" choice was thought to rest with a geographical classification'. The effects of social evolutionary theory were of course reflected in the morphological or typological mode of display in late-nineteenth-century museums – the Pitt-Rivers Museum in Oxford being the most famous example. E. B. Tylor, keeper of the Pitt-Rivers Museum, stressed the importance of collection and the study of material culture for tracing the 'development of civilisation and the laws by which it is governed' (Van Keuren 1989: 26). Tylor thought that the fossil record for human cultural history was disclosed through man's physical, artefactual remains. But such displays were much more difficult to produce, and may have been more difficult for the general public to understand.

The 'naturalness' of geographical classification depends upon an assumption about the rootedness of genealogical connection (cf. Malkki 1992). This assumption also seems to be at work as a principle for ordering many nineteenth-century ethnographic collections. The experience of collection as part of exploration, trade, missionary, diplomatic, and other activities that took Europeans all over the world not only as the subjects of colonial powers but also (as was the case with Norwegians) as employees, perhaps fostered that vision. Motivations among these various categories may have been different, but their collective efforts certainly harmonised with the mood of Norwegian nationalism around the turn of the century. It was as if in contributing to this miniature world in the museum, the diverse actors were also staking a claim to their own national territory (cf. Prösler 1996: 34).

Despite the union with Sweden, Kristiania could have its Ethnographic Museum like every other self-respecting European state – and indeed enjoyed the active patronage of King Oscar II. The museum was installed in a specially commissioned art-nouveau building, which opened to the public in 1904. The geographical layout is evident from Nielsen's guide published for the opening. Africa was in Room I, India in Room II, the Pacific and South-east Asia in Room III, East Asia in Room IV, and America in Room V (Nielsen 1904). The rooms were further divided among different peoples, and the showcases divided to show various crafts among neighbouring peoples. Nielsen retained references to the most important donors to each section in his guide, reinforcing the sense that such an ethnographic collection was simultaneously part of a local social system at this time (see also Nielsen 1907).

The Norwegian collection was reassigned to the Norwegian Folk Museum in 1907, shortly after the end of the union with Sweden. Nielsen's strong repudiation of Daa's inclusion of the Norwegians together with other populations of the world represented in the museum evinces the hierarchisation of difference that developed during the process of mapping and modelling the world. Once Norway achieved nation-statehood in 1905, there was room to separate Norwegians from the rest of the world again.

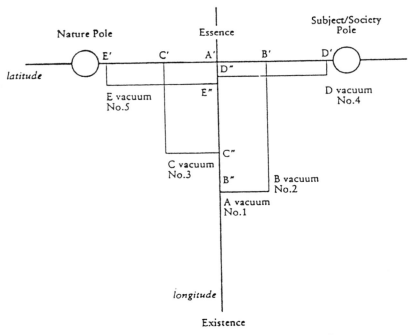

Figure 4 Latour's variable geometry for the ontology of mediators

Nielsen set the pace of acquisition that was continued by Ole Solberg, who succeeded him in 1916, until the Second World War. This acquisitions policy was not, however, matched by the development of social anthropology as a separate discipline (one of the social sciences) from the museum, as occurred in Britain and elsewhere. The Institute of Anthropology, as mentioned earlier, became separate from the museum only in 1967/8, although the younger generation of students that entered the museum after the war had little time for old-style museum anthropology. They wanted to do ethnographic fieldwork, which was where they saw the future of the discipline. The historical nature of the collections was particularly troublesome to anthropologists working within a synchronically oriented frame of reference. The problem resembles that analysed in Latour's (1993: 86) diagram of the 'variable geometry for the ontology of mediators'. Museum specimens acquire layers of meaning in their trajectories *out* of context. For this reason, the means of their acquisition, naming, deployment, and so on – their impurities in so far as they are conceived as specimens of this or that ethnic group – become part of their 'non-modern' ethnography, in Latour's terms.

Consider how objects, once separated from their place of origin, are associated with other artefacts as part of their translation into new contexts. The Bedamini collection, for example, contrasts sharply with earlier collections in being ethnographically well documented. However, the life-sized model of a Bedamini male, which is intended as a modern mediator of ethnographic knowledge, belongs to a much older genre. Kirschenblatt-Gimblett (1991: 398–9) describes how 'wax models as a form of three dimensional anatomical illustration were commonly used to teach medicine and were featured in anatomical displays open to the public. With the rising interest in racial typologies and evolution, Sarti's Museum of Pathological Anatomy in London during the mid-nineteenth century, and others like it, became the place to exhibit culturally constructed anatomical pathologies.' These included 'parts of a Moorish woman's anatomy', missing links in the evolutionary sequence (such as wax figures of African 'savages' with tails), and wax tableaux of ethnographic scenes. As early as 1797, Peale had completed wax figures for 'a group of contrasting races of mankind' that included natives of North and South America, the Sandwich Islands, Tahiti, and China. The faces were thought to have been made from life casts. The figures were kitted out with appropriate clothing and artifacts. Half a century later (1849), the Gallery of All Nations in Reimar's Anatomical and Ethnological Museum in London featured the 'varied types of the Great Human Family'.

As Kirschenblatt-Gimblett observes, the Gallery of Nations idea, which had served as the organising principle for books devoted to customs, manners, religions, costumes, and other ethnographic topics since the late sixteenth century, was easily adapted to the display of ethnographic specimens. This is scarcely surprising in view of the prevailing biblical-ethnologial paradigm, with its search for the origins of peoples and nations. A logical spin-off was the monographic display. Nathan Dunn's Chinese collection, installed in Peale's museum in 1838 and moved to London in 1841, purported to show a 'perfect picture of Chinese life'. Kirschenblatt-Gimblett argues that the attention in this description to the individuation of the faces reflects a more general preoccupation with types and the notion of physiognomy as the key to moral character. People were fascinated not only by the ethnographic artefacts but also by the physiognomies on display.

Apart from the full-sized Finn mentioned by Nielsen in his description of the museum in 1886, figures seem to have been used in displays from the very inception of the museum. It was unclear exactly when the fourteen ethnological wax heads in glass boxes entered the museum;[9] photographs of former exhibitions indicate that they were sometimes

Figure 5 Fourteen wax heads in glass boxes on the central staircase of the Ethnographic Museum in Oslo

used on figures in life groups. However, they apparently lacked documentation and had been stored on top of cupboards in the students' attic rooms at the museum. Even if they were made in the mid nineteenth century at the height of interest in the varied types of the Great Human Family, they arrived in Oslo much later (in 1923). Contemporary reactions to these things tend towards revulsion: they are viewed as unfortunate anachronisms in the enlightened world of anthropology today. They are, in a sense, exemplary quasi-objects: things without history (see Latour 1993: 70). The wax heads' trajectories differ in detail but not in substance from that of the Bedamini figure, specially commissioned for the Oceania exhibit put up in 1984. Once that exhibit was dismantled to make way for a temporary exhibits' gallery, the figure went into storage in one of the depots.

My argument is that the conventional way of exhibiting (mediating, in Latour's terms) the collections after the Second World War deliberately suppressed information about the collectors and circumstances of collection, and glossed over the presence of such essential props as the Bedamini dancer figure. Paradoxically, the figure was carefully made by the Norwegian sculptor Arve Rønning in collaboration with the anthropologist-collector Arve Sørum. This middle ground is exactly the part that has been downplayed in modern museology, perhaps because it connects so intriguingly with earlier and differently positioned essays in interpreting and mediating human variety. If so, then it is a brilliant example of purification in Latour's sense: purification of history, of the networks of connections between museum and the world from which it was collected, and of our physical devices created to display artefacts collected elsewhere. These shy and retiring confections connect the collections in an extraordinary historical ethnography that is usually present without comment, as though unfit for public consumption.

Genealogical collection

Having examined the genealogical basis of an ethnographic collection, let us now consider the genealogical graphic which became so much identified with *social* anthropology during the first half of the twentieth century. The genealogical diagram representing Sid Askrig's family has not been purified of its ethnographic context, but subtly refers to an anthropological context – kinship studies – whilst pursuing quite a different kind of analysis. This genealogical figure enables anthropologists to take in the kinship connections of the main protagonists, in this ethnography of world views in Wanet, at a glance. The point is that we do not need to be kinship specialists to use the diagram. We don't need to know the ins and outs of the debate between adherents of formal or translation-in-words approaches to the analysis of kinship terminologies (see Parkin 1996). If we want to know where the connecting lines come from (apart from the short answer: 'Nigel, who collected them'), then we inevitably come back to the question 'How did he collect them?' Independently of the particular handbook or manual he may have used, we owe the connecting lines to Rivers (1968: 98), who was the first to systematise the genealogical method as part of social anthropological inquiry.[10]

It was, of course, L. H. Morgan who made the distincion between classificatory and descriptive systems of kinship terminology famous in the mid nineteenth century, during his work among the Iroquois as early as 1846. In this pre-evolutionary, ethnological phase of his work, Morgan was grappling with the question of the peopling of America (Stocking 1990: 721). Morgan was collecting materials illustrative of the institutions of the Iroquois when he uncovered 'a system of relationship for the designation and classification of kindred ... unique and extra-ordinary ... wholly unlike any other'. He found that descriptive kinship terminology was not universal, but distinctive for ancestral Aryan, Semitic, and Uralian language groups (Strathern 1992a: 16). Hence, the question of kinship classification was meshed into families of languages, thus connecting with linguistic ethnology, which (as we have seen) relied very heavily on a 'genealogical method' to reconstruct origins of nations and peoples.

Rivers's reconfiguration of the genealogical method scaled down the chronology, and enabled the separation of kin terminology from what he saw as being objective blood relations. Malinowski's fieldwork revolution brought with it modifications, especially his insistence on studying the 'flesh and blood' rather than the 'algebra' of kinship. British mono-graphs after the First World War amply demonstrated that kinship was more than terminology. The emphasis on ethnographic context trickled through to museum presentations after the Second World War.

The collection of kinship terminologies, like the collection of ethno-graphic artefacts, thus owed much to the perception, derived from philology, of the genealogical connectedness of mankind. As we have seen, the systematisation of ethnographic collections could proceed on a geographical basis (as it did in Christiania); indeed, this classification seemed more 'natural' than what proved the rather unwieldy typological system of classification at the Pitt-Rivers Museum. By the end of the nineteenth century, ideas were shifting: the Norwegian collection left the Ethnographic Museum for the Norsk Folkemuseum in 1907. As the collections expanded, the need to distinguish between exhibition and depot arose. Whilst exhibitions gradually came to use the life-group style, selecting objects to present a purified vision of a timeless ethnographic scene, so culture became inextricably associated with geographical region, leaving history as an unattended residue. That history may take various forms: the conventional archive, dealing with the relations between place of origin and museum; but also the history of props such as the figures used to present artefacts in contemporary (or 1970s-style) life groups.

The systematisation and comparison of kinship systems received a great impetus from Rivers's genealogical method. Leach's (1961b: 2) scathing reference to 'butterfly collecting' draws attention to the parallel between museum taxonomies and the invisible people they made materialise, and the designation (by Radcliffe-Brown) of whole societies as patrilineal or matrilineal on the basis of their descent principle. The graphic representation of genealogies drew upon an established genre, pedigrees (family trees), the tree of Jesse, phylogenies, and philological diagrams (see Maher 1983), which all share a common preoccupation with a specific notion of ancestry and descent that is certainly not human or universal in scope. When we draw genealogical diagrams we are also drawing upon a local (European) historical notion and translating other notions into that model. The genealogical figure is an apparently timeless artefact, as Bourdieu (1977: 38) observed, creating as it does a spatial diagram that can be taken in at a glance, *uno intuito*, and scanned indifferently from any point in any direction. And here I disagree with Kirschenblatt-Gimblett (1991), who says that there are intangibles (and she names kinship among them) that resist appropriation. Genealogical collection is one of the ways we do indeed bring kinship, as an object of relations, back home with us.

My view is that visual representation is actually part of what constitutes kinship for us. And here I do not mean kinship terminologies – kin terms and the various ways in which they can be combined, but rather how Rivers believed 'that systems of relationship are bodies of dry fact the accuracy of which, especially when collected by the genealogical method . . . is about as incapable of being influenced by bias, conscious or unconscious, as any subject that can be imagined' (quoted in Firth 1968: 19). As Firth observes, 'the great question is what these "bodies of dry fact" really mean in their principles of arrangement and in their social context' (Firth 1968: 19). For Rivers they had, as Firth (p. 21) has put it, an 'obvious biological referent'. Parkin's (1996: 87) assertion that 'Genealogical reckoning is not merely convenient but almost unavoidable in kinship analysis, and is used in practice even by those who would argue that it does not necessarily correspond to the way particular peoples see their own kinship system' skates over this referent. Indeed, he tries to persuade us that since 'category and genealogy ... belong not to different sorts of society but to different contexts even in the typical Western society, *there is perhaps less objection to admitting that the parallel may be found elsewhere too*' (p. 97; emphasis added).

I think, however, that Rivers's transformation of pedigree into genealogical method fundamentally altered its theoretical status, and that the visual representation of genealogy was a critical step in this process. It fixed birth as the defining moment of kinship, and fixed the instruments for its recording accordingly. By ignoring the work of instrumentation, and conflating science with nature, we ignore a major contribution to taking the measure of other peoples, sizing them up by rendering them commensurable and by creating measuring standards that did not exist before (Latour 1993: 113). The method *enabled* the kinds of comparisons and debates which followed. The visual nature of the genealogical diagram is absolutely central to the way kinship came to be conceived by anthropologists. This visualisation undoubtedly facilitated winnowing the social from the biological in kinship studies, and holding the biological referent steady.

As Latour (1993: 54) has put it, 'Social scientists did not really believe in religion or popular consumption. They did believe in science, however, from the bottom of their scientistic hearts.' Certainly anthropologists such as Rivers and Malinowski saw themselves as scientists, and thought of what they were doing as science. Biological facts could be considered part of 'science' and therefore something that anthropologists did not (need to) go into. *Genealogical reckoning is not merely convenient but almost unavoidable in kinship analysis*. If this way of reckoning kinship was convenient and unavoidable, visualising it diagrammatically did more than faithfully reflect the facts of life. The diagram has, as I have argued elsewhere, its own historicity, making it an anything but neutral instrument.

In shaping the Bedamini figure, a similar mediatory operation is performed, only this time with respect to the dance, time, and space. If we shift our focus slightly, the figure itself (the apparently self-effacing part of the ensemble) has its own trajectory, its own theory. The product of collaboration between an artist in Oslo and an anthropologist after fieldwork among the Bedamini in 1984, the figure is obviously distinct from any Bedamini person (although based on a photograph of one), and from the Bedamini as ethnography (Sørum 1991). And yet the figure somehow stands for the Bedamini in order to bring certain artefacts back to life in the museum. The figure enables us to visualise a

geographically situated cultural group, but it relies upon a physiologi-
cally specific model to do so. And of course such physical specificity
makes sense only against a spectrum of diversity. There is something
familiar about the model.

Among the wax heads in Oslo is the head of a Papua, one of the
nineteenth-century types in the Gallery of All Nations already discussed.
The connecting lines of the genealogy lie behind these types, just as they
inform the Bedamini figure, and it is therefore these invisible lines that
represent the greatest theoretical challenge. These lines, together with
self-effacing figures like the Bedamini dancer, represent the silent
constructions by means of which we display our collections. By recognising their historical connections, we can begin perhaps to reconnect
the collected in the museum and in the academy. At the same time, we
should not only officially recognise but also investigate the theoretical
complexity submerged in the hybrid figures that enable purified definitions of particular fields.

The genealogical connection between ethnographic collections, and
the collection of kinship systems by social anthropologists, gives pause
for thought about the biological/social divide within kinship. The life
histories of artefacts *out* of their original contexts are an inevitable part
of their modern ethnographies, connecting rather than separating the
museum from the world; privileging the original point of production, in
that ethnography corresponds with the purification of data characteristic of incomplete modernity in anthropology. Presentation (or translation) of that purified vision of peoples and cultures evoked, in its turn,
a legion of mediatory forms adding yet another awkward layer of
ethnography.

Dealing with those awkward layers has been a major challenge for
recent ethnographies of both museum collections and kinship. Just as
museum purists recoil at the thought of ethnographic artefacts being
polluted by the hands of sailors, explorers, missionaries, and traders, so
kinship purists are loath to concede that the hard work of kinship
undermines the privileged referent of procreation. The issue of authenticity seems to be as immediate for the study of kinship as it is in the
museum. Both draw upon the pedigree model, which, with its radical
prunings and excisions, was as much involved in cutting the network as
cognatic kinship ever was.

Despite Latour's compelling argument for focusing on hybrids, he
seems nonetheless to maintain the categories Nature and Society, 'only
as a final end, not as a beginning' (1993: 79). In focusing on a
genealogical diagram and a museum prop as emblematic of the middle
kingdom, it has been difficult to sustain the division between the social

and the material as this has polarised the academy and the museum. The middle ground that opens up between these two collectivities, institutions, or fields constitutes, in all its complexity, one of contemporary anthropology's cutting edges. If genealogical thinking was an assumption common to the Bedamini figure and the genealogical diagram, then seeing kinship theory *together with* museum collections properly complicates the polarisation of academy and museum. Questioning the biological/social divide in kinship studies should also presage new interest in material and visual figures of relations.

Notes

My sincere thanks to Janet Carsten, Anthony Cohen, two anonymous readers for Cambridge University Press, and Ann Christine Eek.

1 My own experience of this divide has involved teaching British kinship theory in Portugal (1983–7), and writing it up in the Netherlands (Bouquet 1993a; see also 1996a); making exhibitions in Lisbon (Bouquet and Freitas Branco 1988; Bouquet 1991, 1992), Leiden (Bouquet 1993b, 1995), and Oslo (Bouquet 1996b).

2 Such connections do *not* always appear intrinsically desirable, as Edwards and Strathern argue (this volume), and as I describe for the Department and Museum of Anthropology in Oslo. This is one reason for taking issue with their (and Schneider's 1984: 193) use of the term 'Euro-American', which I have criticised elsewhere (Bouquet 1993a: 23). I mistrust the way this relational term backgrounds Europe (Euro-) to America.

3 I carried out what almost amounted to a piece of ethnographic fieldwork (as senior visiting research fellow and lecturer) at the invitation of IMA, the Institute and Museum of Anthropology, University of Oslo, Norway, 1995–6. I should like to express my gratitude to IMA for their generous hospitality, and to the then Head of Department Professor Ingrid Rudie in particular, for presenting me with such a challenge.

4 Anthony Cohen's introduction before the award of an honorary DSc degree to Fredrik Barth in Edinburgh, on 24 October 1996, was fascinating in claiming Barth entirely for *social* anthropology (especially emphasising the ethnographic fieldwork tradition). I would like, in a way, to claim Barth for museum anthropology, too. Although unmentioned in Cohen's speech, Barth was also Director of the Ethnographic Museum in Oslo for over a decade.

5 There were, of course, exceptions to the rule. See Klausen 1957; Sørensen 1972; Klausen and Sorum 1993.

6 'Academy' is used in a generalised way here. The reality of the Oslo situation was more complicated, with Jos. Falkenberg, who was based at the Museum, specialising in Australian kinship *and* making ethnographic collections after the Second World War (see Falkenberg 1948, 1962). However, Falkenberg was a member of the senior generation by this time, although he remained at the Museum after the Institute's move to Blindern.

7 Ames (1992), for example, characterises material culture as a dead duck floating upside down in the backwaters of social anthropology worldwide by 1954.
8 As observed during the teaching of an introductory course in cultural anthropology at Utrecht University, the Netherlands, January 1997.
9 Information concerning the date of entry of the wax models to the museum – in 1923 as a gift from a wholesaler in Hamburg – surfaced only in 1997. I therefore retain in their description here something of the mystery in which the heads were originally enshrouded.
10 Even if the initial purpose of the genealogical method, developed during the 1898 Torres Straits expedition, was different (i.e. about charting migration processes), it had significantly altered by the time he described and analysed Toda kinship and social organisation (Rivers 1906). The point about Rivers's method is that he scaled down the vast abysses of nineteenth-century 'ethnological time' to the more modest temporal requirements of the emerging 'ethnographic present'.

Bibliography

Abrahams, R., 1990. 'Plus ça change, plus c'est la même chose?', *Australian Journal of Anthropology* 1: 131–46, special issue, 'On the Generation and Maintenance of Person', ed. W. Shapiro.

Ahern, E. M., 1975. 'The Power and Pollution of Chinese Women', in M. Wolf and R. Witke (eds.), *Women in Chinese Society*. Stanford, CA: Stanford University Press.

Aijmer, Goran, 1992. 'Introduction: Coming into Existence', in G. Aijmer (ed.), *Coming into Existence: Birth and Metaphors of Birth*. Gothenberg: IASSA.

Ames, M., 1992. *Cannibal Tours and Glass Boxes: The Anthropology of Museums*. Vancouver: University of British Columbia Press.

Anderson, B., 1991 (1983). *Imagined Communities: Reflections on the Origin and Spread of Nationalism*. London: Verso.

Appadurai, A. (ed.), 1986. *The Social Life of Things: Commodities in Cultural Perspective*. Cambridge: Cambridge University Press.

Astuti, R., 1994. '"Invisible" Objects: Funerary Rituals among the Vezo of Western Madagascar,' *Res: Anthropology and Aesthetics* 25: 111–22.

1995. *People of the Sea: Identity and Descent among the Vezo of Madagascar*. Cambridge: Cambridge University Press.

1998. '"It's a Boy", "It's a Girl!" Reflections on Sex and Gender in Madagascar and Beyond', in M. Lambek and A. Strathern (eds.), *Bodies and Persons: Perspectives from Africa and Melanesia*. Cambridge: Cambridge University Press.

Atkinson, J. M., 1990. 'How Gender Makes a Difference in Wana Society', in J. Atkinson and S. Errington (eds.), *Power and Difference: Gender in Island Southeast Asia*. Stanford, CA: Stanford University Press.

Atkinson, J. M. and S. Errington (eds.), 1990. *Power and Difference: Gender in Island Southeast Asia*. Stanford, CA: Stanford University Press.

Attungana, P., 1986. Address to Alaska Eskimo Whaling Commission, trans. J. Nageak. Repr. in *Uiñiq: The Open Lead* 1(2): 16ff.

Austen, J., 1995 (1813). *Pride and Prejudice*. Harmondsworth: Penguin.

Barnard, A. and A. Good, 1984. *Research Practices in the Study of Kinship*. London: Academic Press.

Barnes, J. A., 1961. 'Physical and Social Kinship', *Philosophy of Science* 28: 296–9.

1967. 'Genealogies', in A. L. Epstein (ed.), *The Craft of Social Anthropology*. London: Social Sciences Paperbacks in association with Tavistock Publications.

1973. 'Genetrix : Genitor :: Nature : Culture?' in J. Goody (ed.), *The Character of Kinship*. Cambridge: Cambridge University Press.

Barnes, R., 1974. *Kédang: The Collective Thought of an Eastern Indonesian People*. Oxford: Clarendon Press.

Battaglia, D., 1992. 'The Body in the Gift: Memory and Forgetting in Sabarl Mortuary Exchange', *American Ethnologist* 19: 3–18.

Beattie, J. H., 1964. 'Kinship and Social Anthropology', *Man* 64: 101–3.

Bloch, M., 1971a. *Placing the Dead: Tombs, Ancestral Villages, and Kinship Organisation in Madagascar*. London: Seminar Press.

1971b. 'The Moral and the Tactical Meaning of Kinship Terms', *Man* n.s. 6(1): 79–87.

1973. 'The Long and the Short Term: The Economic and Political Significance of the Morality of Kinship', in J. Goody (ed.), *The Character of Kinship*. Cambridge: Cambridge University Press.

1993. 'Zafimaniry Birth and Kinship Theory', *Social Anthropology* 1, pt 1B: 119–32.

1995. 'Malagasy Kinship and Kinship Theory', in B. Champion (ed.), *L'étranger in Time*. Réunion: Presses Universitaires de la Réunion.

Bloch, M. and J. Parry, 1982. 'Introduction', in M. Bloch and J. Parry (eds.), *Death and the Regeneration of Life*. Cambridge: Cambridge University Press.

Bodenhorn, B., 1989. 'The Animals Come to Me; They Know I Share: Iñupiaq Kinship, Changing Economic Relations and Enduring World Views on Alaska's North Slope', unpublished PhD thesis, University of Cambridge.

1990. 'I'm Not the Great Hunter; My Wife Is: Iñupiat and Anthropological Models of Gender', *Etudes/Inuit/Studies* 14(1–2): 55–74.

1993. 'Gendered Spaces, Public Places: Public and Private Revisited on the North Slope of Alaska', in B. Bender (ed.), *Landscapes: Politics and Perspectives*. Oxford: Berg.

1997. 'Person, Place and Parentage: Ecology, Identity and Social Relations on the North Slope of Alaska', in S. A. Mousalimas (ed.), *Arctic Ecology and Identity*. Budapest: International Society for Trans-Oceanic Research.

n.d. *Documenting Iñupiat Family Relations in Changing Times*. Report prepared for the North Slope Borough Commission on Iñupiaq History, Language and Culture and the Alaska Humanities Forum, Barrow, Alaska, June 1988.

Boon, J., 1974. 'Anthropology and Nannies', *Man* n.s. 9: 137–40.

1990. 'Balinese Twins Times Two: Gender, Birth Order, and "Household" in Indonesia/Indo-Europe', in J. Atkinson and S. Errington (eds.), *Power and Difference: Gender in Island Southeast Asia*. Stanford, CA: Stanford University Press.

Bouquet, M., 1986. '"You Cannot be a Brahmin in the English Countryside": The Partitioning of Status and Its Representation within the Farm Family in Devon', in A. P. Cohen (ed.), *Symbolising Boundaries: Identity and Diversity in British Cultures*. Manchester: Manchester University Press.

1991. 'Images of Artefacts: Photographic Essay', *Critique of Anthropology* 11(4): 333–56.

1992. 'Framing Knowledge: The Photographic 'Blind Spot' between Words and Things', *Critique of Anthropology* 12(2): 139–207.

1993a. *Reclaiming English Kinship: Portuguese Refractions of British Kinship Theory.* Manchester: Manchester University Press.

1993b. *Man-Ape/Ape-Man: 'Pithecanthropus' in het Pesthuis, Leiden.* Leiden: Nationaal Natuurhistorisch Museum.

1995. 'Exhibiting Knowledge: The Trees of Dubois, Haeckel, Jesse and Rivers at the *Pithecanthropus* Centennial Exhibition', in M. Strathern (ed.), *Shifting Contexts: Transformations in Anthropological Knowledge.* London: Routledge.

1996a. 'Family Trees and Their Affinities: The Visual Imperative of the Genealogical Diagram', *Journal of the Royal Anthropological Institute* n.s. 2: 43–66.

1996b. *Sans og samling . . . hos Universitetets Etnografiske Museum/Bringing It All Back Home . . . to the Oslo University Ethnographic Museum.* Oslo: Scandinavian University Press.

Bouquet, M. and J. Freitas Branco, 1988. *Melanesian Artefacts, Postmodernist Reflections/Artefactos melanésios, reflexões pós-modernistas.* Lisbon: IICT/ Museu de Etnologia.

Bourdieu, P., 1977. *Outline of a Theory of Practice.* Cambridge: Cambridge University Press.

Broch-Due, V., 1993. 'Making Meaning out of Matter: Perceptions of Sex, Gender and Bodies among the Turkana', in V. Broch-Due, I. Rudie, and T. Bleie (eds.), *Carved Flesh/Cast Selves: Gendered Symbols and Social Practices.* Oxford: Berg.

Broch-Due, V. and I. Rudie, 1993. 'Carved Flesh – Cast Selves: An Introduction', in V. Broch-Due, I. Rudie, and T. Bleie (eds.), *Carved Flesh/Cast Selves: Gendered Symbols and Social Practices.* Oxford: Berg.

Broch-Due, V., I. Rudie, and T. Bleie (eds.), *Carved Flesh/Cast Selves: Gendered Symbols and Social Practices.* Oxford: Berg.

Bromham, D., R. Dalton and J. C. Jackson (eds.), *Philosophical Ethics in Reproductive Medicine.* Manchester: Manchester University Press.

Burch, E. S., Jr., 1975. *Eskimo Kinsmen: Changing Family Relationships in North-west Alaska.* New York: West Publishing.

1988. 'Modes of Exchange in North-West Alaska,' in T. Ingold, D. Riches, and J. Woodburn (eds.), *Hunters and Gatherers (2): Property, Power and Ideology.* Oxford: Berg.

Burghart, Richard, 1996. *The Conditions of Listening: Essays on Religion, History and Politics in South Asia,* ed. C. J. Fuller and Jonathan Spencer. Delhi: Oxford University Press.

Busby, Cecilia, 1997a. 'Of Marriage and Marriageability: Gender and Dravidian Kinship', *Journal of the Royal Anthropological Institute* n.s. 3: 21–42.

1997b. 'Permeable and Partible Persons: A Comparative Analysis of Gender and Body in South India and Melanesia', *Journal of the Royal Anthropological Institute* n.s. 3: 261–78.

Butler, J., 1990. *Gender Trouble: Feminism and the Subversion of Identity.* London: Routledge.

1993. *Bodies That Matter: On the Discursive Limits of 'Sex'.* New York: Routledge.

Cannell, F., 1990. 'Concepts of Parenthood: The Warnock Report, the Gillick Debate, and Modern Myths', *American Ethnologist* 17: 667–86.

Carrithers, M., S. Collins, and S. Lukes (eds.), 1985. *The Category of the Person: Anthropology, Philosophy, History.* Cambridge: Cambridge University Press.

Carsten, J., 1995a. 'The Substance of Kinship and the Heat of the Hearth: Feeding, Personhood, and Relatedness among Malays in Pulau Langkawi', *American Ethnologist* 22: 223–41.

1995b. 'The Politics of Forgetting: Migration, Kinship and Memory on the periphery of the Southeast Asian State', *Journal of the Royal Anthropological Institute* n.s. 1: 317–35.

1997. *The Heat of the Hearth: The Process of Kinship in a Malay Fishing Community.* Oxford: Clarendon Press.

Carsten, J. and S. Hugh-Jones (eds.), 1995. *About the House: Lévi-Strauss and Beyond.* Cambridge: Cambridge University Press.

Cassell, M. S., 1988. 'Farmers of the Northern Ice: Relations of Production in the Traditional North Alaskan Iñupiat Whale Hunt', *Research in Economic Anthropology,* 10: 89–116.

Chapman, W. R. 1985. 'Arranging Ethnology: A. H. L. F. Pitt-Rivers and the Typological Tradition', in G. Stocking (ed.), *Objects and Others: Essays on Museums and Material Culture.* Madison: University of Wisconsin Press.

Cheal, D., 1988. *The Gift Economy.* London: Routledge.

Chen, C., 1985. 'Dowry and Inheritance', in J. Hsieh and Y. Chuang (eds.), *The Chinese Family and Its Ritual Behavior.* Taipei: Institute of Ethnology, Academia Sinica.

Clifford, J., 1988. *The Predicament of Culture: Twentieth-Century Ethnography, Literature, and Art.* Cambridge, MA: Harvard University Press.

Cohen, A. P. (ed.), 1982. *Belonging, Identity and Social Organisation in British Rural Cultures.* Manchester: Manchester University Press.

Cohen, M., 1976. *House United, House Divided: The Chinese Family in Taiwan.* New York: Columbia University Press.

Collier, J. F., 1988. *Marriage and Inequality in Classless Societies.* Stanford, CA: Stanford University Press.

Collier, J. F. and M. Rosaldo, 1981. 'Politics and Gender in Simple Societies', in S. Ortner and H. Whitehead (eds.), *Sexual Meanings: The Cultural Construction of Gender and Sexuality.* Cambridge: Cambridge University Press.

Collier, J. F. and S. J. Yanagisako (eds.), 1987. *Gender and Kinship: Essays towards a Unified Analysis.* Stanford, CA: Stanford University Press.

Coombe, R., 1994. 'Challenging Paternity: Histories of Copyright' [review article], *Yale Journal of Law and the Humanities* 6: 397–422.

Coombes, A. E., 1988. 'Museums and the Formation of National and Cultural Identities', *Oxford Art Journal* 11(2): 57–68.

Cucchiari, S., 1981. 'The Origins of Gender Hierarchy', in S. Ortner and H. Whitehead (eds.), *Sexual Meanings: The Cultural Construction of Gender and Sexuality.* Cambridge: Cambridge University Press.

Cussins, C., 1997. 'Quit Snivelling, Cryo-Baby: We'll Decide Which One's Your Mama', in R. E. Floyd-Davis and J. Dumit (eds.), *Cyborg Babies: From Techno Tots to Techno Toys.* New York: Routledge.

Daa, L. K., 1855. *Utsigt over etnologien.* Christiania: Steenske Bogtrykkeri.

1870. *Skisser fra Lapland, Karelstranden og Finland.* Christiania: Selskabet for Folkeopplysningens Fremme.

Daniel, E. Valentine, 1984. *Fluid Signs: Being a Person the Tamil Way*. Berkeley and Los Angeles: University of California Press.

Das, Veena, 1976. 'Masks and Faces: An Essay on Punjabi Kinship', *Contributions to Indian Sociology* 10(1): 1–29.

Davis, D. and S. Harrell (eds.), 1993. *Chinese Families in the Post-Mao Era*. Berkeley and Los Angeles: University of California Press.

De Boeck, F., 1994. 'Of Trees and Kings: Politics and Metaphor among the Aluund of Southwestern Zaire', *American Ethnologist* 21(3): 451–73.

DeGlopper, D., 1995. *Lukang: Commerce and Community in a Chinese City*. Albany: State University of New York Press.

Delaney, C., 1986. 'The Meaning of Paternity and the Virgin Birth Debate', *Man* n.s. 21(3): 494–513.

Descola, P. and G. Palsson (eds.), 1996. *Nature and Society: Anthropological Perspectives*. London: Routledge.

Douglas, M., 1968. 'The Relevance of Tribal Studies', *Journal of Psychosomatic Research* 12: 21–8.

Drummond, L., 1978. 'The Transatlantic Nanny: Notes on a Comparative Semiotics of the Family in English-Speaking Societies', *American Ethnologist* 5(1): 30–43.

Dumont, Louis, 1994 (1966). 'North India in Relation to South India', in Patricia Uberoi (ed.), *Family, Kinship and Marriage in India*. Delhi: Oxford University Press.

Edwards, J., 1993. 'Explicit Connections: Ethnographic Enquiry in North-West England', in J. Edwards, S. Franklin, E. Hirsch, F. Price, and M. Strathern (eds.), *Technologies of Procreation: Kinship in the Age of Assisted Conception*. Manchester: Manchester University Press.

1995. 'Gametes Need Names', paper read to Royal Anthropological Insitute, London, May.

1998. 'The Need for a "Bit of History": Place and Past in English Identity', in N. Lovell (ed.), *Locality and Belonging*. London: Routledge.

Edwards, J., S. Franklin, E. Hirsch, F. Price, and M. Strathern, 1993. *Technologies of Procreation: Kinship in the Age of Assisted Conception*. Manchester: Manchester University Press.

Eekelaar, J. and P. Šarčevič, 1993. *Parenthood in Modern Society: Legal and Social Issues for the Twenty-first Century*. International Society of Family Law. Dordrecht: Nijhoff.

Errington, S. 1989. *Meaning and Power in a Southeast Asian Realm*. Princeton, NJ: Princeton University Press.

1990. 'Recasting Sex, Gender and Power: A Theoretical and Regional Overview', in J. M. Atkinson and S. Errington (eds.), *Power and Difference: Gender in Island Southeast Asia*. Stanford, CA: Stanford University Press.

Evans-Pritchard, E. E., 1940. *The Nuer: A Description of the Modes of Livelihood and Political Institutions of a Nilotic People*. Oxford: Clarendon Press.

1945. *Some Aspects of Marriage and Family among the Nuer*. Lusaka: Rhodes–Livingston Institute.

1951. *Kinship and Marriage among the Nuer*. Oxford: Clarendon Press.

Falkenberg, J., 1948. *Et steinalderfolk i var tid*. Oslo: Norli.

1962. *Kin and Totem: Group Relations of Australian Aborigines in the Port Keats District*. Oslo: Oslo University Press.

Faure, D. and H. Siu (eds.), 1995. *Down to Earth: The Territorial Bond in South China*. Stanford, CA: Stanford University Press.

Feeley-Harnik, G., 1991. 'Finding Memories in Madagascar', in S. Küchler and W. Meliot (eds.), *Images of Memory*. Washington, DC: Smithsonian Institution Press.

Fei, X., 1946. 'Peasantry and Gentry: An Interpretation of Chinese Social Structure and Its Changes', *American Journal of Sociology* 52: 1–17.

Finch, J., 1989. *Family Obligations and Social Change*. Cambridge: Polity.

Firth, R., 1963. 'Bilateral Descent Groups: An Operational Viewpoint', in I. Schapera (ed.), *Studies in Kinship and Marriage*. London: Royal Anthropological Institute.

1968. 'Rivers on Oceanic Kinship', in W. H. R. Rivers, *Kinship and Social Organisation*. London: Athlone; New York: Humanities Press.

Forde, Daryll, 1963. Letter: 'On Some Further Unconsidered Aspects of Descent', *Man* 63: 12–13.

Fortes, M., 1949. *The Web of Kinship among the Tallensi*. Oxford: Oxford University Press.

1958. 'Introduction', in J. Goody (ed.), *The Developmental Cycle in Domestic Groups*. Cambridge: Cambridge University Press.

1969. *Kinship and the Social Order*. Chicago: Aldine.

1974. 'The First Born', *Journal of Child Psychology and Psychiatry* 15: 81–104. (Repr. in Fortes, *Religion, Morality and the Person: Essays on Tallensi Religion*. Cambridge: Cambridge University Press, 1987.)

1977. 'Custom and Conscience in Anthropological Perspective', *International Review of Psycho-Analysis* 4: 127–54. (Repr in Fortes, *Religion, Morality and the Person: Essays on Tallensi Religion*. Cambridge: Cambridge University Press, 1987.)

Fox, J., 1971. 'Sister's Child as Plant: Metaphors in an Idiom of Consanguinity', in R. Needham (ed.), *Rethinking Kinship and Marriage*. London: Tavistock.

1980 ed. *The Flow of Life: Essays on Eastern Indonesia*. Cambridge, MA: Harvard University Press.

1987. 'The House as a Type of Social Organisation on the Island of Roti', in C. Macdonald (ed.), *De la hutte au palais: sociétés 'à maison' en Asie du Sud-Est insulaire*. Paris: CNRS.

Fox, R., 1967. *Kinship and Marriage*. Harmondsworth: Penguin.

Franklin, S. 1996. 'Making Transparencies: Seeing through the Science Wars', *Social Text* 46–7: 141–56.

1997. *Embodied Progress: A Cultural Account of Assisted Conception*. London: Routledge.

1998. 'Making Miracles: Scientific Progress and the Facts of Life', in S. Franklin and H. Ragoné (eds.), *Reproducing Reproduction: Kinship, Power, Technological Innovation*. Philadelphia: University of Pennsylvania Press.

Franklin, S. and H. Ragoné, 1998a ed. *Reproducing Reproduction: Kinship, Power, and Technological Innovation*. Philadelphia: University of Pennsylvania Press.

1998b. 'Introduction', in S. Franklin and H. Ragoné (eds.), *Reproducing*

Reproduction: Kinship, Power, and Technological Innovation. Philadelphia: University of Pennsylvania Press.

Freedman, M., 1958. *Lineage Organisation in Southeastern China*. London: Athlone.

1979. *The Study of Chinese Society*. Stanford, CA: Stanford University Press.

Freeman, J. D., 1961. 'On the Concept of the Kindred', *Journal of the Royal Anthropological Institute* 91: 192–220.

1970. *Report on the Iban*. London: Athlone.

Friis, J. A., 1871. *En sommer i Finmarken, russisk Lapland og Nordkarelen: skildringer af land og folk*. Christiania: Cammermeyer.

Fruzzetti, Lina, Ákos Östör, and Steve Barnett, 1992 (1982). 'The Cultural Construction of the Person in Bengal and Tamilnadu', in Á. Östör, L. Fruzzetti, and S. Barnett (eds.), *Concepts of Person: Kinship, Caste, and Marriage in India*. Delhi: Oxford University Press.

Fuller, C. J. (ed.), 1996. *Caste Today*. Delhi: Oxford University Press.

Gallin, B. and R. Gallin, 1985. 'Matrilateral and Affinal Relationships in Changing Chinese Society', in J. Hsieh and Y. Chuang (eds.), *The Chinese Family and Its Ritual Behavior*. Taipei: Institute of Ethnology, Academia Sinica.

Gates, H., 1996. *China's Motor: A Thousand Years of Petty Capitalism*. Ithaca, NY: Cornell University Press.

Gay-y-Blasco, P., 1997. 'A Different Body? Desire and Virginity among Gitanos', *Journal of the Royal Anthropological Institute* n.s. 3(3): 517–35.

Geertz, H. and C. Geertz, 1975. *Kinship in Bali*. Chicago: University of Chicago Press.

Gellner, E., 1957. 'Ideal Language and Kinship Structures', *Philosophy of Science* 24: 235–42.

1960. 'The Concept of Kinship', *Philosophy of Science* 27: 187–204.

Gewertz, D., 1984. 'The Tchambuli View of Persons: A Critique of Individualism in the Works of Mead and Chodorow', *American Anthropologist* 86: 615–29.

Ginsburg, F. and R. Rapp, 1991. 'The Politics of Reproduction', *Annual Review of Anthropology* 20: 311–43.

1995 ed. *Conceiving the New World Order: The Global Politics of Reproduction*. Berkeley and Los Angeles: University of California Press.

Gjessing, G. and M. Krekling Johannessen, 1957. *De hundre ar: Universitetets Etnografiske Museums historie, 1857–1957*. Oslo: Forenede Trykkier.

Goodenough, W., 1970. 'Epilogue: Transactions in Parenthood', in V. Carroll (ed.), *Adoption in Eastern Oceania*. Honolulu: University of Hawaii Press.

Goody, E. N. 1982. *Parenthood and Social Reproduction*. Cambridge: Cambridge University Press.

Goody, J. 1958 ed. *The Developmental Cycle in Domestic Groups*. Cambridge: Cambridge University Press.

1973 ed. *The Character of Kinship*. Cambridge: Cambridge University Press.

1990. *The Oriental, the Ancient and the Primitive*. Cambridge: Cambridge University Press.

Gough, Kathleen, 1971. 'Nuer Kinship: A Re-Examination.', in T. O. Beidelman (ed.), *The Translation of Culture*. London: Tavistock.

Guemple, L., 1965. 'Saunik: Name Sharing as a Factor Governing Eskimo Kinship Terms', *Ethnology* 4(3): 323–35.

1972. 'Eskimo Band Organisation and the DP Camp Hypothesis', *Arctic Anthropology* 9(2): 80–112.

1986. 'Men and Women, Husbands and Wives: The Role of Gender in Traditional Inuit Society', *Etudes/Inuit/Studies* 10(1–2): 9–24.

1988. 'Teaching Social Relations to Inuit Children', in T. Ingold, D. Riches, and J. Woodburn (eds.), *Hunters and Gatherers (2): Property, Power and Ideology*. Oxford: Berg.

Hannerz, U., 1992. 'The Global Ecumene as a Network of Networks', in A. Kuper (ed.), *Conceptualising Society*. London: Routledge.

Haraway, D. J., 1989. *Primate Visions: Gender, Race and Nature in the World of Modern Science*. London: Routledge.

1991. *Simians, Cyborgs and Women: The Reinvention of Nature*. London: Free Association Books.

1997. *Modest_Witness@Second_Millennium.FemaleMan©_Meets_OncoMouse™: Feminism and Technoscience*. New York: Routledge.

Hayden, C., 1995. 'Gender, Genetics, and Generation: Reformulating Biology in Lesbian Kinship', *Cultural Anthropology* 10(1): 41–63.

1998. 'A Biodiversity Sampler for the Millennium', in S. Franklin and H. Ragoné (eds.), *Reproducing Reproduction: Kinship, Power, and Technological Innovation*. Philadelphia: University of Pennsylvania Press.

Heinrich, A., 1963. 'Personal Names, Social Structure and Functional Integration.' Anthropology and Sociology Papers 27. Department of Sociology and Welfare, Montana State University.

Heinrich, A., and R. L. Anderson, 1971. 'Some Formal Aspects of a Kinship System', *Current Anthropology* 12(4–5): 541–8.

Hirsch, E., 1993. 'Negotiated Limits: Interviews in South-East England', in J. Edwards, S. Franklin, E. Hirsch, F. Price, and M. Strathern (eds.), *Technologies of Procreation: Kinship in the Age of Assisted Conception*. Manchester: Manchester University Press.

Holck, P., 1993. *Den fisiske antropologi i Norge: Fra Anotomisk Institutts historie 1815–1990*. Antropologiske Skrifter 3. Department of Anatomy, University of Oslo.

Holy, Ladislav, 1979a. 'The Segmentary Lineage Structure and Its Existential Status', in L. Holy (ed.), *Segmentary Lineage Systems Reconsidered*. Queen's University Papers in Social Anthropology 4. Belfast: Department of Social Anthropology, Queen's University.

1979b. 'Nuer Politics', in L. Holy (ed.), *Segmentary Lineage Systems Reconsidered*. Queen's University Papers in Social Anthropology 4. Belfast: Department of Social Anthropology, Queen's University.

1996. *Anthropological Perspectives on Kinship*. London: Pluto.

Howell, S., 1995. 'Rethinking the Mother's Brother: Gendered Aspects of Kinship and Marriage among the Northern Lio, Indonesia', *Indonesia Circle*, 67: 293–317.

Howell, S. and M. Melhuus, 1993. 'The Study of Kinship; the Study of Person; a Study of Gender?' in T. del Valle (ed.), *Gendered Anthropology*. London: Routledge.

Hsieh, J., 1985. 'Meal Rotation', in J. Hsieh and Y. Chuang (eds.), *The Chinese Family and Its Ritual Behavior*. Taipei: Institute of Ethnology, Academia Sinica.

Hutchinson, S., 1996. *Nuer Dilemmas: Coping with Money, War and the State*. Berkeley and Los Angeles: University of California Press.

Jenness, D., 1985. *Dawn in Arctic Alaska*. Chicago: University of Chicago Press.

Johnson, M., 1989. 'Did I Begin?' *New Scientist*, 9 December: 39–42.

Karp, I. and S. B. Lavine (eds.), 1991. *Exhibiting Cultures: The Poetics and Politics of Museum Display*. Washington, DC: Smithsonian Institution Press.

Kelly, Raymond, 1985. *The Nuer Conquest*. Ann Arbor: University of Michigan Press.

Kirschenblatt-Gimblett, B., 1991. 'Objects of Ethnography', in I. Karp and S. D. Lavine (eds.), *Exhibiting Cultures: The Poetics and Politics of Museum Display*. Washington DC: Smithsonian Institution Press.

Klausen, A. M., 1957. *Basket-Work Ornamentation among the Dayaks*. Oslo: Forenede Trykkerier.

Klausen, A. M. and A. Sørum (eds.), 1993. *Under tropens himmel – Den store norske oppdager Carl Lumholz*. Oslo: Tiden Norsk Forlag.

Kuper, A., 1982. 'Lineage Theory: A Critical Retrospect', *Annual Review of Anthropology* 11: 71–95.

1988. *The Invention of Primitive Society: Transformations of an Illusion*. London: Routledge.

1991. 'Anthropologists and the History of Anthropology', *Critique of Anthropology* 11(2): 125–42.

Lambek, M., 1998. 'Body and Mind in Mind, Body and Mind in Body: Some Anthropological Interventions in a Long Conversation', in M. Lambek and A. Strathern (eds.), *Bodies and Persons: Comparative Perspectives from Africa and Melanesia*. Cambridge: Cambridge University Press.

Lambek, M. and A. Strathern (eds.), 1998. *Bodies and Persons: Comparative Perspectives from Africa and Melanesia*. Cambridge: Cambridge University Press.

Lambert, Helen, 1996. 'Caste, Gender and Locality in Rural Rajasthan', in C. J. Fuller (ed.), *Caste Today*. Delhi: Oxford University Press.

Latham, R., 1850. *The Natural History of the Varieties of Man*. London: John van Vorst.

Latour, B., 1993. *We Have Never Been Modern*, trans. C. Porter. London: Harvester Wheatsheaf.

Law, J., 1994. *Organising Modernity*. Oxford: Blackwell.

1996. 'Traduction/trahison: Notes on ANT', in R. Chia (ed.), *Into the Realm of Organisation: Essays for Robert Cooper*. London: Routledge.

Leach, E. R., 1961a. *Pul Eliya: A Village in Ceylon: A Study of Land Tenure and Kinship*. Cambridge: Cambridge University Press.

1961b. 'Rethinking Anthropology', in *Rethinking Anthropology*. London: Athlone.

1962. 'On Certain Unconsidered Aspects of Double Descent Systems'. *Man* 62: 130–4.

1967. 'Virgin Birth', *Proceedings of the Royal Anthropological Institute*: 39–49.

Lévi-Strauss, C., 1969. *The Elementary Structures of Kinship*. London: Eyre and Spottiswoode.

Lewis, G., 1980. *Day of Shining Red: An Essay on Understanding Ritual*. Cambridge: Cambridge University Press.

Lukes, S., 1973. 'Individualism, Types of', in P. P. Weiner (ed), *Dictionary of the History of Ideas*. New York: Scribner.

Luton, H., 1986. 'Wainwright, Alaska: The Making of Iñupiaq Cultural Continuity in a Time of Change', unpublished PhD thesis, University of Michigan.

MacCormack, C. and M. Strathern (eds.), 1980. *Nature, Culture and Gender*. Cambridge: Cambridge University Press.

Macdonald, S., 1997. *Reimagining Culture: Histories, Identities and the Gaelic Renaissance*. Oxford: Berg.

Macfarlane, A., 1986. *Marriage and Love in England: Modes of Reproduction 1300–1840*. Oxford: Blackwell.

1987. *The Culture of Capitalism*. Oxford: Blackwell.

Macintyre, M., 1995. 'Violent Bodies and Vicious Exchanges: Personfication and Objectification in Melanesia', *Social Analysis* special issue. 'Persons, Bodies, Selves, Emotions', ed. J. Morton and M. Macintyre, 37: 29–43.

Maher, J. P., 1983. 'Introduction', in K. Koerner (ed.), *Linguistics and Evolutionary Theory: Three Essays by August Schleicher, Ernst Haeckel and Wilhelm Bleek*. Amsterdam: John Benjamin.

Malinowski, B., 1929. *The Sexual Life of Savages*. New York: Harcourt, Brace and World.

1930. 'Kinship', *Man* 30(2): 19–29.

1960 (1927). *Sex and Repression in Savage Society*. London: Routledge and Kegan.

Malkki, L., 1992. 'National Geographic: The Rooting of Peoples and the Territorialisation of National Identity among Scholars and Refugees', *Cultural Anthropology* 7(1): 24–44.

Mandelbaum, David G., 1970. *Society in India*, vol. II: *Change and Continuity*. Berkeley and Los Angeles: University of California Press.

Marriott, McKim, 1969 (1955). 'Little Communities in an Indigenous Civilisation', in McKim Marriott (ed.), *Village India: Studies in the Little Community*. Chicago: University of Chicago Press.

1976. 'Hindu Transactions: Diversity without Dualism', in Bruce Kapferer (ed.), *Transaction and Meaning: Directions in the Anthropology of Exchange and Symbolic Behaviour*. Philadelphia: Institute for the Study of Human Issues.

Marriott, McKim and Ronald Inden, 1977. 'Toward an Ethnosociology of South Asian Caste Systems', in Kenneth David (ed.), *The New Wind: Changing Identities in South Asia*. The Hague: Mouton.

Marshall, M., 1977. 'The Nature of Nurture', *American Ethnologist* 4(4): 643–62.

Martin, E., 1987. *The Woman in the Body: A Cultural Analysis of Reproduction*. Boston: Beacon.

1988. 'Gender and Ideological Differences in Representations of Life and Death', in J. Watson and E. Rawski (eds.), *Death Ritual in Late Imperial and Modern China*. Berkeley and Los Angeles: University of California Press.

1991. 'The Egg and the Sperm', *Signs* 16(3): 485–501.

Mauss, M., 1966. *The Gift: Forms and Functions of Exchange in Archaic Societies*, trans. I. Cunnison. London: Cohen and West.

Mayer, Adrian C., 1960. *Caste and Kinship in Central India: A Village and Its Region*. Berkeley and Los Angeles: University of California Press.

McKinnon, S., 1995. 'Houses and Hierarchy: The View from a South Moluccan Society', in J. Carsten and S. Hugh-Jones (eds.), *About the House: Lévi-Strauss and Beyond*: Cambridge: Cambridge University Press.

Middleton, K., in press. 'The Rights and Wrongs of Loin-washing', *Taloha: Revue de Musée d'Art et d'Archéologie* [issue on gender in Madagascar].

n.d. a. 'Memory, Alliance, and Landscapes of Power in the Karembola (Madagascar)'.

n.d. b. 'Tomb-work, Body-work: Gender, Ancestry, and Reproduction among the Karembola of Madagascar'.

n.d. c. 'Female Rivalry in Kachin-type Marriage: A Case-study from Madagascar'.

Milton, K., 1979. 'Male Bias in Anthropology?' *Man* n.s. 14: 40–54.

Mol, A. and J. Law, 1994. 'Regions, Networks and Fluids: Anaemia and Social Topology', *Social Studies of Science* 24: 641–71.

Moller, Joanne, n.d. [1994]. 'Locating "the Inside": Women, Milk and the House in Kumaon, North India'. Unpublished manuscript.

Moore, H. L., 1988. *Feminism and Anthropology*. Cambridge: Polity.

1993. 'The Differences Within and the Differences Between', in T. del Valle (ed.), *Gendered Anthropology*. London: Routledge.

1994. *A Passion for Difference*. Cambridge: Polity.

Morgan, L. H., 1870. *Systems of Consanguinity and Affinity in the Human Family*. Washington, DC: Smithsonian Institution Press.

Morris, R., 1995. 'All Made Up: Performance Theory and the New Anthropology of Sex and Gender', *Annual Review of Anthropology* 24: 567–92.

Needham, R., 1962. *Structure and Sentiment: A Test Case in Social Anthropology*. Chicago: University of Chicago Press.

1971a. 'Remarks on the Analysis of Kinship and Marriage', in R. Needham (ed.), *Rethinking Kinship and Marriage*. London: Tavistock.

1971b. 'Introduction', in R. Needham (ed.), *Rethinking Kinship and Marriage*. London: Tavistock.

Nielsen, Y., 1886. *Handbook for Travellers in Norway*. Christiania: Cammermeyer.

1904. *Forer i Universitetets Ethnografiske Museum*. Christiania: W. Fabritius.

1907. *Universitetets ethnografiske samlinger, 1857–1907: en historiske oversigt over deres tilblivelse, vaekst og udvikling*. Christiania: W. C. Fabritius.

Ortner, S., 1974. 'Is Female to Male as Nature Is to Culture', in M. Rosaldo and L. Lamphere (eds.), *Women, Culture and Society*. Stanford, CA: Stanford University Press.

1981. 'Gender and Sexuality in Hierarchical Societies: The Case of Polynesia and Some Comparative Implications', in S. Ortner and H. Whitehead (eds.), *Sexual Meanings: The Cultural Construction of Gender and Sexuality*. Cambridge: Cambridge University Press.

Ortner, S. and H. Whitehead, 1981. 'Introduction: Accounting for Sexual

Meanings', in S. Ortner and H. Whitehead (eds.), *Sexual Meanings: The Cultural Construction of Gender and Sexuality*. Cambridge: Cambridge University Press.

Östör, Ákos, Lina Fruzzetti, and Steve Barnett (eds.), 1992. *Concepts of Person: Kinship, Caste, and Marriage in India*. Delhi: Oxford University Press.

Paige, K. and J. Paige, 1981. *The Politics of Reproductive Ritual*. Berkeley and Los Angeles: University of California Press.

Parkin, R., 1996. 'Genealogy and Category: An Operational View', *L'Homme* 139 (July–Sept.): 87–108.

1997. *Kinship: An Introduction to the Basic Concepts*. Oxford: Blackwell.

Pasternak, B., 1972. *Kinship and Community in Two Chinese Villages*. Stanford, CA: Stanford University Press.

Peletz, M., 1995. 'Kinship Studies in Late Twentieth-Century Anthropology', *Annual Review of Anthropology* 24: 343–72.

Pitt-Rivers, J., 1973. 'The Kith and the Kin', in J. Goody (ed.), *The Character of Kinship*. Cambridge: Cambridge University Press.

Potter, S. and J. Potter, 1990. *China's Peasants: The Anthropology of a Revolution*. Cambridge: Cambridge University Press.

Pound, C., 1995. 'Imagining Information: The Complex Disconnections of Computer Networks', in G. Marcus (ed.), *Technoscientific Imaginaries: Conversations, Profiles, and Memoirs*. Chicago: Chicago University Press.

Price, F. V., 1981. 'Only Connect? Issues in Charting Social Networks', *Sociological Review* 29: 283–312.

Prösler, M., 1996. 'Museums and Globalisation', in S. Macdonald and G. Fyfe (eds.), *Theorising Museums: Representing Identity and Diversity in a Changing World*. Oxford: Blackwell.

Rabinow, P., 1996a. 'Artificiality and Enlightenment: From Sociobiology to Biosociality', *Essays on the Anthropology of Reason*. Princeton, NJ: Princeton University Press.

1996b. *Making PCR: A Story of Biotechnology*. Chicago: Chicago University Press.

Radcliffe-Brown, A. R., 1950. 'Introduction', in A. R. Radcliffe-Brown and D. Forde (eds.), *African Systems of Kinship and Marriage*. London: Oxford University Press for the International African Institute.

Ragoné, H., 1994. *Surrogate Motherhood: Conceptions in the Heart*. Boulder, CO: Westview.

1998. 'Incontestable Motivations', in S. Franklin and H. Ragoné (eds.), *Reproducing Reproduction: Kinship, Power, Technological Innovation*. Philadelphia: University of Pennsylvania Press.

Raheja, Gloria Goodwin and Ann Grodzins Gold, 1994. *Listen to the Heron's Words: Reimagining Gender and Kinship in North India*. Berkeley and Los Angeles: University of California Press.

Rapport, N., 1993. *Diverse World Views in an English Village*. Edinburgh: Edinburgh University Press.

Reissland, Nadja and Richard Burghart, 1988. 'The Quality of a Mother's Milk and the Health of Her Child: Beliefs and Practices of the Women of Mithila', *Social Science and Medicine* 27(5): 461–9.

Richards, R. J., 1992. *The Meaning of Evolution: The Morphological Construction* and *Ideological Reconstruction of Darwin's Theory*. Chicago: University of Chicago Press.

Riles, A., 1994. 'Representing In-between: Law, Anthropology and the Rhetoric of Interdisciplinarity', *University of Illinois Law Review* 1994: 597–650.

1996. 'The Actions of Fact', unpublished PhD thesis, University of Cambridge.

Rivers, W. H. R., 1906. *The Todas*. London: Macmillan.

1968 (1910). 'The Genealogical Method of Social Anthropological Inquiry', *Kinship and Social Organisation*. London: Athlone; New York: Humanities Press.

Rivière, P., 1974. 'The Couvade: A Problem Reborn', *Man* n.s. 9: 423–35.

Rosaldo, M., 1974. 'Woman, Culture, and Society: A Theoretical Overview', in M. Rosaldo and L. Lamphere (eds.), *Woman, Culture, and Society*. Stanford, CA: Stanford University Press.

Rousseau, T., 1970. *L'adoption chez les esquimeaux tununermiut*. Quebec: Centre des Etudes Nordiques, Université Laval.

Sacks, K., 1979. *Sisters and Wives: The Past and Future of Sexual Equality*. London: Greenwood.

Saladin D'Anglure, B., 1986. 'Du foetus au chamane: la construction d'un "troisième sexe" inuit', *Etudes/Inuit/Studies* 10(1–2): 25–113.

Sax, William S., 1990. 'Village Daughter, Village Goddess: Residence, Gender, and Politics in a Himalayan Pilgrimage', *American Ethnologist* 17: 491–512.

1991. *Mountain Goddess: Gender and Politics in a Himalayan Pilgrimage*. New York: Oxford University Press.

Schneider, D. M., 1968. *American Kinship: A Cultural Account*. Englewood Cliffs, NJ: Prentice-Hall.

1972. 'What Is Kinship All About?' in P. Reining (ed.), *Kinship Studies in the Morgan Centennial Year*. Washington DC: Anthropological Society of Washington.

1980. *American Kinship: A Cultural Account*, 2nd edn. Chicago: University of Chicago Press.

1984. *A Critique of the Study of Kinship*. Ann Arbor: University of Michigan Press.

Schneider, D. M. as told to Richard Handler, 1995. *Schneider on Schneider: The Conversion of the Jews and Other Anthropological Stories*, ed. Richard Handler. Durham, NC: Duke University Press.

Schneider, D. M. and K. Gough (eds.), 1961. *Matrilineal Kinship*. Berkeley and Los Angeles: University of California Press.

Schweitzer, P., n.d. 'Kreuzpunkt am Rande der Welt: Kontaktgeschichte und sozial Verhaltnisse der siberischen Eskimo zwischen 1650–1920', unpublished PhD thesis, University of Vienna.

Scott, J., 1988. 'Trend Report: Social Network Analysis', *Sociology* 22: 109–27.

Seaman, G., 1981. 'The Sexual Politics of Karmic Retribution', in E. Ahern and H. Gates (eds.), *The Anthropology of Taiwanese Society*. Stanford, CA: Stanford University Press.

Segalen, M. (ed.), 1991. *Jeux de familles*. Paris: Presses de C.N.R.S.

Shelton, A., 1994. 'Cabinets of Transgression: Renaissance Collections and the Incorporation of the New World', in John Elsner and Roger Cardinal (eds.), *The Cultures of Collecting*. London: Reaktion Books.

Shimizu, Akitoshi, 1991. 'On the Notion of Kinship', *Man* n.s. 26(3): 377–403.

Simpson, R., 1994. 'Bringing the "unclear" Family into Focus: Divorce and Remarriage in Contemporary Britain', *Man* n.s. 29: 831–51.

Singleton, V. and M. Michael, 1993. 'Actor-networks and Ambivalence: General Practitioners in the UK Cervical Screening Programme', *Social Studies of Science* 23: 227–64.

Sørensen, S. A., 1972. 'The Flying Ship in Indonesia', in *Ethnographic Museum, University of Oslo, Yearbook 1972*. Oslo University Press.

Sørum, A., 1991. 'The Forked Branch', unpublished PhD thesis, University of Trondheim.

Southall, A., 1971. 'Ideology and Group Composition in Madagascar', *American Anthropologist* 73: 144–64.

   1986. 'The Illusion of *Nath* Agnation', *Ethnology* 25: 1–20.

Spiro, M. E., 1968. 'Virgin Birth, Parthenogenesis and Physiological Paternity: An Essay in Cultural Interpretation', *Man* n.s. 3: 242–61.

Stack, C., 1974. *All Our Kin: Strategies for Survival in a Black Community*. New York: Harper and Row.

Stafford, C., 1995. *The Roads of Chinese Childhood: Learning and Identification in Angang*. Cambridge: Cambridge University Press.

Stanworth, M. (ed.), 1987. *Reproductive Technologies: Gender, Motherhood and Medicine*. Cambridge: Polity.

Stocking, G. W. 1971. 'What's in a Name? The Origins of the Royal Anthropological Institute (1837–71)', *Man* n.s. 6(3): 369–90.

   1985 ed. *Objects and Others: Essays on Museums and Material Culture*. Madison: University of Wisconsin Press.

   1990. 'Paradigmatic Traditions in the History of Anthropology', in R. C. Olby, G. N. Cantor, J. R. R. Christie, and M. J. S. Hodge (eds.), *Companion to the History of Modern Science*. London: Routledge.

Stolcke, V., 1995. 'Talking Culture: New Boundaries, New Rhetorics of Exclusion in Europe', *Current Anthropology* 36: 1–24.

Strathern, A. and M. Lambek, 1998. 'Introduction: Embodying Sociality: Africanist–Melanesianist Comparisons', in M. Lambek and A. Strathern (eds.), *Bodies and Persons: Comparative Perspectives from Africa and Melanesia*. Cambridge: Cambridge University Press.

Strathern, M., 1981. *Kinship at the Core: An Anthropology of Elmdon, Essex*. Cambridge: Cambridge University Press.

   1982. 'The Place of Kinship, Class and Village Status in Elmdon, Essex', in A. P. Cohen (ed.), *Belonging: Identity and Social Organisation in British Rural Cultures*. Manchester: Manchester University Press.

   1984. 'Domesticity and the Denigration of Women', in D. O'Brien and S. Tiffany (eds.), *Rethinking Women's Roles: Perspectives from the Pacific*. Berkeley and Los Angeles: University of California Press.

   1988. *The Gender of the Gift: Problems with Women and Problems with Society in Melanesia*. Berkeley and Los Angeles: University of California Press.

   1992a. *After Nature: English Kinship in the Late Twentieth Century*. Cambridge: Cambridge University Press.

1992b. *Reproducing the Future: Essays on Anthropology, Kinship and the New Reproductive Technologies.* Manchester: Manchester University Press.

1992c. 'Parts and Wholes: Refiguring Relationships in a Postplural World', in A. Kuper (ed.), *Conceptualising Society.* London: Routledge.

1993. Review of Kath Weston, *Families We Choose: Lesbians, Gays, Kinship,* Man n.s. 28(1): 195–6.

1995. *The Relation: Issues in Complexity and Scale.* Prickly Pear Pamphlet no. 6. Cambridge.

1996. 'Cutting the Network', *Journal of the Royal Anthropological Institute* n.s. 2: 517–35.

1998a. 'Surrogates and Substitutes: New Practices for Old?' in J. Good and I. Velody (eds.), *The Politics of Post-modernity.* Cambridge: Cambridge University Press.

1998b. 'Divisions of Interest and Languages of Ownership', in C. Hann (ed.), *Property Relations: Renewing the Anthropological Tradition.* Cambridge: Cambridge University Press.

Thomas, N., 1991. *Entangled Objects: Exchange, Material Culture, and Colonialism in the Pacific.* Cambridge, MA: Harvard University Press.

1994. 'Licensed Curiosity: Cook's Pacific Voyages', in J. Elsner and R. Cardinal (eds.), *The Cultures of Collecting.* London: Reaktion Books.

Thompson, S., 1988. 'Death, Food and Fertility', in J. Watson and E. Rawski (eds.), *Death Ritual in Late Imperial and Modern China.* Berkeley and Los Angeles: University of California Press.

Trawick, Margaret, 1992 (1990). *Notes on Love in a Tamil Family.* Berkeley and Los Angeles: University of California Press.

Uberoi, Patricia (ed.), 1994. *Family, Kinship and Marriage in India.* Delhi: Oxford University Press.

Valeri, V., 1994. 'Buying Women but Not Selling Them: Gift and Commodity Exchange in Huaulu Alliance', *Man* n.s. 29: 1–26.

Van Keuren, D., 1989. 'Cabinets and Culture: Victorian Anthropology and the Museum Context', *Journal of the Behavioural Sciences,* 12: 26–39.

Vasavi, A. R., 1994. '"Hybrid Times, Hybrid People": Culture and Agriculture in South India', *Man* n.s. 29(2): 283–300.

Vatuk, Sylvia, 1969. 'Reference, Address, and Fictive Kinship in Urban North India', *Ethnology* 8: 255–72.

1975. 'Gifts and Affines in North India', *Contributions to Indian Sociology* n.s. 9(2): 155–96.

1992 (1982). 'Forms of Address in the North Indian Family: An Exploration of the Cultural Meaning of Kin Terms', in Á. Östör, L. Fruzzetti, and S. Barnett (eds.), *Concepts of Person: Kinship, Caste, and Marriage in India.* Delhi: Oxford University Press.

Vermeulen, H. F., 1993. 'Ethnography and Ethnology in the Late Eighteenth and Early Nineteenth Century: The German Tradition and the Ethnological Society of London'. Paper presented at Association of Social Anthropologists Decennial Conference, Oxford, July.

Vermeulen, H. F. and A. A. Roldán, 1995. 'Introduction: The History of Anthropology and Europe', in H. F. Vermeulen and A. A. Roldán (eds.),

Fieldwork and Footnotes: Studies in the History of European Anthropology.
London: Routledge.

Viveiros de Castro, E., 1998. 'Cosmological Deixis and Amerindian Perspectivism', *Journal of the Royal Anthropological Institute* n.s. 4(3): 469–88.

Wagner, R., 1977. Foreword, in B. Clay, *Pinikindu: Maternal Nurture, Paternal Substance*. Chicago: University of Chicago Press.

Watson, J., 1975 'Agnates and Outsiders: Adoption in a Chinese Lineage', *Man* n.s. 10(2): 293–306.

    1982. 'Chinese Kinship Reconsidered: Anthropological Perspectives on Historical Research', *China Quarterly* 92: 589–622.

    1986. 'Anthropological Overview: The Development of Chinese Descent Groups', in P. Ebrey and J. Watson (eds.), *Kinship Organisation in Late Imperial China*. Berkeley and Los Angeles: University of California Press.

    1988. 'The Structure of Chinese Funerary Rites', in J. Watson and E. Rawski (eds.), *Death Ritual in Late Imperial and Modern China*. Berkeley and Los Angeles: University of California Press.

Watson, R., 1985. *Inequality among Brothers: Class and Kinship in South China*. Cambridge: Cambridge University Press.

    1986. 'The Named and the Nameless: Gender and Person in Chinese society', *American Ethnologist* 13(4): 619–31.

Watson, R. S. and P. B. Ebrey (eds.), 1991. *Marriage and Inequality in Chinese Society*. Berkeley and Los Angeles: University of California Press.

Weiner, A., 1985. 'Inalienable Wealth', *American Ethnologist* 12: 210–27.

Weston, K., 1991. *Families We Choose: Lesbians, Gays, Kinship*. New York: Columbia University Press.

    1995. 'Forever Is a Long Time: Romancing the Real in Gay Kinship Ideologies', in S. Yanagisako and C. Delaney (eds.), *Naturalizing Power: Essays in Feminist Cultural Analysis*. New York: Routledge.

Williams, Brackette F., 1995. 'Classification Systems Revisited: Kinship, Caste, Race, and Nationality as the Flow of Blood and the Spread of Right', in S. Yanagisako and C. Delaney (eds.), *Naturalizing Power: Essays in Feminist Cultural Analysis*. New York: Routledge.

Wolf, A., 1985. 'Introduction: The Study of Chinese Society on Taiwan', in J. Hsieh and Y. Chuang (eds.), *The Chinese Family and Its Ritual Behavior*. Taipei: Institute of Ethnology, Academia Sinica.

Wolf, M., 1972. *Women and the Family in Rural Taiwan*. Stanford, CA: Stanford University Press.

    1974. 'Chinese Women: Old Skills in a New Context', in M. Rosaldo and L. Lamphere (eds.), *Woman, Culture and Society*. Stanford, CA: Stanford University Press.

    1985. *Revolution Postponed: Women in Contemporary China*. Stanford, CA: Stanford University Press.

Woodburn, J., 1982. 'Egalitarian Societies', *Man* n.s. 17: 431–51.

Yan, Y., 1996. *The Flow of Gifts: Reciprocity and Social Networks in a Chinese Village*. Stanford, CA: Stanford University Press.

Yanagisako, S. J., 1979. 'Family and Household: The Analysis of Domestic Groups', *Annual Review of Anthropology* 8: 161–205.

    1987. 'Mixed Metaphors: Native and Anthropological Models of Gender and

Kinship', in J. F. Collier and S. J. Yanagisako (eds.), *Gender and Kinship: Essays Towards a Unified Analysis*. Stanford, CA: Stanford University Press.

Yanagisako S. J. and J. F. Collier, 1987. 'Towards a Unified Analysis of Gender and Kinship', in J. F. Collier and S. J. Yanagisako (eds.), *Gender and Kinship: Essays Towards a Unified Analysis*. Stanford, CA: Stanford University Press.

Yanagisako, S. J. and C. Delaney 1995a ed. *Naturalizing Power: Essays in Feminist Cultural Analysis*. New York: Routledge.

1995b. 'Naturalising Power' in S. J. Yanagisako and C. Delaney (eds.), *Naturalizing Power: Essays in Feminist Cultural Analysis*. New York: Routledge.

Yang, M., 1994. *Gifts, Favors and Banquets: The Art of Social Relationships in China*. Ithaca, NY: Cornell University Press.

Zimmerman, Francis, 1988. *The Jungle and the Aroma of Meats: An Ecological Theme in Hindu Medicine*. Berkeley and Los Angeles: University of California Press.

Index

actor networks 162–3, 165n29, 165–6n30
adoption
  and Chinese kinship 52, 53–4n4
  among Iñupiat 2, 139–49, 147–8n13,
    148nn14, 15
  and kinship 145
  Rajasthani relatedness 21, 22, 77–80,
    87–8, 89
  and sense of belonging in English
    families 156
affection and Rajasthani kinship 22
affinity
  in Chinese kinship 38, 39, 41
  and consanguinity in Rajasthan 75
  in Indian kinship 73
  among Malays of Langkawi 103n12
  see also marriage
agnates, Karembola attitudes to 113–17,
    126n9
alienation, and gifts, in surrogacy 159,
    165n22
Alltown (Lancashire)
  biological factors in sense of belonging
    154–7
  and kinship 88
  residents' sense of belonging 151–2
  social and biological factors in English
    relatedness 25, 28
American kinship 6–7, 8, 9
  and concept of blood 130
analytical frameworks, women and children
    omitted from 17–18
Anatomical and Ethnological Museum
    (London), Gallery of All Nations 181
ancestors, nurturing, in Rajasthan 81–3,
    84, 85
ancestry, paternal origins among
    Karembola 113
anthropology
  kinship's importance 2–3
  material factors: parallels with kinship
    studies 29–31
  practice, and ethnography 30

social and material factors, divisions
    between 30–1, 167–70, 172–3
  trends relating to kinship and biology in
    local contexts 4–5
  see also social anthropology
association and belonging 151, 152–3
asymmetric alliance among Karembola
    19–20
autonomous decision-making among
    Iñupiaq children 136, 141, 148n15
awareness, Nuer views 58

Barnard, A. and A. Good 6, 33, 172
Barnes, J. A. 6, 19, 35n4, 105, 107, 110,
    116, 121, 126n10, 172
Barrow (Alaska) (Iñupiaq settlement)
    128–9, 132, 133, 139, 146
Barth, Fredrik 170, 189n4
Baruya relatedness, social factors 26
Bedamini dancer figure (in Oslo) 169, 170,
    171, 174, 182, 184, 187–8
Belcher Island (eastern Canada) 139
belonging 150–3
  and biological factors 154–7
  categories among Iñupiaq 131–2
  collective, among Iñupiaq 128–9, 131
  and mediating 153–7, 158
  sense among families 154–7
biblical pedigrees 173
biblical tradition and ethnography 175
biological factors
  and belonging 154–7
  and kinship 21–4, 25–9, 150; divided
    from social factors 167, 188–9;
    limitations upon 157–61
biology
  and Iñupiaq kinship 1–2, 130–1, 141,
    142–3
  and kinship 3, 4–5, 6, 8–11, 144–5; in
    America 6–7, 9; relationship affected
    by technology 12–13
  and relatedness 33
  see also nature

208

siblingship
among Iñupiat 135–6
among Karembola 113–17, 126n9; and
gender differences 123
in Rajasthan, as adoptive act 78–9
among Trukese 36n11
social anthropology
and kinship, parallels between 167–70,
171
purification and translation practices
within 168, 174–5, 183
see also anthropology
social culture, importance in anthropology
6
social exhaustion as limitation on kinship
159–60
social factors
in anthropology, parallels with kinship
studies 29–31
and kinship 21–4, 25–9, 31–3, 150;
divided from biological factors 167,
188–9
as limitations upon kinship 157–61
and material factors, division in
anthropology 167–70, 172–3
social practices and kinship 4–5, 6
social relations and individuals among
Iñupiat 130, 131–2
social stability, impact on study of kinship
2, 3
social structure, Evans-Pritchard's views 56
social upheavals, effects on Nuer
relatedness 55–7, 63
soil, role in Nuer relatedness 24
soron'anake ritual 103n16
Sørum, Arve (Norwegian anthropologist-
collector) 170, 183
spears, powers (Nuer views), 24, 65–6
state intervention in Chinese kinship 50
step-siblings, interrelatedness with families
154–5, 157
Strathern, A. and M. Lambek 5, 34, 34n2
Strathern, M. 3, 8–10, 12, 18, 19, 26, 29,
33, 89n3, 91, 100, 106–7, 108, 110,
115, 121, 124, 125n2, 130, 142, 145,
147n3, 172, 185
substance and relatedness 21–4
substance sharing and sustenance,
Rajasthani relatedness 83–5, 86
Sudanese People's Liberation Army, views
of blood feuds and effects on Nuer
relatedness 68
surrogacy 149–50, 159
and kinship 28, 36n13
sustenance and substance sharing,
Rajasthani relatedness 83–5, 86

sweat as blood (Nuer views) 58

Tallensi relatedness, unilineal descent
groups 91
Tamils and purity 85
technological developments, effects on
knowledge 9–13
teenagers, status among Iñupiat 134
translation practices and purification
practices in social anthropology 168,
174–5, 184
Trukese
created kinship 34n1
sibling relationships 36n11, 79
tsimahaivel'oñe, functions in Karembola
funeral practices 118–20, 123,
126–7n12

unilineal descent
and cognatic kinship 29
and kinship, controversies over 97–8,
100, 103n15
among Vezo 174; and effects of death
99–101
unilineal descent groups, concept 91, 93
unilineal kinship and bilateral kinship
15–16
uterine families and Chinese kinship 51–2
Utqiagvik, see Barrow

variable geometry for ontology of
mediators (Latour) 181, 182
Vezo 174
and gender 36n10
village kinship in Rajasthan 21

Wainwright (Alaska) 132, 133, 136, 139
water
as food in Rajasthan 78, 83, 84
importance in blood feuds among Nuer
66–7
wax models in museum collections 182–4,
188, 190n9
wedding customs in China 39–41
and laiwang cycle 44–7
and yang cycle 41–2, 43–4
Weston, K. 12, 142–3
whales, importance for Iñupiat 129, 132–3
wife-giving and wife-taking
among Karembola 20, 109–11
in Indian kinship 73
women
adulthood through childbirth among
Nuer 58
exogamous status on marriage in
Rajasthan 76–8, 80, 82